D1171305

Works of Music

Works of Music

An Essay in Ontology

Julian Dodd

OXFORD
UNIVERSITY PRESS

OXFORD
UNIVERSITY PRESS

Great Clarendon Street, Oxford OX2 6DP

Oxford University Press is a department of the University of Oxford.
It furthers the University's objective of excellence in research, scholarship,
and education by publishing worldwide in

Oxford New York

Auckland Cape Town Dar es Salaam Hong Kong Karachi
Kuala Lumpur Madrid Melbourne Mexico City Nairobi
New Delhi Shanghai Taipei Toronto

With offices in

Argentina Austria Brazil Chile Czech Republic France Greece
Guatemala Hungary Italy Japan Poland Portugal Singapore
South Korea Switzerland Thailand Turkey Ukraine Vietnam

Oxford is a registered trade mark of Oxford University Press
in the UK and in certain other countries

Published in the United States
by Oxford University Press Inc., New York

British Library Cataloguing in Publication Data
Data available

Library of Congress Cataloging in Publication Data
Dodd, Julian.
    Works of music / Julian Dodd.
        p. cm.
    Includes bibliographical references and index.
    ISBN-13: 978–0–19–928437–5 (alk. paper)
    ISBN-10: 0–19–928437–7 (alk. paper)
    1. Music—Philosophy and aesthetics.   I.   Title.
    ML3800.D594 2007
    781.1'7—dc22   2006036280

Typeset by Laserwords Private Limited, Chennai, India
Printed in Great Britain
on acid-free paper by
Biddles Ltd., King's Lynn, Norfolk

ISBN 978–0–19–928437–5

10 9 8 7 6 5 4 3 2 1

To Eleanor, with love

Acknowledgements

This book has taken a while. I first started thinking about the ontology of music in the Summer of 1999 and, since then, have benefited enormously from discussing my ideas with numerous friends and colleagues. Many thanks go the people who attended my papers at three British Society of Aesthetics conferences in Oxford, and to those who came to talks by me at the universities of Bolton, Dundee, East Anglia, Lancaster, Manchester, Maribor, Wales (Cardiff), and Warwick. It was also a great pleasure to be invited (along with Ben Caplan, Robert Howell, Carl Matheson, and Guy Rohrbaugh) to take part in a symposium on the ontology of art at the 2006 American Philosophical Association Pacific conference in Portland, Oregon.

I am especially grateful to those people who have given up their time to comment on my work or to talk to me informally about it. Particular thanks go to Helen Beebee, Ben Caplan, Norman Geras, Peter Goldie, Robert Howell, Sam King, Peter Lamarque, Jerry Levinson, Andy McGonigal, Michael Morris, Stefano Predelli, Guy Rohrbaugh, Michael Scott, the late (and sadly missed) Bob Sharpe, Graham Stevens, Kathleen Stock, and an anonymous referee for Oxford University Press. My greatest debt, however, is to David Davies, who read through two versions of the book and gave me pages of rigorous, careful, and sympathetic comments. Such selflessness is rare indeed in a profession that is not as carefree as it once was.

A first draft was completed with the benefit of a year's research leave funded by the University of Manchester's Faculty of Social Sciences and the Arts and Humanities Research Council. I am grateful to both institutions.

Earlier versions of some of the material in this book has already appeared in print. Specifically, Chapters 3–7 contain work based upon my 2000, 2002, 2004, and 2005 published material. I thank the British Society of Aesthetics for granting me permission to use material from these articles.

Finally, this book would have taken longer still to produce, had my working and home environments not been so supportive. The philosophers at the University of Manchester are my friends as well as my colleagues: it's been a pleasure to talk philosophy with them over a coffee or (better still) a pint. As for Susan and Eleanor: I'd just like to thank them for putting up with me.

J. D.

April 2006

Contents

Introduction

Wynton Marsalis composed *In This House, On This Morning* in 1992. But what is the nature of the thing he composed? This, in essence, is the ontological question that I address in this book. As such, it should be distinguished from another question with which I am not concerned: namely, 'What is it for such an entity to count as music?'. This latter question is a plea for a piece of *conceptual analysis*: an analysis of the concept of music that will help us to determine, for example, whether something is a piece of music rather than mere noise. The ontological question is unconcerned with such matters: its correct answer, by contrast, will enlighten us as to the kind of entity musical works are. Such enlightenment, at any rate, is what this book seeks to provide.

Having disentangled this ontological question from the question of the correct application of the concept of music, we can, in fact, decompose it into two discrete inquiries. First of all, there is what we may call *the categorial question*: the issue of which ontological category works of music belong to. Someone addressing this question is engaged in a project of ontological classification, with a view to revealing musical works to be concrete particulars, properties, sets, types, or some such. But, of course, merely assigning musical works to an ontological category does not tell a fully satisfying story about their nature. Such a story must also include an answer to *the individuation question*: an account of the identity conditions of musical works. The ontologist of music should thus provide something informative of the form 'Work W and work W^* are numerically identical if and only if...', or else explain why no such account can be forthcoming.

In what follows, I shall motivate, elaborate, and defend one particular theory concerning the ontological nature of works of music: what I shall call *the simple view*. This account comprises two theses, constituting answers to the categorial question and the individuation question respectively. Its answer to the categorial question is *the type/token theory*. This states that a musical work is a type whose tokens are datable, locatable patterns of sounds: sound-sequence-events, in other words. More specifically, such a work is a *norm*-type (i.e. a type that admits of properly and improperly formed tokens);[1] and its tokens can include performances and playings of it, but also sound-sequence-events brought about in ways other than by the actions of sentient beings.[2] The simple view's second constituent thesis—its account of musical works' identity conditions—is what may be termed *sonicism*. Characterized informally, sonicism states that musical works are types of sound-sequence-event 'pure and simple' (Levinson 1980b: 64): that is, that they are entities individuated purely in terms of how they sound.[3] According to the sonicist, all that is required for W and W^* to be one and the same work of music is that they be acoustically indistinguishable; hence it is possible for one and the same work to be composed by multiple composers at different times, and by means of the production of scores that specify different instrumentation (as long as this difference does not make for a difference in sound). More precisely, the sonicist claims that W and W^* are numerically identical works of music if and only if they have the same acoustic properties normative within them: that is, if and only if how W should sound is identical to how W^* should sound.[4]

What of the simple view's scope? I take it to apply to *all* works of pure, instrumental music—that is, to jazz works in addition to fully notated classical pieces—and to works composed for recording purposes as well

---

[1] This point has its origin in the work of Nicholas Wolterstorff (1980: 58). My account owes much to his illuminating study, although it differs substantially from Wolterstorff's views in several key areas.

[2] Performances are sound-sequence-events produced by the actions of musicians using musical instruments. Playings are sound-sequence-events produced by actions of a different kind. Examples of playings include sound-sequence-events produced by the placement of a disc in a CD player and the pressing of the 'play' button, and sound-sequence-events produced by the setting going of a player piano. I shall defend the thesis that works can have tokens that are neither performances nor playings in §1.5.

[3] The version of sonicism I shall defend—what Stephen Davies calls 'timbral sonicism' (2001: 64)—will be more precisely formulated in Ch. 8. The timbral sonicist, in contrast to her 'pure' counterpart, insists that a work's tone colour—as well as its standard melodic, rhythmic, harmonic, dynamic, and articulational properties—features in an account of its individuation.

[4] This formulation of sonicism should not be taken to suggest that there is *just one* determinate way in which a musical work should be performed. Musical works, as we shall see in §1.5, invite interpretation by performers: a work's score does not precisely determine in every respect how a performance should sound.

as to works composed for performance.[5] Every work of pure instrumental music is a (norm-) type of sound-sequence-event.

So why should we accept the simple view? I argue that both of its constituent theses are *prima facie* correct, and that there are no objections to it sufficiently strong, nor alternative theories sufficiently convincing, to justify giving up what is the default position in the ontology of music. In Chapter 1 I claim that the first constituent thesis of the simple view—the type/token theory—is the most natural way of explaining the *repeatability* of works of music: the fact that they are items that can have multiple sound-sequence-events as occurrences. *In This House, On This Morning* is the thing that its various performances and playings are *of*, and the most plausible way of construing this 'occurrence of' relation is to treat it as another manifestation of the relation that obtains between a type's tokens and the type itself. Certainly, it is a mistake to suppose that the one–many relation holding between a work and its occurrences can be better explained by treating it as the same relation as that obtaining between a set and one of its members, or that holding between a property and one of its instances.

The idea that the repeatability of musical works can be captured by regarding them as types of sound-sequence-occurrence is, then, an intuitive one. Additionally, we shall see that the fact that work and performance stand to each other as type and token nicely explains how it is possible to listen to a work *by* listening to a performance of it. The fact remains, however, that neither the ontological nature of types, nor the nature of the relation that they bear to their tokens, is well understood. Chapters 2 and 3 seek to put this right by addressing these metaphysical questions head on, a project I take to have two clear benefits. First, it enables us to determine the type/token theory's philosophical commitments. The claim that works of music are types of sound-sequence-occurrence is difficult to assess until these commitments have been brought out into the open. Second, and relatedly, much of the work undertaken in the ontology of

---

[5] What of the music of pure improvisation, such as that played in Keith Jarrett's *Köln Concerts*? Here I agree with Stephen Davies (2001: 15) that such music making does not involve the performance of a musical work. True enough, someone might listen to a recording of one of Jarrett's improvisations and attempt to reproduce it, perhaps even adding some improvisational flourishes of her own; but this is insufficient to show that the original improvisation is itself a work. Unlike genuine works, free improvisations are not regarded as blueprints for performances, and our interest in them lies in their immediacy rather than in their potential repeatability. Pure improvisations, then, inasmuch as they are not musical works, fall outside the scope of the simple view.

music has, alas, tended to be cocooned from work done in mainstream analytical metaphysics, something that has contributed to the continued marginalization of aesthetics. By giving the type/token distinction an extended treatment, I hope to buck this trend, and thereby continue the process—begun by writers such as Jerrold Levinson (1980b, 1990c) and Nicholas Wolterstorff (1980)—of returning the ontology of art to its rightful place at the core of the analytic metaphysical tradition.[6]

So what *are* the philosophical commitments that must be made by a type/token theorist? If the conclusions drawn in Chapters 2 and 3 are correct, works of music, if types, are abstract, unstructured, and both modally and temporally inflexible (i.e., incapable of having intrinsic properties other than those they have actually, and incapable of change in their intrinsic properties over time). Perhaps more significantly still, I argue, against Levinson (1980b, 1990c), that any treatment of works of music as types will inevitably end up committed to the thesis that such works exist eternally (i.e. at all times): a position I call *musical Platonism*. However, Chapters 4 and 5 argue that these consequences need not worry us and, in so doing, provide a catalyst for developing the type/token theory further. Two such developments are worthy of note at this stage. First of all, our talk of works as being structured—talk exemplified in claims that a work contains, ends on, or begins with, an A minor chord—must be reinterpreted according to Wolterstorff's theory of 'analogical predication' (1980: 61–2). The predicate 'ends with an A minor chord', when applied to a work, expresses the property *being such that a sound-event cannot be a properly formed token of it unless it ends on an A minor chord*. Such a predication sees us apply the predicate to the work all right; it is just that this predicate expresses a different, though related, property to that which it expresses when applied to one of its occurrences. Second, and perhaps most controversially, Chapter 5 develops an account of composition as (creative) *discovery* that is compatible with musical Platonism. Since works of music exist eternally, the process by which Marsalis composed In This House, On This Morning cannot have ended with the bringing of this work into existence. This compositional process was, I suggest, a creative one that is in some respects akin to a mathematician's uncovering of a proof or a scientist's uncovering of a theory. Nothing in

---

[6] Other key contributors to this process of reintegration include Ben Caplan and Carl Matheson (2004, 2006), Gregory Currie (1989), David Davies (2004), Robert Howell (2002), Stefano Predelli (1995, 2001), and Guy Rohrbaugh (2003).

the phenomenology of composition determines that we should view it as creation rather than discovery, and no feature of our appreciation of music, or indeed of its composers, is compromised by the Platonist account.

Having said this, and having granted the type/token theory's status as the default position on the categorial question, it would, nonetheless be defeated, if other ontological theories could equally well explain works' repeatability whilst assuaging more of our pre-theoretic intuitions. For this reason, Chapters 6 and 7 examine the two leading contemporary competitors to the type/token theory: the view of works of music as historical individuals (or, as I prefer to put it, *continuants*), and the conception of such works as compositional actions (whether these actions are construed, following Currie (1989), as action-types, or, following David Davies (2004), as action-tokens). What I refer to as *the continuant view* fails adequately to explain what the repeatability of a work of music consists in. In taking the relation between a work and one of its performances to be a specific form of that obtaining between an object and one of the items upon which it depends for its existence (the mysterious relation of *embodiment*), the continuant view ends up as, at best, obscure.

The two versions of the conception of works of music as compositional actions fare no better. Currie's 'action-type hypothesis' (1989: 8) can allow that works of music are repeatable, of course: they are types, after all. But the problem is that, in taking them to be types whose tokens are acts of composition rather than sound-sequence-occurrences, Currie cannot explain how the such things can be heard in their entirety: as we shall see in §7.2.3, according to Currie, the thing that is heard by an audience is not the work as a whole but a mere constituent of it. Davies too has to explain away the idea that musical works are audible, but this is not all. He must also motivate and defend his position against the strong intuition that musical works are things that stand in a one–many relation to their performances, rather than being identical with the datable, locatable processes by which they were composed. This is a tall order and one, ultimately, that Davies cannot deliver.

Ultimately, then, the type/token theory is the best available answer to the categorial question. It enables us to explain the nature of musical works' repeatability, and does so whilst being minimally disruptive of our pre-philosophical instincts. This conclusion having been reached, the individuation question takes centre stage. Granted that works of music are types whose tokens are sound-sequence-occurrences, how are they individuated? The answer to this question that I recommend—a version of sonicism—stands to the individuation question as the type/token theory stands to the categorial question. For the obvious thing to say is that works are numerically identical just in case they are acoustically indistinguishable; and this intuition, I argue, is supported by an equally intuitive account of the nature of our aesthetic appreciation: (moderate) musical empiricism. The basic thought behind the latter theory is that a work's aesthetic properties may all be appreciated by merely listening to it; and the view is fine-tuned into a supervenience thesis: the claim that a work's aesthetic properties supervene on its acoustic properties (together with the category of artwork to which it belongs). With this view in place, together with the idea that the ontological nature of works reflects our aesthetic practice, sonicism follows swiftly. If a work's aesthetic properties are all present in its acoustic appearance, then we need look no further than this appearance when providing identity conditions for pieces of music. There is no more to the individuation of such works than how they sound.

One thing that follows from the sonicist's way of individuating musical works is that such works are coarser-grained than many contemporary aestheticians would have it (Levinson 1990c: 221). Given the truth of sonicism, two composers who produce scores that instruct performers to produce sequences of sounds that are qualitatively indistinguishable thereby compose the same work. And this holds even if the composers' respective scores specify that different instruments be used in the production of such sounds (e.g. if one score specifies a piano and the other a Perfect Timbral Synthesizer), and even if the composers are situated at vastly different points in the history of music.

The weight of opinion amongst aestheticians has it that both of these consequences are false, thereby revealing acoustic indistinguishability to be only necessary, and not sufficient, for work-identity. Two composers, it is claimed, can compose acoustically indistinguishable works that are yet manifestly distinct. With a view to demonstrating this contention, counter-examples to the sonicist proposal fall into two categories. Philosophers whom we may term *instrumentalists* appeal to cases designed to show that compositions composed for different instruments, even if sonically indistinguishable, count as numerically distinct; while *contextualists* construct examples intended to prove that, although composers working in distinct musico-historical contexts may compose sonic *sound-alikes*, they cannot be said to compose one and the same work. So whilst the sonicist will say that the cases appealed to by her opponents are really examples in which two composers compose the same work in different epochs, or by specifying different means of sound production, such explanations are argued to be illegitimate by the contextualist and the instrumentalist respectively.

So why is the sonicist's way of describing such cases under threat? Significantly, there is a common form to the most credible arguments offered by the instrumentalist and the contextualist. The idea, in essence, is that a composer's specification of a work's instrumentation, or a composer's occupancy of a set of co-ordinates in musico-historical space, is determinative of many of the work's artistic, aesthetic, and expressive properties (Levinson 1990c: 22; 1980b: 76); and, hence, that if two composers are working in distinct musico-historical contexts, or if they compose their works for different instruments, their compositions—even if acoustic doppelgängers—will inevitably differ with regard to such properties, and so, by Leibniz's Law, fail to be identical.

It is this form of argument that is the main focus of Chapters 8 and 9. In my view, the examples taken to demonstrate that works of music may differ aesthetically without differing acoustically prove no such thing. They are either ill-formed or else can be explained away in a manner consistent with sonicism. There is, I contend, no genuine case in which acoustic indistinguishability fails to make for work-identity. Sonicism—the *prima facie* position on the individuation question—emerges unscathed. What this means, of course, is that both elements of the simple view stand undefeated. In the ontology of music, simplicity rules.

1

The Type/Token Theory
Introduced

1.1 Introduction

As I explained in the Introduction, the simple view that it is the business
of this book to defend comprises two theses: the type/token theory and
sonicism. The former—an answer to the categorial question—has it that
a musical work is a type whose tokens are sound-sequence-events (i.e.
datable, locatable patterns of sounds). The latter—an answer to the individuation question—claims that work-identity consists in acoustic indistinguishability. According to sonicism, when it comes to the individuation of
works of music, all that matters is how they sound.

The purpose of the present chapter is twofold: to provide an initial
motivation for the simple view's first constituent thesis, and then to begin
the process of developing and defending it. To this end, I shall present the
view of musical works as types of sound-sequence-event as the *face-value*
theory: the account that is *prima facie* correct and must be accepted as long
as it is not defeated. Two kinds of defeat are conceivable: the type/token
theory could face objections to which it has no adequate reply; and it could
face rival theories that do a better job of explaining the relevant phenomena
whilst doing justice to our pre-theoretic intuitions about works of music
and our relation to them. In my view, however, the type/token theory is
both defensible and the best value theory available. This chapter makes a
start on demonstrating this conclusion.

After a brief introduction to the type/token theory, I shall consider some
of the familiar rival accounts in the ontology of music, before going on to

elaborate it in such a way as to fend off what might at first seem to be quick and easy objections. By the present chapter's end, a kind of philosophical base camp will have been reached. Many of the usual suspects (i.e. the familiar rivals to the type/token theory) will have been rounded up and dispatched, and we will be confident in the type/token theory's position as the face-value theory on the categorial question. Having gained such a foothold, Chapters 2 and 3 will offer a detailed account of the ontological nature of types: a project that will reveal works of music, *qua* types, to be unstructured, unchanging, and, most significantly of all, eternally existent entities. Chapters 4 and 5 will defend these consequences before, in Chapters 6 and 7, I offer critiques of what I regard as the type/token theory's most serious rivals: the view of musical works as continuants; and the family of views that takes such works to be compositional actions.[1] With this, the defence of the type/token theory will have reached completion.

1.2 Motivating the Type/Token Theory: Repeatability

Works of music exist. True sentences such as

(1) *In This House, On This Morning* is a suite,

(2) Bartok's Fifth Quartet sets people's nerves on edge,[2]

(3) *Straight, No Chaser* is dynamic,

and

(4) Marsalis composed *In This House, On This Morning*

have as constituents singular terms that refer to such items. And true sentences such as

(5) There are more than thirty symphonies composed by Mozart,

and

(6) Exactly one of Bruckner's symphonies was unfinished,

see us quantifying over them. So what kind of thing are they?

---

[1] The former view is explicitly taken by Rohrbaugh (2003), and suggested by Predelli (forthcoming) and Michael Morris (forthcoming); the latter approach is taken by Currie (1989) and David Davies (2004).

[2] I owe this example to Wolterstorff (1970: 251).

The answer that I recommend is that a work of music is a species of abstract (i.e. non-spatially located) entity: that is, a type whose tokens are concrete patterns of sounds. Significantly, in taking musical works to be types rather than, say, sets, we commit ourselves to a distinctive view of how such works are individuated. For, in Ian Rumfitt's words, the identity of a type is determined, not by which tokens actually exist, but by 'the *condition* which a token meets or would have to meet in order to instantiate it' (1993: 448).[3] As we shall see presently, this feature of the type/token theory nicely enables it to capture the fact that works have their performances, playings, and other occurrences inessentially.

Before we get on to this, however, it is important that we appreciate how swiftly the type/token theory emerges as a neat solution to a puzzle concerning the ontological nature of works of music. For the perplexing thing about musical works—as opposed to, say, paintings—is that they are *repeatable*. According to the standard view, at least, the ontological story about paintings is fairly open and shut: paintings are physical objects.[4] A painting can, of course, be copied—a forger, for example, might produce a work that succeeds in reproducing the original's visual array—but such copies are works distinct from the original. Musical works, by contrast, have the possibility of multiple occurrence built in to them. A symphony can be performed or played over and over again, and, crucially, such performances and playings are not mere copies of it, but *occurrences* of it: items that make the work manifest. Whereas a copy of a painting is another work that resembles the original, a symphony's performances are the very means by which we encounter the symphony itself. Symphonies, and works of music generally, are in this sense intrinsically repeatable; and the appeal of the type/token theory lies in the fact that it elegantly explains what this phenomenon of repeatability consists in.

Taking note of this one–many relationship that obtains between a work of music and its occurrences, a reconstruction of the thinking that leads to the type/token theory begins by making the plausible assumption that this repeatability is explicable in terms of the ontological category to which

---

[3] Though sufficient for my present purposes, this account of the way in which types are individuated will be amended—in order to deal with the phenomenon of norm-types—in §1.5 below.

[4] This standard view of the ontological nature of paintings has been challenged by P. F. Strawson (1974), who argues that all artworks are types. At this stage, I have no wish to take sides on this issue: I introduce it only as a heuristic device to convey the problem raised by musical works' repeatability.

such works belong. Specifically, it is suggested that the best explanation of a musical work's repeatability takes such a work to be a *generic entity*: that is, something whose ontological category supports instantiation.[5] We are then invited to treat musical works as types because, in doing so, we thereby provide a familiar and plausible explanation of the nature of the relation holding between a work and its occurrences. The relation obtaining between a work of music and its occurrences is just that obtaining between a type of sound-sequence-occurrence and its tokens. Rather than being a queer relation of *embodiment*, it turns out to be just one more example of the familiar relation that holds, for instance, between the word 'table' and its token inscriptions and utterances.

But this is not all. Musical works, besides being repeatable, are also audible. When listening to a performance of a work of music, one thereby listens to the work performed. As Wolterstorff puts it, '[i]n listening to a symphony one hears two things at once, the symphony and a performance thereof' (1980: 41); indeed, one hears the symphony *by* hearing the performance (1980: 40–1). A further benefit of the type/token theory is that it smoothly explains how such *indirect listening* is possible: hearing a work by hearing a performance of it is a matter of hearing a type of sound-event by virtue of hearing one of its token patterns of concrete sounds. The token stands proxy for the type, and thereby enables one's perceptual experience to 'pass through' the token, and so relate the listener to the type lying behind it.

At this point, an analogy with what Quine terms 'deferred ostension' (1969: 39–41) may help the point to stick. To use Quine's own example, one may explain the abstract singular term 'alpha' by pointing at an instance of the letter on a blackboard and saying 'That is alpha'; and the explanation works because, in pointing at the concrete token, one thereby indirectly demonstrates the type that lies behind it. It is the token's presence before one in space that enables the pointing gesture to pick out the type for which the token stands proxy, and it does not matter that 'the abstract object … which is the letter alpha does not contain the ostended point, nor

---

[5] This use of 'generic' is borrowed from Richard Wollheim (1968: 91). The thought that musical works' repeatability should be explained by treating them as generic entities is denied by those who take such works to be continuants. But when it comes to this issue, the proof of the pudding is in the eating: as we shall see in Ch. 6, Rohrbaugh's denial (2003) that musical works are generic entities prevents him from adequately explaining what the repeatability of such works amounts to.

any point' (Quine 1969: 40). The presence of one of the type's concrete tokens ensures that demonstrative reference to the type is secured.

Well, as for demonstrative reference, so for perceptibility. The type/token theorist in the ontology of music can use the conceptual apparatus of the type/token distinction in an analogous way to explain how it is possible to listen to a work of music by listening to one of its performances. Just as the demonstration of a letter-type is secured by one of its tokens being present in space before one, so one may listen to a type of sound-event by virtue of listening to one of its token performances or playings. As in the case of demonstrative reference via deferred ostension, the presence of a token secures the obtaining of a relation between a person and a type. Hearing a performance of a work just *is* to hear the work *in* performance; and the reason why this is so is that the work stands behind a performance of it in exactly the same way that a letter-type stands behind its concrete tokens.

This, then, is the way in which the apparatus of the type/token theory enables us to explain how we may listen to a work by listening to one of its performances. But it is unlikely that leaving things here will be enough to convince the more naturalistically inclined philosopher. For types are abstract entities, which, as I use the term, means that they have no location in space; and an objector might question whether such entities are the kinds of things that can be heard, even indirectly. Specifically, it may be alleged that types, since they are not located in space, cannot impinge upon our sensory surfaces: being abstract in the sense introduced above, they are causally inert and hence can play no part in the concrete causal process that ends with an auditory experience. Given that the objects of perception *must* be things that enter into this process, and that types' abstract status precludes them from doing so, musical works, if types, cannot be things that are themselves heard.

One response to this objection would be to grant it and, as a result, to retreat to the thesis that only *performances* of works of music can be heard. But such a move would be both counter-intuitive and unnecessary. It would be counter-intuitive because, as we have seen Wolterstorff suggest already, it is surely a datum that works of music are things that we can listen to. We hear *works* performed; we do not merely hear performances of them. Someone who had clearly listened attentively to a performance of *In This House, On This Morning,* but who nonetheless insisted that she had never heard the work, would be looked upon with bewilderment by her fellow concert-goers. An ontological proposal that had as a consequence that such a person had spoken truly should only be adopted *in extremis*.

Thankfully, such a desperate move is not forced upon the type/token theorist. Before getting too carried away with the objection currently under consideration,[6] we should first of all unpack it. Its key claim, of course, is that types of sound-event cannot themselves be perceived because, lacking location in space, they cannot enter into causal relations, and hence cannot figure in the causal process that ends with an auditory experience. But at this point, we would do well to remember that the question of what it is for an entity to enter into causal relations requires very careful handling. Indeed, it only *seems* obvious that abstract (i.e. non-spatial) entities cannot be causally efficacious, once a couple of controversial philosophical assumptions have been made. When these assumptions are (rightly) questioned, the idea that certain *abstracta* may yet be causally active, and hence be numbered amongst the objects of perception, turns out to be harmless.

With a view to laying bare the assumptions in question, we may start by remarking that it is *events*, rather than objects (material or otherwise), that are primarily related as cause and effect.[7] Objects *can* be said to be causes, but only by virtue of somehow participating in an event: that is, by figuring in the thing that *does* the causing and, so to speak, 'acts as the elbow in the ribs' (Bennett 1988: 23).[8] Shem, for example, can be said to have brought about the bruising on Shaun's knee, but only by virtue of participating in an event (i.e. a kicking of Shaun) that had the bruising of Shaun's knee (another event) as its effect. Now, the assumptions made by someone who denies that abstract entities such as types can be causally efficacious would seem to be these: first, that there are clear criteria for whether an entity participates causally in an event; and, second, that it is clear that entities without a spatial location fail to meet these criteria. But in fact, neither assumption is warranted, as we shall now see.

As John Burgess and Gideon Rosen explain (1997: 24), there are a number of ways in which material objects may be involved in events in

---

[6] As R. A. Sharpe does, for example. (1995: 39).

[7] See, e.g., Davidson 1963, 1967a. The remarks of the following two paragraphs rely heavily on the insightful discussion in Burgess and Rosen 1997: 23–5. I was pointed in its direction by Caplan and Matheson (2004: 120).

[8] Although the colourful phrase is Bennett's, he would not agree with the use that it is put to here: he actually denies that events are entities that emit force and hence do the pushing, shoving, and forcing that is found in nature (1988: 22–3).

a way deemed causally efficacious. Some such involvement has the object undergo some intrinsic change (such as in Shem's and Shaun's participation in Shem's kicking of Shaun); other such involvement has the participating object undergo only extrinsic change (as when a stone participates in the event of a smashing of a window); whilst objects are sometimes taken to participate in events in a causally efficacious way, if they fail to change when they could have done so (as when someone tries to kick a boulder into a stream but fails to budge it). What we have here is a pretty shapeless collection of cases of causally relevant participation with no overall criterion that binds them together.

Of course, one could just insist that an entity can participate in an event in a causally efficacious way only if it is the kind of thing that can emit the forces recognized by physics: a position nicely characterized by Burgess and Rosen thus:

Physics tells us how ordinary material bodies act causally. They act by exerting forces of one of four kinds: gravitational, electromagnetic, or weak or strong nuclear. Biographies and novels, species and genera, exert no such forces over and above that of the aggregate of the concrete tokens and organisms pertaining to them. So they do not act causally in the relevant sense—and there's an end on't! (Burgess and Rosen 1997: 25)

But as Burgess and Rosen explain (1997: 25), this way of thinking—though engagingly expressed—is a *non sequitur*. Physics informs us as to the nature of the forces involved in the causal processes that obtain between physical events. What it does *not* do is provide an answer to the *conceptual* question of what it is for an object to participate causally in an event. To answer this question, we must do some philosophy, not physics; and our problem is that no fully developed theory is forthcoming.

A further complication is introduced by the fact that there is no unanimity about how the notion of an event should be explicated. If events are construed along the lines suggested by Jaegwon Kim (1976)—that is to say, as ordered triples of objects, properties, and times—then a natural thing to say is that an object counts as causally efficacious if it is a constituent of a triple that is a causally productive event. But, at a stroke, such a move undercuts the reason for thinking that types, *qua abstracta*, are causally inert and, hence, imperceptible. For there is no conceptual barrier to supposing that *abstracta* may be members of ordered triples; indeed, if, as seems plausible, properties are abstract objects, then Kim himself must accept that *every* event contains an abstract object, namely, a property.

Of course, Kim's particular account of events is not the only item on the menu. A popular alternative is that suggested by Davidson (1969). Concerned that Kim's ontological proposal individuates events too finely—according to Kim, no stabbing can be a killing, no killing can be a murder, no arm raising a signalling, and no birthday party a celebration (1967*b*: 133–4)[9]—Davidson presents a theory of events as things whose only parts are temporal parts. Given this account, talk of an event's having objects, properties, or times as constituents is senseless: events *concern* objects and properties, but a single event may be described in a variety of ways that introduce different objects and different properties.

With such a conception in place, the question of what it is for an object to figure causally in an event becomes cloudier still. The idea that objects count as causes by virtue of *entering into*, or *participating in*, events in a causally relevant way has to be treated metaphorically. Indeed, it seems that all we can say is that an object so participates causally in an event by being *appropriately related* to the said event (Caplan and Matheson 2004: 121); and, naturally, just what it is for a candidate relation between an object and an event to count as 'appropriate' is up for grabs. But at this point, I think that we should reconsider the machinery of the type/token distinction. For one plausible species of appropriate relation would seem to obtain precisely when the participating object is a type and the event one of its tokens. Suppose, for example, that the showing of a film sparked a riot. In this sense, the showing of the film—the event—*concerns* the film every bit as much as does Shem's kicking of Shaun concern Shem and Shaun. The film—the type—participates in the event that causes the riot. But does it do so in a causally relevant way? Ordinary language has it that it does: we are quite happy to speak of films causing riots; the film causes the riot by virtue of being shown. But more than this, philosophy reveals there to be no defensible motive for denying it. As we have noted already, we do not possess a worked out theory of what it is for an object to participate in Davidson-style events in a causally active way. And without there being such a theory that rules out the film's causing the riot, we remain free to say that it does so by virtue of the riot-sparking

---

[9] This objection is actually aimed at the account offered by R. M. Martin, but Martin's views (as presented by Davidson) differ little, if at all, from those of Kim.

event being one of its tokens. (A film, after all, is just a type whose tokens are datable, locatable showings.) It does not matter that the film is an abstract object: it participates causally in a causal process by virtue of one of its tokens being a member of the chain of causally related events. To resist this way of speaking is, I believe, to rely unthinkingly upon the scientism that Burgess and Rosen have unmasked as irrelevant to the point at issue.

The moral for the audibility of works of music, *qua* types of sound-event, should be obvious. A work of music, thus construed, can enter into causal relations derivatively by virtue of being a type of sound-event: a type whose token events can feature as relata of causal relations. Hence, given that the objects of perception are just those things that causally effect how things perceptually seem to us, this means that the type/token theory is not precluded from saying that works of music, in addition to their tokens, may be heard. Far from it. In fact, a work of music, though abstract, can be heard precisely *because* it is a type of whose tokens are performances, playings, and other sound-events that can cause us to have certain auditory experiences. The work itself counts as a *bona fide* object of hearing because the event that initiates the causal chain leading to an auditory experience—a sound-event—is one of its tokens.

The type/token theory thus provides a defensible account of what it is to listen to a work by listening to a performance or playing of it; and the elegance of this account, together with the type/token theory's aforementioned explanation of the nature of musical works' repeatability, serves to make it an attractive answer to the categorial question in the ontology of music. Once we assume that works of music are generic entities—that is, entities with instances—a conception of such works as types seems to follow swiftly.

But perhaps too swiftly, it could be alleged. An entity is generic just in case it is the sort of item that has exemplification built into it as standard. Given this gloss, it is clear that types are not the only generic entities: there are also sets and properties. So why should an acknowledgement that works of music are generic commit us to viewing them as types of sound-event rather than as sets of, or indeed properties of, such events? This is the question that I address in the remainder of this section. It will become evident that there are compelling reasons for preferring the type/token theory to these two alternatives, reasons that help to establish the type/token theory's position as the face-value answer to the categorial question.

Properties, it is true, are generic. A property is an entity that is capable of instantiation by particulars. So could *In This House, On This Morning* be a property of certain sound-sequence-occurrences? No, for two reasons. First, properties are categorially unsuited to be musical works. *In This House, On This Morning* is not a mere feature of a performance of it: a respect in which performances or playings can be alike or differ. It is, by contrast, the *blueprint* for such performances and playings: a thing in its own right. This is reflected in the fact that 'In This House, On This Morning'—like other type-names such as 'The Union Jack' and 'The Ford Thunderbird'–is itself neither a predicate nor a singular term systematically related to such a predicate (as 'happiness' is to 'is happy'). On the contrary, 'In This House, On This Morning' only appears in predicates that are themselves explicitly relational, such as 'is a performance of *In This House, On This Morning*' (Rohrbaugh 2003: 197).

Second, and relatedly, works and their occurrences exhibit a pattern of shared predication characteristic of the type/token model rather than the property/instance model. The following thesis, whose origin lies in the work of Wollheim (1968: 92–3), holds good at the level of *predicates*:[10] if a predicate 'is F' is true of a token in virtue of the token's being a token of a type K, then 'is F' is also true of K. Hence, 'is coloured' and 'is rectangular' are both true of The Union Jack in addition to being true of its tokens.[11] Significantly, the analogous principle concerning the transmission of predicates does *not* hold for particulars and their properties: as Wollheim points out (1968: 93), we do not describe redness as being itself red.

So does the pattern of shared predication between musical works and their performances match the pattern exhibited between types and tokens or that between properties and their instances? The former. Take any predicate true of a performance by virtue of its being a performance of W—predicates such as 'has a $C^\#$ in its seventh measure' or 'ends with an A minor chord'—and the predicate will also be truly applicable to the work itself. This being so, works of music look like being types rather than properties.

What, then, of a set-theoretical approach to the ontology of music? Could *In This House, On This Morning* be the set of its occurrences? Again,

---

[10] Though not, as we shall see in §2.3, at the level of the properties they express.

[11] I capitalize names of types (except when referring to word-types by means of inverted commas).

no, and again for two reasons. First, it is a fact, and a fact explained by the type/token theory, that one can listen to a work by listening to one of its performances; but if musical works were sets, it is quite unclear how this could be so. A set is just an extensional construction from its members, so to listen to the set, one would have to listen to its complete membership; and there is no sense in which, by listening to a single performance of *In This House, On This Morning*, one has thereby listened to every such performance.

Second, there is a modal difference between musical works and sets of sound-sequence-events. Since sets are extensional constructions out of their members, what makes a set *that* set is purely that it has *those* members. Consequently, sets have their members (or lack of them) essentially:[12] no set could have different members from those it has actually. *In This House, On This Morning*, by contrast, does not have its occurrences essentially: it might have had more, fewer, or different performances than it has had actually. There are possible worlds in which *In This House, On This Morning* has more, fewer, or different occurrences than it has actually; but there is no possible world in which the set ω of the work's actual occurrences has more or fewer members; hence the work cannot be ω.

Two possible replies to this objection are available to the supporter of the set-theoretical approach to the ontology of music, but both are seriously undermotivated. First, as Caplan and Matheson point out (2004: 133), one might resist this modal argument's conclusion by taking a Lewisian counterpart-theoretic approach to *de re* modality.[13] But such an approach fixes a high price for identifying works of music with sets of occurrences: along with other commentators, I find it counter-intuitive to suppose that a claim about how things could have stood with α really concerns how things stand with *another* object: a world-bound α-counterpart (Kripke 1980: 45–6). An account of the ontological nature of works of music that avoided such a commitment would be welcome.

---

[12] This point about the identity conditions of sets is well made by, among others, Peter Simons (1982: 198), David Wiggins (1980: 113), and Wolterstorff (1970: 178–80).

[13] See, e.g., Lewis 1968 and 1986. According to such a construal, a property *F* is essential to α just in case both it and all its counterparts are *F*, whilst *F* is accidental to α just in case α is *F* but some of its counterparts are not *F*. With this account in place, demonstrating that it is possible for a work—*qua* set ω of occurrences—to have more, fewer, or different occurrences merely requires us to introduce a counterpart relation that selects as a counterpart of ω at least one set that differs in its membership to ω.

It could, nonetheless, be argued, I suppose, that there need be no such commitment to counterpart theory, if works were identified with sets of actual *and merely possible* occurrences. This, indeed, appears to be the kind of position taken by Nelson Goodman. According to Goodman, 'the work exists as the possibility of a range of (differing) performances, each of which satisfies it' (1968: 41). However, I agree with John McDowell (1980: 210) that the thesis that there are possible but non-occurrent events is no more palatable than the thesis that there are possible but non-existent people. Such a desperate attempt to prolong the life of the set-theoretical approach is not worth the trouble it inevitably brings.

Indeed, this is especially so given the way the type/token theory neatly avoids the difficulties that beset the set-theoretical approach. The crucial difference between types and sets is this: whilst the identity of a set is determined by its membership, the identity of a type, we have noted already, is determined by the condition that something must meet to be one of its tokens. And it is this difference that enables the type/token theory to sidestep neatly the modal problem facing the set-theoretical approach. For, since the identity of a type is determined by the condition that something must meet to be one of its tokens, and not by which tokens actually exist, it follows that types do not have their instances essentially. What makes the type *K that* type is that it lays down a certain condition for something to be one of its tokens; it would still lay down this condition, and so would remain that type, even if fewer, more, or different tokens satisfied it. As a result, the type/token theorist can straightforwardly account for our modal intuitions concerning works and their occurrences without having to take on the kinds of controversial commitments that blight the set-theoretical approach.

Having said this, the history of philosophy is littered with face-value theories that have turned out to be second-best at explaining the relevant data. Not in this case, however. And, with a view to eventually demonstrating the truth of this claim, the next two sections will demonstrate that neither nominalist approaches nor anti-realist accounts of the ontology of music are to be preferred to the type/token theory. A consideration of these competitors will enable us both to further elaborate the thesis that musical works are types of sound-sequence-event and to appreciate the theory's comparative strength.

1.3 Nominalist Approaches to the Ontology of Music

The discussion thus far has presupposed—quite rightly, I shall argue[14]—that musical works, if types, are abstract entities (i.e. entities with no spatial location). Nominalists, naturally, will be unhappy with the type/token theory for just this reason and, as a result, will either claim that such works are really concrete entities, or else argue that our ontology need not include works of music at all. The purpose of this section is to explain why neither of these nominalistic strategies succeeds.[15]

Perhaps the simplest nominalist approach to the ontology of music would have us seek to reduce works to their occurrences. But putting the programme like this merely serves to prompt the question of how this reduction should be characterized. One thing is for sure: we cannot *identify* *In This House, On This Morning* with the sound-sequence-events that we regard as its occurrences: identity is a one–one relation, so the single work cannot be identical with two or more sound-sequence-events. Equally, we cannot privilege one particular occurrence—say, the piece's first complete run-through—as the work. For such events have properties that works do not have, and vice versa: Marsalis composed *In This House, On This Morning*, not a performance of it; and whilst the work itself currently exists, the same cannot be said of the concrete sequence of sounds constituting the piece's first run-through.

In fact, the prospects for identifying a work with its first complete performance are dimmer still. For such an approach fails to address the fact that any satisfactory answer to the categorial question must explain: namely, that works are repeatable. Merely identifying such a work with one of its occurrences fails to explain—indeed, seems to rule out the possibility of explaining—what this repeatability consists in. For even the work's first performance is but a performance *of* the work; and it is mysterious how one such occurrence of the work could be the thing that all such occurrences, including itself, are occurrences of.

Having rejected the idea that works are identical with their occurrences, a would-be nominalist might be tempted by the thought that works are

---

[14] See §2.3 below.

[15] A more sophisticated version of nominalism—a view of musical works as concrete, perduring entities—is discussed, and rejected, in Ch. 6.

somehow *constituted* by them. But what needs to be explained is the precise nature of this constitution. The most plausible such account treats a work's performances, playings, and other occurrences as its temporal stages. However, as we shall see in Chapter 6, two counter-intuitive consequences swiftly ensue: first, that works of music are scattered objects; and, second, that an audience at a performance cannot hear a whole work. If *In This House, On This Morning* has its performances as temporal parts, then an audience listening to such a performance can audit only one stage of the work, and not the work as a whole. Listening to the work in its entirety—listening to the whole work—would require an audience to listen to the totality of its constituent temporal stages.

Presuming that a nominalist will find none of the above theories persuasive, she may, nonetheless, attempt to identify works with their original scores. Such an approach, in denying that musical works are generic entities at all, will, presumably, seek to explain the fact that a work is repeatable in terms of the score being in some sense embodied in, or realized by, sound-sequence-events that accord with it. But it is far from clear what the details of such an account would be and, in any case, the view of works of music as autographed scores faces insuperable objections. First, it is not generalizable: some pieces do not have a score. Second, works of music can survive the destruction of their original scores: if Marsalis's score for *In This House, On This Morning* were to be destroyed, the work itself would not be annihilated; it could, after all, continue to be performed. And finally, musical works have properties that original scores do not: for instance, works, but not scores, can be heard.

It is this final objection that demonstrates the wrong-headedness of the attempt to reduce musical works to scores. Music is a *performance* art; works are composed in order to be listened to by an audience, whether this audience is in a concert-hall or listening to a recording. To identify a work with its score is to fail to see the purpose of music, and is to make a mistake as glaring as that of someone who identified a play with its script or a sculpture with the sculptor's drawings.

Which way could a nominalist now turn? At this point, she may find an *eliminativist* approach attractive. That is to say, she may seek, not to *identify* works of music with concrete particulars, but to eliminate them in favour of *concreta*. On this view, musical works are not genuine denizens of the universe, but fictions enabling us to think and speak more conveniently about performances and playings. And such a nominalist seeks to make her case by showing that true sentences that appear to have us ontologically committed to works of music may be paraphrased in such a way as to reveal such a commitment to be illusory. However, such a project is fraught with difficulties of both a technical and theoretical nature.

It is fair to say that, when it comes to sentences such as

(1) *In This House, On This Morning* is a suite,

the sort of paraphrase recommended by both Richard Rudner (1950) and Jay Bachrach (1971) seems natural enough. That is, the nominalist will be tempted to argue that (1) should be paraphrased as something like

(7) All performances of *In This House, On This Morning* are composed of a succession of short movements,

a sentence whose logical form may, in turn, be represented as

(8) $(\forall x)(x$ is a performance of *In This House, On This Morning* $\rightarrow x$ is composed of a succession of short movements).

But we should be careful not to underestimate the difficulties that this apparently simple style of nominalistic paraphrase presents. For, as we have noted already, the predicate 'is a performance of *In This House, On This Morning*' seems to be explicitly relational, one of its constituents being a singular term referring to a work. Clearly, the nominalist must provide an analysis of this predicate that reveals the appearance of a genuine singular term within the predicate to be illusory.

This, though, is none too easy a thing to do. One option would be to treat 'is a performance of *In This House, On This Morning*', like Quine's 'is-Pegasus' (1948: 8), as an irreducible predicate. But such a move evidently cannot convince us that apparent names of works can be analysed out of all contexts: our understanding of such a Quinean predicate requires us to know the reference of the name from which it is so obviously derived. Bachrach, meanwhile, suggests that we analyse the predicate in terms of the production of scores (1971: 418–20), his favoured strategy representing the logical form of (1) as

(9) $(\forall x)(x$ is a performance for which Marsalis wrote the notation during a certain time in 1992 $\rightarrow x$ is composed of a succession of short movements).

But this proposal fares no better, for it is highly implausible to suppose that apparent talk of works involves talk of the production of scores. In particular, it is possible for someone to understand (1) and yet have no idea who produced the original score and when. Bachrach's suggested paraphrase seems to demand too much knowledge from speakers.

Things get messier still when we consider sentences such as

(2) Bartok's Fifth Quartet sets people's nerves on edge

and

(3) *Straight, No Chaser* is dynamic.

For one thing that is plain is that the nominalist must come up with different styles of paraphrase for (1), (2), and (3). Clearly, someone sincerely uttering (2) need not commit herself to *every* performance of the piece setting people's teeth on edge (Wolterstorff 1970: 251). The claim, rather, is more likely to be that

(10) Most performances of Bartok's Fifth Quartet set people's teeth on edge.

And when it comes to (3), it is clear that the sentence has both descriptive and normative readings, and hence must have two nominalistic paraphrases (Snoeyembos 1979: 383−4). If (3) is read as being merely a statistical claim, then it may be paraphrased as

(11) Most performances of *Straight, No Chaser* are dynamic.

On the other hand, there is a use of (3) that is intended to convey a fact about how performances *ought* to be. Someone uttering (3) in this sense gives voice to a standard that she thinks performances should live up to. Obviously, (11) fails to do justice to the normative reading of (3), a reading that will have to be paraphrased by the nominalist as something like

(12) Any *properly formed* performance of *Straight, No Chaser* is dynamic.

One thing that the discussion thus far suggests is this: even if success-ful nominalistic paraphrases *are* forthcoming, they have a disappointingly 'piecemeal quality' (Loux 1998: 68). Whilst it is plausible to think that (1)−(3) have a common logical form, the nominalist, searching for ways to analyse out our apparent reference to musical works, is forced to treat them as semantically disparate. And this suspicion that the nominalist's response is *ad hoc* is confirmed by a consideration of sentences such as

(4) Marsalis composed *In This House, On This Morning*.

The problem here is that (4) resists all of the paraphrases proposed so far: Marsalis did not compose most, all, or each properly formed performance.

Milton Snoeyembos's response to examples such as (4) is to offer a different style of paraphrase altogether, one which appeals to score-tokens rather than sound-sequence-events (1979: 384). So (4) is paraphrased as

(13) Marsalis created a score (token) of *In This House, On This Morning*,

an approach that has an obvious application to both

(5) There are more than thirty symphonies composed by Mozart

and

(6) Exactly one of Bruckner's symphonies was unfinished.

(5), presumably, will be paraphrased as

(14) There are more than thirty symphonic scores (i.e. score-tokens) created by Mozart,

whilst (6) will come out as

(15) Bruckner failed to finish exactly one of the symphonic scores (i.e. score-tokens) he created.

But besides the worry that this approach is merely an arbitrary move designed to prop up nominalism, (13)–(15) are extremely counter-intuitive paraphrases of (4)–(6) respectively. For the things that are composed by composers are surely *works of music*, not their scores. True enough, Marsalis composed the work *by* producing a score, but the score is not the thing composed: it is a *representation* of the thing composed. Furthermore, as we have noted already, some works do not have scores at all.

Perhaps alternative nominalist paraphrases of (4)–(6) are available, and perhaps the nominalist can come up with other ways of explaining away the apparently relational nature of predicates of the form 'is a performance of φ'; but the piecemeal nature of the nominalist's response neither does justice to our sense that the target sentences exhibit a commonality of form, nor inspires confidence that such further paraphrase will not simply invite further counter-examples.

But this is not the end of the matter. For even if *all* our talk of musical works admitted of nominalist paraphrase, this fact would not demonstrate that such talk failed to commit us ontologically to works of music. Two things need to be stressed. First, the fact (if it is fact) that (1) may be paraphrased as (7) does not of itself indicate that it is (7), rather than (1), that reveals our ontological commitments. Given that (1) and (7) have the same meaning—that what is said in an utterance of one is the same as what is said by an utterance of the other—who is to say that (1) does not, in fact, reveal the hidden ontological commitments in (7)? Indeed, philosophers have, on occasion, argued in just this kind of way. David Lewis, for example, claims that the modal realist's case is made by the fact that we are happy to paraphrase modal sentences in such a way as to render explicit what he takes to be a hidden ontological commitment to possible worlds.[16] The moral Lewis draws is this: we should take such sentences, with their ontological commitments, at face value unless doing so leads to trouble and doing otherwise is known not to (Lewis 1973: 84).

All of which brings me on to my second point. Given that it is *prima facie* the case that (1)–(6) see us referring to, or quantifying over, musical works, we should only abandon this reading if it is shown to be unsustainable. And this certainly has not been done. Indeed, I intend to show the opposite. By the end of Chapter 5, we shall see that nothing need deter us from the natural path of treating the (apparent) names of works at face value: as names of types of sound-sequence-event. Certainly, this position has no consequence more implausible than the thesis that the things composers compose are scores, not works.

1.4 Musical Anti-Realism

An acknowledgement that works of music are repeatable, together with a recognition of the drawbacks of nominalist, set-theoretical, and property-based approaches to the categorial question, makes the type/token theory seem all the more attractive. However, the failure to find concrete, physical entities with which to identify works of music might be taken by some to indicate that we have been misguided in assuming them to be inhabitants

---

[16] 'It is uncontroversially true that things might be otherwise than they are. I believe, and so do you, that things could have been different in countless ways. But what does this mean? Ordinary language permits the paraphrase: there are many ways things could have been besides the way they actually are. On the face of it, this sentence is an existential quantification. It says that there exist many entities of a certain description, to wit "ways things could have been". I believe that things could have been different in countless ways; I believe permissible paraphrases of what I believe; taking the paraphrase at its face value, I therefore believe in the existence of entities that might be called "ways things could have been". I prefer to call them "possible worlds" ' (Lewis 1973: 84).

of the mind-independent world at all. The moral drawn by the follower of the *anti-realist* approach to the ontology of music is that such works are not fully objective denizens of the universe, but mind-dependent entities. But to my mind, this approach, too, is untenable. The remainder of this section is devoted to explaining why this is so.

Let us define *anti-realism* in the ontology of music as the doctrine that works of music are mental entities or, at least, mental constructions. Such a disjunctive definition means that the musical idealism suggested by R. G. Collingwood (1938) and, more recently, by Renée Cox (1986), as well as the constructivist view taken by David Pearce (1988), all count as anti-realist. In my view, however, no version of the view stands up to close scrutiny.

If we focus, to begin with, on the idealist thesis that musical works are to be identified with mental entities of some kind, we will note at once that it has attracted three main objections. First, in what is already emerging as something of a theme, it seems that musical works, if mental entities, would not be the kinds of things that could be heard (Levinson 1980*b*: 63). Second, and relatedly, mental entities are not, it appears, shareable (Levinson 1990*c*: 256; Pearce 1988: 105): an imagined tune before Marsalis's mind, if it is an entity at all, is a distinct entity from a remembered tune before the mind of a listener. If musical works were such mental entities, there would not be one work accessible to us all, but as many works as there were occasions on which a work was imagined, remembered, or otherwise thought about. Finally, there has tended to be a lack of clarity concerning the precise nature of the mental entities with which works of music are identified. Such entities have been claimed to be: imaginary tunes, where such things have been viewed as tunes in the composer's head (Collingwood 1988: 142); 'conceptions' (Cox: 1986: 136); as well as thoughts (Cox 1986: 136). Clearly, if an identification of musical works with mental entities is to stand a chance of convincing us, we need to know in no uncertain terms what the said mental entities are.

It is the latter problem that is the deepest source of idealism's difficulties, for, as we shall see, there is no candidate mental entity available that is suited for being identified with a work of music. For a start, it would be wildly counter-intuitive to identify *In This House, On This Morning* with a mental *event* or *state-token*. Such items, unlike works of music, are demonstrably unrepeatable. To identify the work with, for example, a datable event of Marsalis's imagining of it would be to admit that one and the same work could not be imagined, performed, or played at any other time.

It might be alleged, however, that such a criticism merely undermines a straw man. Collingwood, for one, does not identify works with mental events; he takes works to be *objects of mental acts*. A composer's work of music, he says, is 'something imagined ... [that] exists merely as a tune in his head' (1938: 142). So, according to Collingwood, it seems that imagining a tune—having a tune run through one's mind, in other words—consists in one's standing in some quasi-perceptual relation or other to a certain mental object: a real but mental tune. But immediately, it is hard to see how this position is an improvement upon the doomed attempt to identify musical works with mental state-tokens. For, once again, there is no available explanation of how a mental item before Marsalis's mind can be one and the same entity as a mental item before the mind of someone else. To simply stipulate, as Cox does, for example, that such inner objects 'exist outside the mind of any particular perceiver ... in that they exist in the minds of other perceivers' (1986: 139) is to take for granted the phenomenon that stands in need of explanation. It can only be baffling to be told that a mental tune is an entity that can pop up in more than one mind. If we are to accept the invitation to treat tunes heard by the mind's ear as entities at all, then the entity before my mind's ear would seem to have to be a thing distinct from the entity before yours. As is the case with mental pictures, if such things exist at all, I cannot have yours, and you cannot have mine. Given that this is so, and that identity is a one–one relation, it follows that *In This House, On This Morning* cannot be identified with such an item without provoking a counter-intuitive proliferation of such works.

As if this objection were not serious enough, it in fact serves to introduce a further, deeper worry. For the philosophy of mind upon which Collingwood's ontology of music is predicated—namely, that a tune's running through one's head is a process in which one stands in a quasi-perceptual relation to a real but mental tune—has been decisively refuted by both Wittgenstein (1953: §§363–97) and Gilbert Ryle (1949: ch. 8). Collingwood assumes that the fact that one is imagining, or seemingly hearing, a tune entails that one is 'hearing' a seeming-tune (where placing 'hear' in inverted commas indicates the quasi-perceptual relation believed to obtain between the subject and the mental item).[17] But this transition is no more valid here than in the perceptual case. 'The argument from hallucinations' fails because the fact that Macbeth seems to see a dagger does not entail that he 'sees' a seeming-dagger (Smith and Jones 1986: 98–9), so we should not assume that hearing a tune in one's head is being aware of a seeming-tune.

Furthermore, an ontology of mental tunes can only be mythical, given that neither the nature of such items, nor the kind of relation that subjects are supposed to bear to them, admit of explanation. The notion of an imagined tune gets its appearance of cogency via an intended analogy with heard tunes; but such an analogy cannot be made good: an imagined tune cannot resemble a heard tune because imagined tunes precisely *cannot* be heard—the 'mind's ear' is nothing like its literal counterpart. And when it comes to the question of the relation that the imagining subject is supposed to bear to one of these entities, the intended analogy between running a tune through in one's head and actually hearing it is of little use either. For any likeness between a tune's running though one's mind and hearing it is not a matter of both processes being (quasi-) perceptual. Having a tune run through one's head is in *no sense* perceptual, as is evident in the differences between the two processes. One can only hear what is there to be heard, and one can only hear a tune in situations in which others could do so; neither of these features is true of the phenomenon we call 'running a tune through in one's head'. Imagining a tune, too, unlike hearing it, is subject to the will: it is something one can be told to do (Wittgenstein 1980: §83), and one can, on occasion, *choose* to imagine a certain tune; neither thesis is true of hearing a tune. All in all, the supporter of Collingwood's position is forced to admit that imagined tunes are entities we know not what, to which we are related by a mental act about which we can say next to nothing.

What, then, *is* going on when I run through the first part of *In This House, On This Morning* in my head? In what does the likeness between imagining it and hearing it consist? Just this: that in hearing the tune with my 'mind's ear' I imagine that the tune is being played in my hearing (Ryle 1949: 242). And what this amounts to is this: not standing in some kind of

---

[17] The same assumption is made by Cox when she slides from the truism that someone may remember a work of music to the claim that 'the music of a particular work can exist *in* a perceiver's memory' (1986: 134; my italics). This latter way of putting it is not innocent, since it perpetuates the myth that the mind is a strange place in which mental objects, such as tunes, reside.

relation to ghosts of sounds, but coming up with a series of *abstentions* from producing noises that would be produced, were it to be hummed, sung, or played aloud (Ryle 1949: 255). Following a heard tune and imagining the tune are alike, not because they both involve standing in a relation to an entity (one heard, the other merely mental), but because they are both utilizations of *knowledge* of how the tune goes. Knowing the tune just consists in having such capacities (Ryle 1949: 255).

The upshot for Collingwood's account of the ontology of works of music is thus clear. True enough, his account has difficulty in explaining how musical works could be public and shareable. But the deeper objection is simpler and utterly conclusive: there exist no items of the kind with which he seeks to identify works of music.

This being so, it might be appealing for a would-be idealist to follow Cox in identifying works of music with 'conceptions (of tones, silences and relationships)' (1986: 136) or, as she sometimes puts it, 'musical thoughts' (1986: 138). But this move is no more convincing than that considered previously. If such conceptions and thoughts are *acts of thinking*, then they are datable mental events; and we have already rejected the idea that musical works can be identified with these. So what else could 'thoughts' be? Well, they could be construed as the objects of acts of thinking: propositions. But the problem here is that propositions have tended to be regarded as necessarily existent, mind-independent, and language-independent entities (Loux 1998: 137). On such a view, clearly, thoughts are not mental entities at all, and so can be of no use to the musical idealist. Other philosophers, by contrast, have denied that thoughts are anything other than mental events, rejecting the idea that propositional attitudes relate thinkers to propositions (Prior 1963). Either way, the ontology of mind resolutely refuses to offer up entities suitable for the musical idealist's project.

So what of the more sophisticated anti-realist suggestion that musical works are not mental items, but mental *constructions*? According to Pearce (1988), we should exploit a potential analogy between the ontology of music and constructivism in the philosophy of mathematics. Mathematical objects, so the constructivist's story goes, are brought into being by our mathematical practices. Nonetheless, once created, they have objective, mind-independent properties. If musical works were like this, we would have a neat way of accepting that Marsalis created *In This House, On This Morning* whilst denying that the work inhabits a private mental realm.

Works would be human creations, yet mind–independent entities. As Pearce himself puts it,

A musical work is a (certain kind of) mental construction, created by the activity of the composer. Once created, however, the work has an 'objective' character in that it can be referred to, studied, performed and heard *as* a certain work with such-and-such characteristics. (Pearce 1988: 107; emphasis original)

But such a view remains a mere promissory note unless the ontological nature of such mental constructions is fully explained and defended; and it is telling that precisely this task has not even been attempted by Pearce. We have been told what Pearce thinks musical works might be *like* (viz. numbers-as-construed-by-the-intuitionist), but a simile is not a theory. Until we are told a little more, of a positive nature, about the properties had by such items, the claim that they are created and shareable can only be wish-fulfilment. Types form a long-established ontological category; musical-works-according-to-Pearce do not.

Besides facing this problem, there are two other respects in which Pearce's conception falls short when compared with the type/token theory. First, when it comes to the question of musical works' audibility, Pearce is no better off than Collingwood. The analogy between musical works and numbers breaks down because numbers, unlike works of music, cannot be heard. Pearce nowhere explains how an item characterized purely in terms of an analogy with mathematical objects can be listened to. Given what has been said already, it is plain that the type/token theorist is substantially better off when it comes to satisfying our intuitions concerning the perceptibility of musical works.

Second, Pearce offers no explanation of musical works' repeatability: that is, the one–many relation that holds between works of music and their occurrences. According to the type/token theory, of course, a sound-sequence-event's being an occurrence of *In This House, On This Morning* is a matter of the former being one of the latter's tokens: work and performance instantiate the same relation that obtains between words and their instances and between The Polar Bear (i.e. the type) and polar bears. This relation is familiar and explicable: a token *t* is a token of a type *K* just in case it meets the condition or conditions that something must meet to be a *k*. All Pearce can say, by contrast, is that '*a musical work is explicitly presented by a performance of it*' (1988: 108; emphasis original). This, however, is to label, rather than explain, the phenomenon of a work's repeatability. The type/token theorist suggests that a work's repeatability consists in its being a type whose tokens are sound-sequence-occurrences. Pearce offers no equivalent explanation.

1.5 The Type/Token Theory Elaborated

Our brief survey of some of the type/token theory's rivals has served to reinforce its position as the face-value theory in the ontology of music. None of the other theories discussed so far manages simultaneously to explain satisfactorily the nature of a musical work's repeatability whilst doing justice to the everyday fact that we can listen to (the whole of) such works. This is not to deny that there are other available positions in metaphysical space: the conception of works of music as continuants and the view of such works as compositional actions will be discussed in detail in Chapters 6 and 7 respectively. Nonetheless, a provisional moral can be drawn at this stage: we have yet to come across an objection or an alternative theory that would justify our dispensing with our *prima facie* theory. This being so, we can now go on to develop the type/token theory in more detail, refining and elaborating the claim that works of music are types of sound-event. In particular, it is time to consider in greater depth the nature of the types that are musical works.

In order to see one way in which a properly formulated version of the type/token theory must be developed, it is only necessary to consider the following problem: how is it possible for a performance of a work of music to be anything other than properly formed? How, in other words, can we explain the fact that an amateurish performance can nonetheless count as a performance (albeit flawed) of a work? To be sure, this is a problem that Richard Wollheim—one of the originators of the type/token theory—does not have the resources to solve. For Wollheim holds that some of a work's properties are *definitive* of it:[18] that is, that there are some properties that must be had by any of its token performances and playings (1968: 93). What would such definitive properties be? Presumably, at the very least, they would pertain to the pitches and durations of notes as specified by the work's score. This, however, merely yields the conclusion that any

---

[18] This way of putting it is due to Predelli (1995: 340). Much of my discussion is owed to his penetrating and pellucid article.

performance lacking one of these properties cannot count as a performance of the work in question: in other words, that a work cannot have clumsy or amateurish performances. My committing a single mistake in a performance of 'Never No Lament'—say, playing a G instead of a D, or holding the D for a beat too long—would mean that my performance failed to count as a performance of the piece at all. The obvious moral to draw from all this is: so much the worse for Wollheim's theory. Faulty, amateurish, and—dare one say it—incompetent performances of works are a (regrettable) fact of life; we do not regard them as necessarily failing even to count as performances of the works intended by their technically limited performers.

Of course, the supporter of Wollheim's position could, at this point, just decide to bite the bullet. But I take it that the consequence just elucidated is too outlandish to be plausible. It is akin to a position according to which, strictly speaking, words cannot be misspelt since an incorrectly spelt inscription is not a genuine token of the word in question at all. Surely, we want to say, there can be both incorrect spellings of words and incorrect performances of works of music; the issue can only be whether the type/token theorist can account for this phenomenon.

As it happens, she can. For, following Wolterstorff (1980: 54–8), we may say that works of music are *norm-types*: types that admit of both properly *and* improperly formed tokens.[19] Let us further say that a property F is *normative within* a type K just in case (i) K is a norm-type; and (ii) it is impossible for there to be something that is a properly formed token of K and which lacks F (Wolterstorff 1980: 58). Two things follow from our recognition of the existence of norm-types. First, the schematic account of the individuation of types suggested in §1.2 requires a harmless piece of emendation: the identity of a type is determined by the condition something must meet in order to be one of its tokens, *or—if the type is a norm-type—to be a correctly formed token.* Second, and crucially, if musical works are norm-types, we can explain how works of music, *qua* types, can have incorrect performances in the following way: just as long as the performance does not lack *too many* of the properties normative to the work, it nonetheless counts as a genuine, albeit incorrect, performance. Of course, the question of *how many* normative properties is *too many* does not have a precise answer, and

---

[19] Wolterstorff uses 'kind' where I use 'type', but he accepts that either term is acceptable (1980: 194).

is only capable of elucidation in the light of the discussion of examples. I assume, for instance, that my tenuous grasp of the score of 'Never No Lament' does not automatically disqualify my performances from counting as performances of the piece. An *unrecognizable* performance, on the other hand, is another matter entirely.

At this point, however, a sceptic may have a couple of worries: namely, that talk of a performance's being 'properly formed' implies that there is *just one* correct way of performing a work (a conclusion that is manifestly false); and that the introduction of norm-types is nothing but a purpose-built, *ad hoc* device for propping up the type/token theory. Happily, both fears are groundless. To ease the first worry, we need only appreciate that the condition that a sound-event must meet to be a properly formed token of a work may, in fact, be quite permissive and, as a result, allow a good deal of room for the performer to stamp her performance with her own interpretation. So, for example, a work's score may be unspecific in some of its demands (as was J. S. Bach's *The Art of Fugue* on the piece's instrumentation); or else the demands may be vague (e.g. if scores make use of tempo-words, words concerning articulation, and words such as 'cantabile'). Musical works, *qua* types of sound-event, leave gaps for the performer's interpretation, and hence do not prescribe exactly one correct way of performing them.

When it comes to the concern that norm-types may be *ad hoc* entities, it need only be pointed out that norm-types are common-or-garden entities. True enough, many types do not have a normative element: the type Red Thing, for example, does not have improperly formed tokens. But equally, natural kinds *are* norm-types. There can certainly be improperly formed tokens of The Domestic Dog (*Canis familiaris*): albino dogs and dogs missing an ear or a leg are nevertheless tokens of the type. And it is a truism that, just as long as an inscription is sufficiently close to being correctly formed, it counts as an inscription of a certain word, albeit one of which its author should not feel particularly proud. The moral is this: in claiming works of music to be norm-types, we are not guilty of plucking a notion out of thin air. Norm-types are part of the fabric of the universe.

Musical works are thus norm-types whose tokens are sound-sequence-events. For such a sound-sequence-event to be a properly formed token of a certain work, it must sound a certain way: it must have all of the properties

normative within the type.[20] And for it to count as a token of the work
at all, it should have a sufficient number of those normative properties.
But is *any* sound-sequence-event that possesses a sufficient number of the
properties normative for a work *W* a genuine token of it? Or, alternatively,
in order to count as a token of *W*, must the token also have been *produced*
in a certain kind of way? Specifically, should we hold that only *performances*
can be tokens of works, that a work's tokens must be performances *or*
playings, or that a work can have tokens that are *neither* performances nor
playings? Up to now, I have been assuming that the least restrictive of
these accounts is correct: I have tended to describe a work's tokens as
'sound-sequence-events' rather than as 'performances' or 'performances or
playings'. I shall end this section by briefly explaining this decision.

The most restrictive account of the nature of a musical work's tokens—
the view of such works as *performance*-types—is, to my mind, needlessly
narrow. It would be perverse to deny that a sound-sequence-event produced by playing a compact disc could be a genuine token of *In This House,*
On This Morning. As Wolterstorff explains (1980: 85), in such a situation
we would describe ourselves as hearing the work in the playing, and this
would seem to indicate that the playing is a genuine token of the work.
At this point, however, Wolterstorff resists any temptation to become any
more permissive on the question, taking the preferred position to be that
only performances and playings can be tokens of works, largely as a result
of considering a thought-experiment such as the following.

Suppose, by some gigantic fluke, a sound-sequence were produced
naturally (perhaps by the wind rattling through an empty house) that
was recognizable as a note-for-note facsimile of the sounds indicated by
Marsalis's score for *In This House, On This Morning*.[21] Would not this also
count as an instance of the work? To my mind, there is no harm in
treating such a pattern of sounds as a genuine token of *In This House, On*
This Morning. First, and as Wolterstorff himself argued when considering
the question of whether a work's tokens may include playings as well as
performances, it would seem to be true that the work could be heard in
the concrete sound-pattern, even though this pattern is produced without
the intervention of human actions; once more, there seems little *prima facie*

---

[20] Here I assume the truth of timbral sonicism: that the only properties normative within works of
music are acoustic ones. This claim will be defended in Chs. 8 and 9.

[21] This example is a variation on that discussed by Wolterstorff (1980: 84–8).

reason for denying its status as a genuine token of a piece. Second, we shall see in Chapter 8 that *performance-means properties*—that is, properties concerning how sounds are produced—are not normative within works. All that matters for whether a sound-sequence-event is a properly formed token of a work is how that token sounds. Given that this is so, there is no reason to expect that only sound-sequences produced on musical instruments, or produced by playing recordings of such sound-sequences, can be genuine work-tokens. If what makes a sound-sequence-event a properly formed token of a work has nothing to do with how its constituent sounds are produced, then the idea that a sound-sequence must be a playing or a performance takes on a distinctly gratuitous air.

Nonetheless, Wolterstorff is correct to point out that the position I am recommending has a consequence that might seem counter-intuitive. For if we allow that a work can have tokens that are neither performances nor playings, then it follows that it is possible for a work of music to be tokened before it has been composed (Wolterstorff 1980: 87). By contrast, if we restrict a work's possible tokens to performances and playings, no such consequence ensues. For someone to perform W, she must intend to do so, and a playing of W is a reproduction of sounds that were produced with that intention; so it follows that no performance or playing of W can take place before the work was composed and thereby made available to performers.

Ultimately, though, I doubt whether such considerations should sway a type/token theorist. For, as will swiftly become apparent in Chapter 3, types, of their very nature, are eternally existent entities. Consequently, even someone who takes musical works to be types of performance or of playing has to admit that such works *exist* before they are composed. Now, as we shall see in Chapter 5, this doctrine of musical Platonism turns out to be by no means as implausible as one might fear. But, for now, we need only accept this: that once it is agreed that works are mind-independent to the extent that they pre-exist their composition, it adds nothing *additionally* counter-intuitive to acknowledge that they may be tokened before they are composed (i.e. discovered). Indeed, if *In This House, On This Morning* is sufficiently mind-independent to have existed before Marsalis composed it, it is only natural to think that it could have had instances (of the kind envisaged in our thought-experiment) prior to its composition.

Having decided that a work's possible tokens are not simply limited to performances and playings, we are led towards the following account

of what is required for a sound-sequence-event to be a token of a work
W. In keeping with the fact that musical works are norm-types, for a
sound-sequence-event to be a token of W, it must have a sufficient
number of the properties normative within the type that is W. This is
a reflection of the fact that we identify W, not with the type Sound-
Sequence-Event Produced by Performing or Playing W, but with the type
Sound-Sequence-Event that is Properly Formed just in case it has Each
Property that is Normative Within W.

1.6 Conclusion

According to our refined type/token theory, a work of music is a norm-
type whose tokens are sound-sequence-events. As such, it is the natural
resting-place for a would-be ontologist of music. In stark contrast to those
of its competitors we have examined thus far, the type/token theory
explains the nature of musical works' repeatability in familiar terms, and
can allow for the fact that works of music can be listened to in their
entirety. Having said this, the claim that musical works are types of any
kind will remain schematic as long as the ontological nature of types
remains unexplained. So it is for this reason that the next two chapters
are devoted to elaborating and defending a type ontology. By the end of
Chapter 3, we shall have uncovered the type/token theory's substantial
commitments. Specifically, musical works, *qua* types, will be revealed as
abstract, fixed, unchanging, and eternally existent entities. As we shall see
in Chapters 4 and 5, this makes the identification of musical works with
types of sound-event interesting, controversial, but, for all that, defensible.

2

Types I: Abstract,
Unstructured, Unchanging

2.1 Introduction

We saw in the previous chapter that the type/token theory is the *prima facie* correct answer to the categorial question. Construing such works as types of sound-sequence-event enables us to explain the nature of their repeatability, whilst doing justice to the fact that they are entities in their own right that have their occurrences inessentially. So far, so good. But, of course, assigning musical works to an ontological category can only explain their ontological nature if this category is itself well understood. So it is for this reason that this chapter and the next are devoted to laying out an ontology of types.

Abstracting from the musical case, we shall see that types possess a fascinating combination of features. In the present chapter, types will be revealed as being abstract (i.e. not located in space), unstructured (i.e. without parts), and both modally and temporally inflexible (i.e. items that possess their intrinsic properties necessarily, and which are incapable of change in these properties through time). In Chapter 3, meanwhile, we shall see that types, by their very nature, are eternally existent entities: items that exist at all times. Needless to say, these results place a new complexion upon the type/token theory. Works of music, *qua* types, turn out to be structureless, fixed, unchanging, eternal entities. But not to worry. Chapters 4 and 5 will point out that these consequences turn out to be a very small price to pay for a theory that so nicely explains what it is for a musical work to be capable of multiple instantiation.

2.2 Types Introduced and Nominalism Repelled

Types, though sometimes regarded as 'the Cinderella of ontology',[1] are items to which we find ourselves ontologically committed in our everyday thought and discourse. We talk of types or kinds of things, these things being instances of the type or kind (Wolterstorff 1970: 235–6); and such types may be classed as either natural kinds (such as The Polar Bear, The Daffodil, and The Nightingale's Song) or non-natural kinds (such as the word 'refrigerator', The Union Jack, The Ford Thunderbird, and The Square Cut[2]). Typically, although not always, we refer to types using the institutional 'the', examples of such reference occurring in sentences such as the following:

(16) The Polar Bear is a mammal.
(17) The Ford Thunderbird is a fine car.
(18) The Polar Bear has four legs.
(19) The Daffodil is the Welsh national flower.
(20) The word 'refrigerator' occurs on this page.

Equally, and as we noted in §1.2, we may also refer demonstratively to types by means of deferred ostension. A teacher might point at an inscription of 'refrigerator' on a blackboard, for example, and say '*That* is the word you failed to spell correctly'. In such an example, the teacher uses the demonstrative, 'that', to refer to the word-*type*; but her use of the demonstrative succeeds in picking out this type by virtue of one of its tokens being present before her in space. Finally, we regularly quantify over types in remarks such as

(21) There are many different types of flower found in Wales

and

(22) There are exactly two types of entity in the early Wittgenstein's ontology: facts and things.

All in all, the truth of sentences such as (16)–(22), together with our demonstrative reference to types, indicates that types are genuine denizens of the universe.

---

[1] This phrase is Eddy Zemach's (1970: 239). It is not one with which he agrees.
[2] The Square Cut is a cricketing batting stroke.

That types should be regarded in this way is, of course, a thesis upon which the type/token theory is predicated. The previous chapter's arguments for the type/token theory would constitute, at best, a pyrrhic victory if there turned out to be conclusive reasons for denying types a place in our ontology. Nominalists, of course, take themselves to have just such reasons—reasons presumed to justify the project of paraphrasing away all apparent ontological commitment to such entities—but in the light of the discussion of §1.3, we should view such a project with a sceptical eye. For one thing, even though a nominalist may happily paraphrase (16)–(18) as

(16*) All polar bears are mammals,
(17*) Most Ford Thunderbirds are fine cars,

and

(18*) All properly formed polar bears have four legs

respectively, the piecemeal quality of (16*)–(18*) gives us little reason to expect there to be acceptable nominalistic paraphrases of sentences that evidently resist the three styles of paraphrase employed by the nominalist hitherto. Consider, for example, (19) and (20). To say that The Daffodil is the national flower of Wales is not to say that all, most, or even properly formed daffodils are the national flowers of Wales. The claim being made seems irreducibly to concern a *type* of flower. And the same goes for (20). It may be true that the word 'refrigerator' occurs on a certain page, but the same cannot be true either of all of its tokens, most of its tokens, or any properly formed token.

This is not to say that I wish to commit myself to the thesis that no nominalist paraphrase of (19) or (20) is possible. My point is that the *ad hoc* nature of the nominalist's enterprise offers scant reason to suppose that such successful paraphrases will be forthcoming, and, even if such paraphrases could be found, no grounds for supposing that the realist could not come up with further recalcitrant sentences. Furthermore, as we saw in §1.3, even if such a project of nominalist paraphrase could be completed, it does not follow that the disputed entities do not, in fact, exist. A realist about types—someone who takes there to exist such items—may just as well take (16) to reveal the hidden ontological commitments in (16*). Naturally, *if* there were compelling reasons for taking types to be unfit to enter our ontology, then we would thereby have a reason to regard (16*) as more basic than (16), and thereby revelatory of (16)'s true ontological commitments; but, as we shall see now, no such compelling motivations exist.

I take it that there are two reasons (besides a mere prejudice against *abstracta*) why a nominalist may seek to rid our ontology of types. First, she may think that they are 'creatures of darkness':[3] that is, intensional entities, which have an inherently mysterious ontological nature. Second, she may reject an ontology of types because she believes their identity conditions to be obscure.[4] However, as we shall now see, these objections cut little ice.

Are types really so mysterious? No, and in order to show this, we may remind ourselves of the way in which they differ from sets. Sets, we agreed in §1.2, are constructions out of their instances. From this, two things follow. First, sets have their members (or lack of them) essentially. Sets cannot gain or lose members: a set with different members is a different set. Second, sets are extensional entities. There cannot be two distinct sets that have the same members: set ω = set ξ just in case ω and ξ have the same membership.

Types, unlike sets, are not constructions out of their members.[5] On the contrary, we saw in §§1.2 and 1.5 that the identity of a type is dependent upon the *condition* that something must meet in order to be one of its tokens (or, if the type is a norm-type, by the condition something must meet to be a correctly formed token). As a result, the identity of a type, unlike that of a set, is independent of the existence of any of its instances, and this means that the two features distinctive of sets do not hold of types. First, types do not have their instances essentially: what makes the type K *that* type is that it lays down a certain condition for something to be one of its (properly formed) tokens; that it happens to have the tokens it has is something which has nothing whatsoever to do with its individuation. The Polar Bear, by contrast with the set of polar bears, is something that gains and loses instances. Whilst The Polar Bear's numbers are declining, this truth about the type has no analogue when it comes to the corresponding set. Second, since a type is individuated by the condition an entity must meet to be one of its (properly formed) tokens, it follows that types—unlike sets—are intensional objects. There cannot be two sets that have exactly the same members, but there *can* be two distinct types that have the same

---

[3] This phrase is, famously, Quine's (1955: 188). He applies this epithet to intensions, but I assume that he regards it as applying to intensional entities generally.

[4] This is Quine's complaint about an ontology of possibilia (1948: 4).

[5] *Pace* Haack (1978: 75), and Hugly and Sayward (1981: 184–6).

tokens: as long as the condition something must meet to be a (properly formed) token of K is distinct from the condition that something must meet to be a token of K^*, K and K^* are distinct, even if they share exactly the same tokens.[6]

Types, then, do not share what Quine calls 'the limpid extensionality' of sets (1958: 21), but they are none the worse for that. It is fair to say that the suggested schematic identity conditions for types presuppose that we can, in fact, distinguish between the various conditions that tokens may or may not meet. It is also fair to point out that these conditions are nothing other than *properties*: a condition that something must meet to be a (properly formed) token of a type is, after all, a property or set of properties that it must have. Naturally, at this point, Quineans will smell a rat. For Quine has famously argued that it is impossible to provide non-circular identity conditions for properties (1960: 209); hence, a Quinean will charge the supporter of types with being similarly unable to do the same for his chosen entities.

Well, this may be so, but—in common with most philosophers hostile to nominalism—I deny that a category of entity should *only* be admitted into our ontology once non-circular identity conditions have been supplied. Although puzzle-cases might emerge, our notion of a property is *clear enough* to be usable, and, as a result, so is our notion of a type. Furthermore, although sets admit of the kind of identity conditions beloved by Quine, many other categories do not do so, including the paradigmatic category of *material objects*. As Michael Loux points out (1998: 56), one might be tempted by the idea that non-circular identity conditions for material objects could be formulated by making reference to such objects' spatio-temporal location; except that the identity of such places and times can, it seems, only be grasped in terms of the material objects located at them. What this demonstrates, I contend, is that the mere fact that non-circular identity conditions cannot be provided for items of a given ontological category does not entail that we should not admit such items into our ontology. The slogan 'No entity without identity' (Quine 1958: 23) is not one that we should accept.[7]

---

[6] I take it that the types Renate Creature and Cordate Creature constitute an example of two distinct types with the same tokens.

[7] As we shall see in Chs. 8 and 9, I hold that informative identity conditions *can* be provided for works of music. What I deny is that the inclusion of such works in our ontology is conditional upon such identity conditions being available.

All in all, nominalists have not presented us with a convincing reason why we should embark upon the project of paraphrase; and, in any case, it is a mistake to suppose that coming up with such paraphrases demonstrates that the appearance of ontological commitment to types is illusory. The moral that should be drawn is that we should take our apparent commitment to types at face value, even when—as in the case of (16), (17), and (18)—paraphrases acceptable to the nominalist are unproblematically available.

2.3 Types as *Abstracta*

Types, then, are *bona fide* denizens of our ontology. To identify works of music with types of sound-event is to assign such works to a well-formed ontological category. So let us return to the question that is the concern of this chapter and the next: what kind of thing is a type? Certain distinguishing features of types have already come into view in the context of my initial characterization of the type/token theory in the previous chapter. A type, unlike a set, is an intensional entity whose identity is determined by the condition that something must meet to be one of its tokens (or, if the type is a norm-type, by the condition that something must meet to be a properly formed token). Such conditions are properties, of course, but it is crucial that types be distinguished from properties. As we noted in §1.2, types, by contrast with properties, are things in their own right rather than features of things: a fact revealed by type-names, such as 'The Union Jack' and 'The Ford Thunderbird', being neither predicates nor names systematically related to such predicates. Additionally, types, but not properties, are such that they may be truly ascribed those predicates truly ascribable to their tokens by virtue of these tokens being tokens of the type. The predicate 'is rectangular' is true of The Union Jack in addition to being true of its tokens, but this predicate is not true of the property of being rectangular.

There is, however, much more that can be said about the nature of types besides this. Let us continue with our definition of an *abstract* entity as an entity that is not located in space. One pressing question is whether types are abstract or concrete. In this section I shall defend the standard view of types as *abstracta* against the animadversions of Eddy Zemach (1970, 1989).

At first blush, it would seem to be something of a platitude to regard types as abstract objects. Consider words. The result of uttering or writing down a word—a word-*token*—has a spatial location, but the thing which such an utterance or inscription is of—the word-*type*—is something which is not located anywhere. Likewise, a certain polar bear may be found in London Zoo, but someone who set off to find The Polar Bear (as opposed to any of its tokens) would surely be regarded as having committed a category mistake. There are, however, two alternatives to construing types as abstract entities. One may take types to be concrete, but *scattered*, objects, thinking of a type's tokens as its spatial parts. Or else one may follow Zemach in taking types to be concrete things that are continuants in space (1970: 232): things which, though concrete, have no spatial parts (1970: 239), and which are thus wholly present in space wherever their tokens are to be found (1970: 245). I shall now explain why I take both of these views to be mistaken.

The drawback with the conception of types as scattered objects lies in its counter-intuitiveness. It sounds downright odd to say that part of The Polar Bear is in London Zoo. The animal in the zoo is not *part* of The Polar Bear, though it is, of course, a token of it. Furthermore, to focus for a moment on the thesis that I presently wish to defend—namely, the type/token theory in the ontology of music—it is equally odd to think of a work of music, *qua* type, as a scattered object comprising its spatially scattered performances as parts. Zemach is quite correct in regarding a consequence of this view—that an audience cannot hear a whole work in performance—as its *reductio ad absurdum*:

> If Jones tells me that he heard Beethoven's *Missa Solemnis* last night, he would probably be very insulted if I responded, 'You mean, of course, that you heard a *part* of the *Missa*—you could not have heard it all!' He would rightly protest that he did hear the whole *Missa* indeed (i.e., he did not leave in the middle). (Zemach 1970: 243)

The point here is that it makes little sense to think of types as having spatial parts. An important question, though, is what follows from this. According to the orthodox view that I wish to defend, what follows is that types are not located in space at all, the thought being that an entity without spatial parts cannot be said to be *in* space. This thought, together with a commitment to 'the axiom of localization' (Grossmann 1992: 13)—the thesis that no entity whatsoever can be wholly present at different places at once—seems to rule out the possibility of treating types as concrete, once it is acknowledged that they lack spatial parts.

In Zemach's view, however, the fact that types have no spatial parts indicates, not that they have no spatial location, but that they constitute a (neglected) ontological category: namely, that of repeatable entities that are continuous in space (1970: 239)—that is, that lack spatial parts (1970: 232)—yet which are concrete. According to Zemach, The Polar Bear, *qua* concrete entity, is present wherever there exists a token polar bear. But since The Polar Bear has no spatial parts, it cannot be merely present *in part* wherever there exists a token polar bear; the type can only be *wholly* present wherever it is tokened. As he himself puts it,

> The [P]olar [B]ear has four legs, is white, and weighs about 500 pounds. Had '[T]he [P]olar [B]ear' denoted a property, an abstract entity, or a set, all these statements were wildly false; no property has four legs, no abstract entity is white, and no set weighs 500 pounds. 'The [P]olar [B]ear' does not denote the mereological sum of all polar bears either, for that huge mass of flesh weighs considerably more than 500 pounds and has thousands of legs. The [P]olar [B]ear is therefore a concrete object, as is evidenced by the above properties it has, yet it is also repeatable; you can see *it* in its natural habitat or in a zoo. (Zemach 1989: 69)

By calling The Polar Bear 'repeatable' here, Zemach means that 'it, the whole thing *recurs*' in space (1989: 69). So, in other words, Zemach takes The Polar Bear to be a concrete entity which has no spatial parts and to which, as a result, the axiom of localization does not apply. But to my mind, such an account of the nature of types is poorly motivated and, ultimately, untenable.

Let us first of all consider the question of Zemach's motivation. In the extract above his main argument is that types must be concrete because they have properties that only concrete entities could have. The Polar Bear, for example, would be weightless were it an abstract entity, whilst The Common Elm, were it not a material object, would not be green (Zemach 1970: 240). But such arguments are powerless against a moderately sophisticated version of the orthodox view. Zemach claims that

(18) The Polar Bear has four legs

can only be true, if The Polar Bear is concrete. But if the predicate 'has four legs' means what it standardly means, then (18) cannot be true, even if the type is construed along the lines suggested by Zemach. For if The

Polar Bear is a continuant in space—if, that is, it has no spatial parts—then how can it have legs? Legs are spatial parts and have spatial parts themselves. If the problem is that of explaining how types can share properties with ordinary material things, it is all too clear that Zemach's account of types provides no solution to it.

As a result of considering examples such as these, it soon becomes apparent that much of our everyday talk about types stands in need of philosophical explication. As I mentioned in §2.2, the type-theorist is perfectly entitled to treat claims such as (16)–(22) at face value, as containing a referring expression that denotes a type or as involving quantification over types. But, once the abstract nature of types is accepted and internalized, some of the claims made about types take on a paradoxical appearance. Consider, for example,

(16) The Polar Bear is a mammal,
(17) The Ford Thunderbird is a fine car,

or, for that matter, (18). Can an abstract entity *really* feed its own young, be a car, or have four legs? Examples such as these demonstrate that it can only be mistaken to suppose that types routinely share the properties instantiated by their tokens. Richard Wollheim, for one, fails to see this, claiming that a raft of properties are transmitted from a type's tokens to the type itself: namely, 'all and only those properties that a token of a certain type has necessarily, i.e., that it has in virtue of being a token of that type' (1968: 93). 'The Union Jack', he says, 'is coloured and rectangular, properties which all its tokens have necessarily' (1968: 93). But this remark sees Wollheim failing to appreciate the consequences of his own conception of types as abstract entities (1968: 98). For if The Union Jack is an abstract entity, and if 'coloured' and 'rectangular' express the same properties they do when ascribed to tokens, it cannot be true that The Union Jack is coloured and rectangular. Types cannot have physical properties such as these.

We thus have a paradox. Claims such as (16), (17), and (18) would seem to be true, but, given the fact that types are abstract, it is difficult to see how they could be anything other than false. One way in which a type-theorist could respond to this puzzle would be to take the bull by the horns and argue that such sentences are, indeed, false. The idea would be that the sentences in question, though themselves false, are commonly used by us to convey the truths expressed by

(16*) All polar bears are mammals,

(17*) Most Ford Thunderbirds are fine cars,

and

(18*) All properly formed polar bears have four legs

respectively. The suggestion would be that we commonly utter, for example, (16)—failing to pick up on its falsehood—but that what we are really interested in getting across is the truth of (16*).

This, though, strikes me as being rather implausible. When we say that The Polar Bear is a mammal and has four legs, we surely utter a truth of some kind or other (Wolterstorff 1970: 240). What we have said is of a different order entirely from a claim that The Polar Bear is an invertebrate, or that it has a hundred legs; and the most obvious way of explaining this difference is to say that the former two claims are true, the latter two false. Consequently, given our justified unwillingness to give up the thought that the logical forms of (16), (17), (18), and the rest are as they appear, the only way of solving the puzzle is to accept what Wolterstorff terms the doctrine of 'analogical predication'(1980: 58–62). Since (16), (17), and (18) are each composed of a referring expression (referring to a type) and a predicate, and since (16), (17), and (18) are literally true, it follows that we must accept that the predicates in these sentences express different properties from the properties they express when they are applied to a concrete token. It is not that types and their tokens can share the same *properties*, but that they can share the same *predicates*: predicates that, when applied to types, express properties that are *systematically related* to the properties expressed by these predicates when applied to their tokens.

To elaborate, (16), (17), and (18) are true in the same circumstances as (16*), (17*), and (18*) respectively; and the reason why this is so is that the senses of the predicates in the former sentences are supplied by the respective paraphrases. In (16), 'is a mammal' expresses the property of *being such that something cannot be a token of it unless it is a mammal*; in (17), 'is a fine car' expresses the property of *being such that most of its tokens are/will be fine cars*;[8] and in (18), 'has four legs' expresses the property of *being such*

---

[8] The addition of 'will be' here allows for it to be true—as it surely can be—that the Ford Thunderbird was a fine car in the period of time after it was designed but before any of its tokens were manufactured.

that something cannot be a properly formed token of it unless it has four legs.[9] The beauty of this proposal is that it preserves our intuition that (16)–(22) are true, but in such a way that we need not follow the nominalist in denying that genuine reference to a type, or quantification over types, has taken place.[10] Equally, it captures the fact that we talk about a type *by virtue of* talking about what it would be for something to be one of its tokens, without having us deny that we are really referring to a type at all.

Where does this leave Zemach's alternative conception of types as concrete entities lacking spatial parts? Crucially, the presumed motivation for Zemach's account has been undercut. As we saw earlier, Zemach himself cannot explain the truth of a claim such as

(18) The Polar Bear has four legs,

since, if—as he assumes—the predicate has its usual meaning, only things with spatial parts can satisfy it. Only things bound, not continuous, in space—that is, things with spatial parts—can have legs. Furthermore, we have just noted that the orthodox view of types—once allied to the doctrine of analogical predication—*can* explain how (18) and the like come to be literally true. This semantic fact is both insusceptible to the explanation that Zemach offers and capable of being explained by the orthodox conception of types that he rejects.

But besides being poorly motivated, Zemach's conception of types as *concreta* lacking spatial parts is deeply problematic in itself. First of all, and as we have noted already, there is something deeply counter-intuitive about the idea that types can be concrete entities, literally possessing properties such as *being located in London Zoo, having four legs*, and *weighing 500 pounds*, yet lack spatial parts. For such properties can be possessed only by things that *occupy* space, and this means that such things must be divisible in space. True enough, at this point Zemach could appeal to the self-same doctrine of analogical predication that we introduced a moment ago in order to explain how it can be true that The Polar Bear can lack spatial parts and yet have four legs and weigh 500 pounds. But such a move would thereby undercut the reason for holding his view in the first place. Zemach's conception of types gains what appeal it has by purporting to explain how a type can

[9] In other words, The Polar Bear, like a work of music, is a *norm-type*.

[10] See Wolterstorff 1980: 61, for such an account of analogical predication for works of music and their tokens. Such an account will be argued for in §4.2.

genuinely be four-legged, 500 pounds in weight, and occupy a place in London Zoo. There would be little point in clinging on to this conception if it turned out that it could not allow for types to have such properties.

Equally problematic is Zemach's jettisoning of the axiom of localization. We can, of course, make sense of the idea of a *scattered object*: something whose *parts* are—at a given time—at far-flung points in the universe. But, as Zemach is at pains to point out, this is not his view (1989: 68). To repeat, his claim is not that parts of types such as The Polar Bear are scattered all over the world, but that these types are located—as a whole—in many places at once. And it is just this that is so difficult to accept. How can (the whole of) *one and the same thing* be in New York and London at the same time? As Alex Oliver has remarked (1996: 26–7), it is precisely its denial of the axiom of localization that causes one to question whether an Aristotelian conception of universals is really preferable to the Platonic conception.

Zemach may reply to this by claiming that the localization axiom applies only to ordinary material things, not to types; and he may go on the offensive by alleging that the relationship between a concrete token and a supposedly abstract type can only be mysterious and mystificatory. But to this we can say two things. First, the mere fact that a type may be abstract, yet its instances be concrete, does not mean that the relation obtaining between the type and its instances is obscure. Enough has been said about how a type binds together its tokens—according to whether they meet a certain condition for being a (properly formed) token of that type—to deflect the charge of obscurity. Second, an abandonment of the axiom of localization should be undertaken only *after* the view of types as abstract entities has been demonstrated to be untenable. And we have just seen that the problem that Zemach takes simultaneously to disable the traditional view and to invite his alternative approach does no such thing. If musical works are types, then they are abstract all right.

2.4 Types as Unstructured Entities

If types are abstract—if they have no spatial location—then they have no spatial parts. Neither do types have temporal parts: they are not perduring entities like events or four-dimensional 'worms'.[11] Fairly obviously, types

---

[11] See Sider 2001 for a detailed discussion of four-dimensionalism.

whose tokens are entities lacking temporal parts do not themselves have temporal parts: if polar bears endure, rather than perdure, then we are under no pressure whatsoever to suppose that The Polar Bear is made up of temporal stages. But, equally, types whose tokens are perduring entities should not themselves be viewed as perdurants. Consider The Tango, for instance. This is a type whose tokens are datable, locatable performances. The Tango that I performed yesterday with my partner lasted about three minutes, and was divisible into temporal parts. (Its second half was a bit of a mess.) But The Tango itself has no temporal parts. The type, though existent in time (indeed, as we shall see in Chapter 3, existent at all times), is not itself extended in time; only its tokens are. So it makes no sense to say that the type has temporal parts. If we wish to say that event-types have parts at all (which, as we shall see, I regard as a mistake), we can only say that these parts exist simultaneously.[12]

What I want to argue now is that we should not regard types as being structured in any way. In arguing for this thesis, my first claim is that there is simply no necessity to view types as structured entities. Let us start with the thought that a type K is a way of binding together tokens. The question is: how, exactly, does a type do this? Returning to our starting-point in §2.2 will help. The identity of type K, we have said, is determined by the condition a token must meet if it is to be a token of K (or, if K is a norm-type, by the condition a token must meet to be a well-formed token of K). This, after all, is why the identity of a type—unlike that of a set—is not determined by which tokens actually exist. It is why, for instance, two untokened types can nonetheless be distinct. Well, the condition upon which the identity of K depends is K's property-associate: *being a k* (or, if K is a norm-type, *being a properly formed k*).[13] So it follows that something counts as a token of type K just in case it instantiates this property-associate. K's property-associate specifies how a thing must be, if it is to count as a (properly formed) token of K, and K itself determines what are to count as its (properly formed) tokens by virtue of being the type-associate of this property. So here is my answer to the question of how K binds together its tokens: it does so according to whether they have its property-associate.

---

[12] This point—as applied to works of music—is well made by Lydia Goehr (1992: 2).

[13] This talk of kinds having property-associates is Wolterstorff's (1980: 47–53). As he explains, the associate function is a one–one mapping of properties on to kinds.

Naturally, the type K can be complex in the sense that it determines—via its property-associate in the sense explained above—that a properly formed *token* has to be structured in some way. For example, The Polar Bear determines that any properly formed instance has certain parts (viz. four limbs, two eyes and ears, and so on). But it does not follow that the type itself is ontologically complex, for the type is nothing but an entity which binds together tokens according to whether they instantiate its property-associate. Granted, it might be a tempting thought that K succeeds in binding together its tokens by virtue of being a structured entity that determines that its tokens be structurally isomorphic to it; but, as we have just seen, this conception is not compulsory. Furthermore, the way in which we talk of types as being structured can be plausibly reinterpreted according to the doctrine of analogical predication that we examined in §2.3. For 'The Polar Bear has four legs' to be true, for example, is just for it to be true of The Polar Bear that it is such that something cannot be a properly formed token of it without being four-legged.

Of course, to say that we *need* not view types as structured is not to say that we *must* not. But in order for the case to be made for types being structured, there needs to be a clear, unparadoxical sense to the claim that types have structure; and it is precisely this condition that cannot be met. To see why this is so, let us first of all focus on the case of word-types. The thesis that types can have structure is perhaps at its most natural and intuitive when it comes to words. Words, we tend to think, are just orderings of letters, their structure mirroring the structure of their correctly formed tokens. The word-type 'cat', we are inclined to say, is nothing but the string consisting of 'a' flanked by 'c' and 't' (in that order). The word, so it seems, is a structured type whose parts are letter-types.

Well, this is, indeed, what we have found it natural to say, but it is a position that, ultimately, cannot be explicated without running into serious trouble. To begin with, our problem is that the way in which we explain the structure of word-tokens is simply unavailable to us when it comes to word-types. Since word-types have no spacial location, if 'to the left of', 'to the right of', and the like mean what they standardly mean, then it *cannot* be the case that the word-type 'cat' sees the letter 'a' flanked by the letter 'c' on its left and the letter 't' on its right. Likewise, if 'is made up of' means what it standardly means, then The Polar Bear's being an abstract entity entails that The Polar Bear (by contrast with one of its tokens) cannot be 'made up of' legs, a body, and a head.

Given the argument of §2.3, the obvious moral to take from all this is that predications of structure to tokens and types fall under the doctrine of analogical predication. If 'contains a "c" to the left of an "a"' meant what it standardly means,

(23) The word 'cat' contains a 'c' to the left of an 'a'

would be false. That (23) is true is assured by the fact that the sentence's predicate expresses the property *being such that something cannot be a properly formed token of it unless it contains a 'c' to the left of an 'a'*. And the predicate expresses this property in (23), of course, because (23) shares its truth conditions with

(24) Any properly formed inscription of 'cat' contains a 'c' to the left of an 'a'.

Having said this, such a conclusion might still be resisted by someone faithfully (though naïvely) wedded to the orthographic conception of words: the idea that word-types are strings of letter-types. However, the merest attempt to explain the supposed difference in structure between 'met' and 'meet' along the lines of the orthographic conception leads to intractable problems that even the orthographic conception's most loyal defender would have trouble with (Simons 1982: 196−7).

The difference between 'met' and 'meet', one might suppose, consists in the fact that 'met' contains only one occurrence of 'e', whereas 'meet' contains two. But, given our understanding of what a type is supposed to be, we cannot say this. For 'e' is a type, and types are unique abstract individuals. So, if an entity were to include two *occurrences* of 'e', these occurrences would either have to be *tokens*, or else there would have to be several abstract 'e's, which would have to be occurrences of some higher-level type. But neither option is sustainable. A word-type cannot have a (datable, locatable) letter-token as a constituent: such letter-tokens are constituents of word-tokens, not word-types. Peter Simons is quite right to regard a word-type with a letter-token as one of its parts as 'an impossible hybrid' (1982: 196). But equally, if the two occurrences of 'e' in 'meet' turn out to be tokens of a higher-order type—that is, geometrically identical types that are tokens of a second-order type—it would be impossible to know which of these exactly matching types a given token was a token of. This being so, we would, with justification, suspect that such a proliferation of types was merely an *ad hoc* device designed to stave off absurdity.

But this is not all. A further problem with the idea that word-types are structured stems from the fact that a word's tokens may fall into very different ontological categories. Thus far, we have been presuming that a word's tokens are *inscriptions*: datable, locatable marks that have letter-tokens as constituents. As result of this presumption, we have assumed that word-types, if structured, would have to be as the orthographic conception would have it: strings of letter-types. But a word's tokens include not only inscriptions, but *utterances*: that is, sequences of sounds. Given that this is so, and granted that the leading idea behind thinking of types as structured is that a type is structurally isomorphic with its tokens,[14] it immediately becomes quite unclear just what the structure of a word-type is supposed to be. For how could there be an entity that was structurally isomorphic with both a pattern of marks on a blackboard and a particular sequence of sound-waves? There could not: inscriptions and patterns of sound-waves are too disparate for a word-type to resemble both structurally.

So what sort of a thing is a word, if it is not something that has letters (or sound-types) as constituents? The answer can only be that word-types bind together their tokens according to whether they meet a certain complex, and disjunctive, condition: the word 'cat' is such that: if a token is an inscription, it should be spelt with a 'c' followed by an 'a', and then a 't'; and if a token is an utterance, it should sound like this: kæt.[15] But, as we have just seen, no sense can be made of the idea that the word-type itself has a structure that matches the structure of any well-formed token, since there could not be a thing that was structurally isomorphic with both an inscription and a sequence of sounds. As a result, we must give up the idea that a word-type is a structured entity, replacing it with the conception of a word as a *sui generis* abstract entity individuated by the condition it lays down for something to be one of its tokens. A word's tokens do not '*reflect*' (Kaplan 1990: 98) a

---

[14] Presumably, according to the view of types as structured entities, there is supposed to exist a congruence between a type's constituents and the constituents of any of the type's tokens: for any type K and properly formed token k thereof, K has a type C as a constituent just in case k has a token c of type C as a constituent. Presumably, it is by virtue of the obtaining of such a correlation that a type supposedly determines the sorts of thing that can instantiate it.

[15] So words, too, are norm-types; and it is this that allows for words to be misspelt.

word, if this is taken to suggest that a properly formed token must mirror the word's structure. Words, by contrast with their tokens, have no structure.

Two considerations should lead us to generalize this conclusion to all types. First, types surely form a unified ontological category. If word-types—which seem, after all, to be the most plausible candidates for having structure—are unstructured, then so must be any type. Second, we have already seen how odd it is to view types such as The Polar Bear as having the kinds of parts that their tokens have. Since types are abstract entities, the way in which we characterize the structuredness of a polar bear has no application to the type of which it is a token. Although

(18) The Polar Bear has four legs

is true, it is only true because 'having four legs' takes on a new meaning when applied to a type. Because the type is not located in space, it cannot have legs. So, given this, and that types form a single ontological category, we must treat types as, by their very nature, lacking structure.

2.5 Types as Fixed and Unchanging

Types are often claimed to be fixed and unchanging (e.g. Kaplan 1990: 98; Wolterstorff 1980: 89–90). For an entity to be *fixed* is for it to be *modally inflexible* (Rohrbaugh 2003: 178): for there to exist no possible worlds in which the entity in question differs with respect to the intrinsic properties it has actually. For an entity to be *unchanging* is for it to be *temporally inflexible*: incapable of change in its intrinsic properties over time (Rohrbaugh 2003: 178). The remainder of this chapter is devoted to explaining why types are inflexible in both of these ways.

Before I get on to this substantive task, however, I should note at once that it is only an entity's *intrinsic* properties that are relevant to the question of whether it is modally or temporally flexible. This restriction makes the point that the issue we are concerned with is whether types could have been different, and can undergo change, *in themselves*: an intuitive difference that we mark with our concept of an intrinsic property. On Socrates' death, Xanthippe became a widow, but this was not a genuine change in Xanthippe herself, since *being a widow* is an extrinsic, not an intrinsic, property of an object. The real change that Socrates' death constitutes is a change in Socrates, not in Xanthippe. Likewise, the fact that a type may have had more or fewer tokens, or may differ in the number of its tokens through time, does not indicate that types may genuinely have been different or can change, *in themselves*, through time: the number of tokens a type has, or can have, is determined by matters outside of itself and does not concern its intrinsic nature.[16]

So let us return to the question of whether types are dually inflexible in the sense introduced at the beginning of this section. And let us, in addition, return to the way in which they are individuated. Types, it emerged in the previous section, are ontologically thin entities: they are unstructured items individuated by the condition that something must meet to be one of their (properly formed) tokens. They are just, as it were, token-binders. Given that this is so, the only way in which a type could differ in its intrinsic properties, or could change with respect to such properties through time, would be by laying down a different condition upon potential instances, or by the condition it lays down changing over time. But it follows from the way in which types are individuated that neither of these situations is possible. For if the identity of a type is understood in terms of the condition for being one of its (properly formed) tokens, any type which lays down a different such condition is automatically a different type. Any attempt to describe a type as having changed, or a possible situation in which a type differs from the way it is actually, ends up, at best, as a description of a different type altogether.

An objector, however, will point out immediately that we *do* sometimes talk as if types are capable of both temporal and modal flexibility. For example, one might think that, as modifications were made to its design, The Ford Thunderbird—that is, the type—changed; and it is tempting to suppose that, had its designers thought a little differently, it might have been different. Such claims, however, need to be interpreted carefully. For in my view, apparent cases in which types are modally or temporally flexible can be explained away as cases in which there is more than one (inflexible) type. I shall return to this approach to explaining away the apparent flexibility of

---

[16] Of course, precisely how the distinction between intrinsic and extrinsic properties should be analysed is a substantial, and thorny, philosophical question; but something like the following would seem to be correct: an *intrinsic* property of an object is one the object possesses by virtue of itself, i.e. depending on no other thing (Dunn 1990: 178). And even if this definition requires some fine-tuning, the intrinsic/extrinsic distinction is intuitive enough to grasp by means of the kinds of paradigmatic examples of intrinsic and extrinsic properties that I have just provided.

types in Chapter 4, when I consider the claim that musical works are dually flexible. For now, though, some examples might help the strategy to stick.

Imagine, then, that the designers of the Ford Thunderbird decided to undertake what they called 'a radical overhaul' of the car's design. Perhaps the engine is upgraded, the suspension system changed, and the chassis given a new 'look'. Here, it seems to me, we are under no obligation to regard the single type as having changed, and it is revealing that ordinary language would have us refer to the later design as a 'new version' of the car, or else as a 'Mark 2', or some such. All in all, the most intuitive description of what has gone on here is that a new car has been designed that is *based upon* the original. There are two types here, not one that has changed.

Other cases, however, are a little more complicated. Now imagine that the Ford Motor Company decides merely to increase the length of the Ford Thunderbird's wing mirrors by a quarter of an inch. Here, perhaps, it is less obvious that we should regard the new design as representing a different type of car. Nonetheless, even in cases such as this, we shall see that we have the resources to explain away the thought that the type itself has changed.

So what should we say about such a case? Well, the first thing that should be pointed out is that the example has not yet been adequately described, since we have not yet been told of the nature of the original design's instructions concerning the length of the car's wing mirrors. Specifically, we have no idea whether the original design explicitly allowed for the kind of change in the length of the wing mirrors that has taken place. So let us explore the various options by, first of all, imagining that the decision to increase the length of the car's wing mirrors *was* explicitly allowed for in the original design. (Perhaps the original design said that the length of the wing mirrors should fall within a certain range.) Here we have a case analogous to a composer's use of vague tempo-words in a score: that is to say, we have an instruction that allows the producer of the type's tokens some leeway with regard to the feature in question. In such a situation, it seems to me that the right thing to say is that the decision to increase the car's wing mirrors within the range allowed for by the original design does *not* result in the production of tokens of a different type. The Ford Thunderbird has built into it the idea that its tokens can vary (within a certain range) with respect to the length of their wing mirrors. But neither has the type *changed*, of course. It always has, and always will be, such as to allow for such variation in its tokens. The type is unchanging but *fuzzy* with regard to this feature.

What, then, if the minimal redesign were *not* explicitly allowed for in the original design, either because a determinate length of wing mirror was specified, or because the wing mirrors' length was specified as unregulated, or even not mentioned at all? In such cases, we should revert to our original strategy: namely, that of insisting that the redesign introduces a new car-type (rather than a change in the type). For if the redesign conflicts with the original design (either by contradicting a specific instruction or by introducing a specific instruction where no such thing existed before), then it can only represent a different (albeit closely related) type.

Naturally, at this point, someone attracted to the idea that types may be modally and temporally flexible will insist that it is precisely cases of this kind that add grist to her mill. We *do*, after all, say things like 'Ford have introduced a small change to the Thunderbird'. Ultimately, though, I doubt whether any user of ordinary language would complain if this remark were unpacked as the claim that the company had developed a new type of car based upon the original Thunderbird and sharing its name. Nothing of any importance seems to hang on the idea that types are modally and temporally flexible; and, in any case, the appearance of dual flexibility can be explained away.

2.6 Conclusion

Types, I have argued, are abstract, unstructured, fixed, and unchanging. So we already have a clear idea of some of the commitments involved in the thesis that musical works are types. Crucially, however, this set of commitments is not yet complete. For, as we shall see in the next chapter, types are, by their very nature, eternally existent. As a result, and to return to this book's main concern, if *In This House, On This Morning* is a type of sound-sequence-event, it follows that Marsalis's compositional act could not have literally created the work. The work existed already.

Some, no doubt, will blanche at a conception of musical works as unstructured, fixed, unchanging, and eternally existent *abstracta*. Such philosophers will claim that the type/token theory's cost—in the form of the commitments it imposes upon its propounder—prices it out of the market. Chapters 4 and 5 rebut this suggestion. Once the type/token theory's commitments are properly understood, we can appreciate that its explanation of musical works' repeatability actually comes cheap.

3

Types II: Platonism

3.1 Introduction: Eternal Existence and Timelessness

We saw in the previous chapter that types are fixed and unchanging. But besides possessing these features, types have also tended to be regarded as items that cannot come into or go out of existence (Wolterstorff 1980: 88; Kaplan 1990: 98). But does this mean that types are eternal existents (i.e. that they exist at all times), or does it mean that they exist timelessly (i.e. that they exist but at no time)? Philosophers have been divided on this issue: Kaplan (1990: 98), for example, takes the former view, whilst Rohrbaugh (2003: 193) seems to take the latter. In this chapter I shall argue for, and defend, the thesis that types exist eternally. I shall call this view *Platonism* about types.

To begin with, though, we need to be clear about what the distinction between timeless and eternal existence consists in. A key difference is this. If an entity α exists eternally, *both* the tenseless claim

(25) α exists

and

(26) α exists at all times

are true. By contrast, the thesis that α enjoys timeless existence has it that the truth of (25) renders (26) is *senseless*. If α really is a timeless existent, then (26) makes as little sense as does the claim that the number 2 is everywhere. Indeed, if α exists timelessly, then to say that α exists now makes no more sense than saying that the number 2 is in Manchester.

So why am I so sure that a commitment to the thesis that types neither come into nor go out of existence should lead to us to view types as eternal, rather than timeless, existents? For two reasons.[1] First, treating types as timeless entities problematizes the very idea of coming into certain kinds

---

[1] Here I follow the enlightening discussion of eternality and timelessness in Carruthers 1984: 4–7.

of epistemic contact with such things. If, for example, words (i.e. word-types) cannot be said meaningfully to exist-at-a-time, then they cannot be understandable-at-a-time. For a word to be understood at t, it must exist *to be* understood at t. Likewise, assuming musical works to be types, if such types existed timelessly, then how could they be composed, performed, or listened to at various times? If an audience is to listen to a work, *qua* type, at t, then the work must be present at t: it must be available to be heard at that time.

But this is not all. For the plain fact is that a sentence ascribing eternal existence to a type, a sentence such as

(27) The Ford Thunderbird exists now, has always existed, and will always exist

does not have the patent senselessness of the claim that the number 2 is everywhere. The point about (27) is not that it makes no sense, but that it is controversial. We can make sense of it all right. If we are to be convinced that, contrary to its appearance, (27) is senseless, then we need an argument to do the job.

The problem, however, is that no such argument would seem to be forthcoming. One might, I suppose, take the senselessness of (27) to follow from the fact that the types are *changeless* (or, at least, temporally inflexible in the sense explicated in §2.5). But such reasoning would be mistaken. For although it may be plausibly argued that there cannot be time without change—that is, that a universe in which nothing underwent change would be a timeless universe—it does not follow from this that any changeless thing must be a timeless thing. As Carruthers explains (1984: 6), we can perfectly well imagine a changeless object being surrounded by changing things and, hence, existing through the times of these changes. Once it is granted that types coexist with things that change, there is no obstacle to supposing that they exist changelessly yet eternally. So, given the aforementioned objections to conceiving of types as timeless entities, my conclusion is this: to deny that types can come into existence or cease to be is to commit oneself to their existing at all times. Types exist eternally. Or so I shall argue in this chapter.

3.2 Types and Properties

No type can come into or go out of existence, and hence types—all types—exist eternally. Why do I think this? To see why, let us, first of all, follow Wolterstorff (1980: 47) in introducing the *associate* function, which is a one-to-one mapping of properties on to kinds. For any property *being a k*, the value of this function is K, the property's type-associate, and every type is the associate of exactly one property. Now for the answer to our question. Types exist eternally because a type's existence at a time t is guaranteed by the existence at t of the property of which it is the associate, and because all properties exist eternally. That is to say, the conclusion that types are eternal existents follows from

(28) For any type K and any time t, K exists at t, if its property-associate, *being a k*, exists at t, [2]

and

(29) All properties exist at all times.

I shall now set about defending both (28) and (29).

Someone who certainly accepts (28) is Wolterstorff (1980: 51), but, oddly, he does not explain his confidence in it.[3] I say 'oddly' because, as it happens, (28) is extremely plausible. To see why, consider the following example. It is *being a (well-formed) polar bear*—and nothing else—that determines the identity of its type-associate: The Polar Bear. Just as long as this property exists at t, there exists at t a condition that a thing would have to meet in order to be a (well-formed) token of The Polar Bear; and just as long as there exists such a condition at t, the type exists at t. Nothing else is required. Remember that, by contrast to the set of polar bears, The Polar Bear is not dependent for its existence upon its instances. All that is necessary is that there be a condition that something must meet in order to be one of the type's (well-formed) tokens. The moral is this: if a type's property-associate exists at a time, the type itself cannot but exist at that time.

So much for (28). How can we explain our confidence in (29): the claim that any property exists eternally (if it exists at all)? Let us start by noting that properties cannot come in or out of existence: a doctrine that follows from a highly intuitive theory concerning the existence conditions of properties.

---

[2] If K is a norm-type, then the property with which it is associated, properly speaking, is *being a properly formed k*. Such complications matter little, though: as we shall see, the considerations determining that properties exist eternally apply across the board.

[3] In fact, Wolterstorff also holds that

(28*) For any type K and any time t, K exists at t *only if being a k exists at t.*

And he is quite right to do so. A type exists at t only if, at t, there exists a condition that something must meet to be one of K's tokens; and this condition is nothing but the type's property-associate.

The theory in question, simply stated, is that a property F exists at t if and only if there is some time t^* such that t^* is either before, after, or identical with t, and at which it is (metaphysically) possible for F to be instantiated. And the reason why this entails that properties do not come into or go out of being is this: if it is ever the case that there is some time (past, present, or future) at which it is possible for something to be F, it is always the case; and it if is ever false, it is always false (Wolterstorff 1970: 161). Of course, there are two ways in which we may explain the fact that there is no time at which *being a k* comes into or goes out of existence: it may be true because the property exists at all times, or it may be true because the property exists timelessly. But, as with the case of types themselves, it is clear which option should be taken, and for analogous reasons. For one thing, it is hard to understand how a property could come to be instantiated at a time, if it did not exist *at* that time. The nature of instantiation is difficult enough to explain without committing ourselves to the idea that a property can be instantiated by an object at t and yet the property not exist at the time at which its instantiated. Second, it makes sense to describe properties, no less than it does types, as existing at times. People may need to be convinced that properties exist at all times, but they can certainly understand this claim.

Let us now return to our favoured account of the existence conditions of properties. Why is this account so intuitive? The reason is that it enables us to steer between a Scylla and a Charybdis. Scylla is the doctrine of transcendent properties. According to this conception, properties are what Michael Dummett has termed 'self-subsistent objects': objects that can be referred to, or thought about, without our needing to refer to, or think about, concrete entities. Properties, thus conceived, are not intrinsically *of* (Dummett 1986: 261) particulars at all, a view that opens up the possibility of there being properties that are necessarily uninstantiated (properties such as *being a round square*). With such a conception in place, however, it becomes hard to conceive of how a particular could come to *have* a property. On this view, properties and their instances, so it seems, occupy different realms, and, as a result, instantiation is rendered utterly mysterious: 'a very big deal: a relation between universals and particulars that crosses realms' (Armstrong 1989: 76). Once the conceptual tie between properties and particulars is severed, it cannot be repaired.

Charybdis, to veer to the other extreme, is the idea that properties exist only at times at which they are actually instantiated: a view that has properties switching in and out of existence as they have, and then cease to have, any instances. This view, I take it, is intrinsically implausible. If everything were healthy at t, there would be nothing diseased at t, but there would still be such a thing as disease.[4] To be diseased is to be a certain a way. Although, in our example, nothing is actually that way at t, it is not that that way of being has gone out of existence; it is just that nothing happens to be that way.

The view I recommend neatly avoids both of these extremes, conceptually tying properties to particulars whilst ensuring that they exist at all times. A property *is* essentially the kind of thing that is capable of being instantiated, and so properties are not self-subsistent, and instantiation is not a queer relation that crosses ontological realms. Crucially, though, this consequence is achieved without having to hold, with Charybdis, that properties switch in and out of existence as they come to be, and then fail to be, instantiated.

Of course, this construal of the existence conditions of properties is not the *only* way of steering between Scylla and Charybdis. Indeed, at first blush, two alternative accounts may seem attractive. The first is propounded by Armstrong, who achieves a conceptual tie between universals and particulars by denying that there can be uninstantiated universals, though in such a way as also to rule out the possibility of a property's coming or ceasing to be. In Armstrong's view, a property F exists at t just in case there exists a time t^* such that t^* is either before, after, or identical to t, and F is instantiated at t^* (1989: 75–82).[5] So as long as *being a k* is instantiated at some time, there is no time at which it does not exist. This being so, Armstrong's account too avoids the transcendent conception of properties in such a way as to commit him to their eternal existence.

Given these similarities between my favoured account and Armstrong's, one might think that there would be little to choose between them; but, in fact, the existence conditions for properties recommended by Armstrong yields an uncomfortable result. As Robert Howell has pointed out, the denial that there exist properties that are *contingently* uninstantiated in the whole course of the universe seems hard to motivate (2002: 114). Presumably, Armstrong would stick out his chin in the wake of such criticism, but the crucial point to appreciate is that the very notion of a

---

[4] *Pace* Aristotle, as quoted by Loux (1998: 46).   [5] A view that I once seconded (2000: 436).

property would seem to grant that contingently uninstantiated properties exist. As Levinson has put it (1992*b*: 658–9), a property is simply a way that something can be, where a way of being is just a mode of existence available to (that is to say, *possible for*) things (1992*b*: 658). Alternatively, we may think of a property as a condition that something can meet. This plainly does not require that all such conditions actually be met by something at some time.

No doubt, at this point Armstrong would charge me with treating properties as transcendent, as 'floating free from things' (1989: 97). But such an accusation would be unfair. It is true that my favoured account of properties' existence conditions has it that properties have no spatial location: a contingently uninstantiated property has no *place* to exist and, given that both instantiated and uninstantiated properties fall under the same ontological category, it follows that all properties are similarly abstract. However, this localization issue should be distinguished from the question of whether properties are free-floaters in the damaging sense that concerns us. Properties would float free from things in this sense if they were self-subsistent—if, in other words, they were not intrinsically *of* things—but this is precisely what I deny.

Just to be absolutely clear about this, an avoidance of the transcendent conception of properties, together with its attendant problems, only requires us to tie properties *conceptually* to instances. That is to say, we need only have an account that has as a consequence that to *think* of a property is to *think* of something's having it (Levinson 1992*b*: 658–9). It is, I contend, precisely this conceptual dependence that is explained by the account of the existence conditions of properties that I favour: to think of a property is to think of something's having it *precisely because* properties are essentially instantiable (at some time or other). To suppose, as Armstrong seems to, that a property depends for its existence upon the actual existence of an instance (at some time) is to insist on more than suffices for the underpinning of the conceptual connection between properties and their instantiation. Consequently, since the kind of conceptual connection mentioned by Levinson is a direct consequence of my view, and since it avoids the counter-intuitiveness of Armstrong's account, I take it that it should be preferred. Properties are—dare one say it?—Platonic without being denizens of Platonic heaven. The Platonism I espouse does away with such a realm.

So much for the views of Armstrong. The second alternative way of avoiding Scylla and Charybdis, like the position I recommend, ties the existence of properties to the possibility of their instantiation, but does so in a slightly more circumscribed way. In short, the idea is that a property exists at a time just in case it is possible for it to be instantiated at that time or at some earlier time. More precisely, the claim is that a property F exists at t just in case there is a time t^* such that t^* is either before or identical to (but not after) t, and it is possible for F to be instantiated at t^*. Since the existence of F is tied to the possibility of its being instantiated, F is not a self-subsistent entity; and since F, once it is instantiated, cannot go out of existence, this account too avoids the absurd consequence that F can switch in and out of existence. Crucially, however, properties, thus construed, *can* come *into* existence: a property comes to exist at the time when it is first possible for it to have an instance. For example, as I write, there is, and has been, no time at which it has been possible for something to be a child born in 2050; so, if this second alternative suggestion is correct, it follows that the property *being a child born in 2050* has not existed up to now but will come into existence at that date.

So what is to be said for this second option? One might, I suppose, think it intuitive that the property *being a child born in 2050* does not exist until the time indicated. After all, it might be insisted, if it is metaphysically impossible now for anything to be a child born in 2050, in *what sense* can the property in question presently exist? But the answer to this question is easy once we appreciate that a property is simply a condition that something must meet in order to be of a certain kind (in this case, a child born in 2050). It is, of course, true that nothing that presently exists can be a child born in 2050; but it does not follow from this that *the condition* something must meet to be a child born in 2050 does not itself exist. Indeed, this claim has the odour of a category mistake about it. Of course, *the condition* exists; it is just that nothing can meet it until 2050.

But this is not the only reason for preferring a conception of properties as eternal existents to an account that holds that they exist only from the time at which they are first capable of being instantiated. To adapt a point made by Michael Loux (1998: 46–7), the very same semantic considerations that prompt us to posit the existence of properties also prompt us to suppose that these properties exist *before* it was possible for them to be instantiated. A realist about properties argues that both true *and false* sentences of the form

(30)   *a* is *F*

commit us to the existence of the properties expressed by their predicates. Whether 'F' expresses a property or not cannot depend on the truth-value of (30); so, given that (30) would commit us to the existence of a property if true, it must do so if false. But now let us return to the case of *being a child born in 2050*. Specifically, let us imagine that someone, in 2007, becomes confused about what year it is and says, of a newly born child:

(31) Amy is a child born in 2050.

Given the style of argument that I have just set out, it follows that the believer in properties must accept that the falsehood of (31), as uttered in 2007, commits us to viewing (31) as expressing a property at this time. An utterance of (31), even in 2007, is false by virtue of Amy failing to instantiate *being a child born in 2050*; and for this to be so, the property in question must exist. We thus have a counter-example to the claim that a property exists at a time just in case there is a time (present or past) at which it is possible for it to be instantiated.

I noted earlier that there is a principled philosophical reason for denying the existence of properties that cannot be instantiated at *any* time (past, present, or future): such properties would be self-subsistent, and, as such, their existence would render instantiation mysterious. Predicates such as 'is a round square', then, must be regarded as recalcitrant predicates that do not express properties. But, crucially, there exists no such principled reason for denying that *being a child born in 2050* exists now. After all, my proposed account of the existence conditions of properties—namely, that a property exists at a time just in case there is some time or other at which it is possible for it to be instantiated—entails that *being a child born in 2050* exists in 2007, and yet does so whilst preserving the idea that properties are conceptually tied to particulars. Furthermore, we have seen already that the idea that properties exist eternally seems quite natural once properties are (correctly) thought of as conditions that items must meet to be tokens of a certain type.

My conclusion, then, is that neither Armstrong's account of the existence conditions of properties, nor this second alternative account, is to be preferred to the account I propose. And what this means is that the avoidance of Scylla and Charybdis requires us to embrace the idea that properties exist eternally.

As with properties, so with their type-associates. Given the truth of (28) and (29), types exist eternally and, like their property-associates, exist just in case there is some time at which it is possible for them to be instantiated. So whilst The Round Square does not exist, we can acknowledge this whilst accepting that there can be types that, as a matter of contingent fact, go untokened during the whole course of the universe. The counter-intuitiveness that attached to Armstrong's account of the existence conditions of properties, and hence to an Armstrongian account of the existence conditions of types, is thereby avoided.

Given the fact that the dependence of a property upon its instantiation need only be conceptual, and that this may follow from an account that has the existence of a property dependent merely upon its *instantiability*, one criticism of this conception of types may be dispensed with immediately. It is clearly mistaken to suppose that viewing types as eternally existent thereby places them in some kind of Platonic heaven (Kaplan 1990: 111). As I have just noted in connection with the case of properties, the literal content to the claim that an entity is a denizen of Platonic heaven is that we can refer to, or think about, such a thing without needing to refer to, or think about, concrete entities. Frege, for example, in infamously placing propositions in a 'third realm' (Frege 1918: 45), thinks of them as being independent of language and language-use in just this way. The problem for Frege now becomes an analogue of the problem facing the supporter of transcendent properties: if propositions are not intrinsically *of* utterances, it is unclear how an utterance can come to express a proposition.

Are types self-subsistent in Dummett's sense? Well, we have seen that they are eternal entities and exist before they are tokened, but this is a different issue. For although a type is not existentially dependent upon actually being tokened, it is nonetheless *conceptually* tied to its tokens in exactly the way in which Frege's propositions fail to be tied to utterances. (Indeed, it is no accident that Dummett's emendation of Frege's position (1986: 260−1) has it that propositions should be thought of as types of utterance.) A type, such as The Polar Bear, is precisely not a ghostly inhabitant of some mythical Platonic realm, but something that we can think of only as a kind of concrete particular. For although it is not dependent for its existence on the existence of its tokens, it would not exist, were there not a time at which it was possible for it to be tokened. The Polar Bear is, in this sense, intrinsically *of* polar bears.

Another example may help. Consider, once more, The Square Cut. This is a cricketing batting stroke and, as such, is a type of thing done with a cricket bat. Of course, that this is so does not entail that The Square Cut depends for its existence upon cricket bats. It would be extremely odd to insist that if every cricket bat in the world were destroyed, The Square Cut would cease to exist. Nonetheless, this batting stroke is *conceptually dependent* upon cricket bats: we can only think of it as something done by a person *with a bat*. This combination of relations—namely, conceptual dependence upon and existential independence of—is precisely what is distinctive of the relation that holds between a type and its tokens. The close conceptual dependence of a type upon its tokens ensures that types are not self-subsistent. The charge that we have placed types in Platonic heaven cannot be made to stick.

That said, an opponent of Platonism about types will worry about what seems to be the sheer counter-intuitiveness of the idea that types exist eternally. Is it really the case that The Polar Bear or—more implausibly still—The Ford Thunderbird existed at the time of the Big Bang? The remainder of this chapter is devoted to replying to these objections. In the course of the ensuing discussion we will, inevitably, revisit (28) and (29).

Although the idea that types exist eternally might attract a good deal of dissent, opposition to the thought that *natural* kinds are eternal existents may be dissipated by taking care not to conflate the question of whether a type exists at a time t with the distinct question of whether it has, or indeed could have, any tokens at t. My account of the existence conditions of types, remember, rides on the back of my account of the existence conditions of properties: a type, like a property, exists at t just so long as there is some time or other at which it is possible for it to be tokened; and it is compatible with this account that the type be incapable of being instantiated at t itself.

Nonetheless, it might be alleged that it is absurd to believe The Polar Bear to have existed at the time of the Big Bang. But what would be the harm in thinking that it did? True enough, the type had no tokens then, but this is irrelevant to the question of whether the type itself existed then. The identity of a type is fixed by the condition that a token must meet in order to be a (well-formed) token of that type. Given that this is so, there is no reason to deny that The Polar Bear existed at the time of the Big Bang. After all, we know what condition a token would have had to meet at that time in order to be a (well-formed) polar bear. It was just that nothing met (or, perhaps, even could have met) that condition at that time. Nevertheless, given that this condition is a property, given that properties exist eternally, and given that this property cannot exist without its type-associate existing, it follows that the type exists at that (and every) time.

It is noticeable, however, that this example has concerned the existence conditions of The Polar Bear: a *natural* type (= kind). A philosopher prepared to acknowledge that natural kinds exist eternally may still be unwilling to accept that non-natural types, such as The Ford Thunderbird or The Jet Engine, were anything other than brought into being in the twentieth century. For types such as these would seem to be paradigmatically *man-made*. The Jet Engine, we want to say, was *invented* by Frank Whittle; he was the person who created it.

To a certain extent, the force of this objection can be dispelled by explicating the concept of invention, and by holding fast to the distinction between a type's existence conditions and the question of whether it has any tokens. For let us say this: 'the inventor of K' is used, not to refer to the person who (*per impossibile*) supposedly brought the type K into existence, but to the person who first conceived of K, and whose grasp of its concept was responsible for the creation of its first token. The Jet Engine (the type) has always existed; Frank Whittle, brilliant as he was, could not have brought this entity into existence. Types are not the sorts of thing that can be brought into being by anyone. Nevertheless, Frank Whittle counts as The Jet Engine's inventor because his creative act was the origin of the process that ended with the creation of the first (token) jet engine.

This is fine as far as it goes, but an opponent of this thesis may, nonetheless, have an objection of an altogether more theoretical nature. It might be suggested that types such as The Jet Engine and The Ford Thunderbird are what Jerrold Levinson has termed *indicated types* (Levinson 1980b: 80–1). An indicated type is a type in which there figures ineliminably a datable, locatable process of *indication*: a process (such as the drawing up of plans or the production of a score) by which human beings set out the condition that must be met by the type's properly formed tokens (Levinson 1990c: 259–61). Such a type, Levinson suggests, is ontologically tethered to this indicative act (1990c: 216). Now, motivated by the intuition that it is essential to the identity of The Ford Thunderbird that it was indicated by the Ford

Motor Company in 1957 (in other words, that a qualitatively identical car indicated by a rival company, or by the Ford Motor Company at a different time, would be a different car from the Thunderbird), Levinson states:

The Ford Thunderbird is not simply a pure structure of metal, glass, and plastic. … The Ford Thunderbird … is a metal/glass/plastic structure-as-indicated (or -determined) by the Ford Motor Company on such and such a date. (Levinson 1980b: 81)

The car, then, is not the pure type, ψ,[6] that we pre-theoretically suppose it to be, but ψ *tethered to a certain act of indication*: a conception Levinson fleshes out by representing this indicated type as 'ψ-as-indicated-by-the Ford Motor Company-in-1957' (1980b: 81).[7]

For my present purposes, we may ignore Levinson's erroneous assumption that types can be themselves structured. The important feature of his proposal is his view that The Ford Thunderbird is an indicated type. For Levinson takes such a type to exist only from the time t at which the relevant act of indication takes place (1980b: 79–80); and, in support of Levinson, Howell has suggested—*pace* (29)—that the reason why this is so is that an indicated type's property-associate does not exist before t (Howell 2002: 109–15). Clearly, if Howell is right in thinking this, then, given the truth of (28*)—namely, that a type exists at t only if its property-associate exists at t—it follows that the indicated type itself does not exist before t either.

Needless to say, this objection, were it correct, could have important ramifications for the ontology of music. For, as we shall see in Chapter 5, Levinson argues—against the simple view that I recommend—that musical works are indeed indicated types tied to the time of their composition. If Levinson is right about this, and if Howell is right about the property-associates of indicated types, then musical works do not pre-exist their composition. However, in the next section I shall take issue with Howell's views: we shall see that even the property-associates of indicated types are eternal. So, given the correctness of (28), Platonism about types stands (and works of music—if types of *any* kind—exist eternally).

---

[6] 'ψ' names the pure abstract entity that, intuitively, we would identify with the car (-type). As has been noted already, Levinson takes ψ to be itself structured; my disagreement with him on this matter does not undermine his thesis that the type is indicated.

[7] As we shall see in §9.2, Levinson modifies this notion of an indicated type, but, given our current concern, harmlessly so.

3.3 The Eternal Existence of Properties Reconsidered

The starting-point for Howell's attack on (29) is a distinction between
pure and *impure* properties. Impure properties, by contrast with their pure
cousins, are properties whose specification includes reference to a concrete
entity: properties such as *being a son of Abraham Lincoln* and *being older than
Elliott Carter.* Another such impure property is the property-associate of
the indicated type that Levinson and Howell presume to be The Ford
Thunderbird: *having the structure determined by ψ and being produced in a way
that is properly connected to The Ford Motor Company's 1957 act of indication.*[8] It
is precisely these impure properties that Howell denies are eternal.

So why does Howell take this view? The answer lies in the following,
apparently intuitive thought: that such properties do not exist until the
entities they essentially involve have come into existence. *Being a son of
Abraham Lincoln,* according to Howell, only came into existence once
Lincoln himself was born, and he takes a similar moral to apply to *having the
structure determined by ψ and being produced in a way that is properly connected
to The Ford Motor Company's 1957 act of indication.* Of such a time-tethered
property, Howell asks:

How can it already have existed in, say, 1600—or at the moment of the Big
Bang—when the specific, concrete entities to which it essentially relates had not
yet themselves come into existence? To suppose that it can would be like supposing
that your signature—not just ink marks geometrically congruent to it, but actual
marks that attest to *you,* to your own personal identity—could exist a million years
before you do, or that the set consisting of last night's thunderstorm and today's
gusting of the wind could pre-exist both these events. (Howell 2002: 112–13)

But we should not lose our heads here. The threat seemingly posed by Howell's remarks about signatures and sets is relatively easily deflated. First of all,
the suggestion that it is *obviously* absurd to take my signature to pre-exist
me may be countered once we remind ourselves that by 'signature' here
we mean *signature-type*: the abstract object that my signature-tokens instantiate. Presumably, this too is an indicated type: *X-as-produced-by-Julian Dodd*
(where *X* is the inscriptional type). Now, what *would* be absurd would be to

---

[8] According to an indicated type-theorist, tokens can only be tokens of an indicated type, if they are
appropriately related to the act of indication that, supposedly, brought the indicated type into existence
(Howell 2002: 112). For more on this, see §§5.2 and 7.1 below.

claim that this type could have been *tokened* before I was born. Only marks made by me can count as tokens of my signature. But it does not follow from this that the signature-type did not exist before I did. To think that such a conclusion follows is, once more, to confuse the question of what it is for a type to be tokened with the distinct question of what it is for the type itself to exist. However, it seems to me that the force of Howell's question—how 'actual marks' that attest to me could pre-exist me—relies upon precisely this conflation. For what are such 'actual marks' but signature-tokens? Of course, no 'actual marks'—that is to say, concrete tokens—made a million years ago could be examples of my signature. But pointing this out does not undermine the claim that the type itself existed a million years ago.

Furthermore, the analogy between properties and sets is misleading. The reason why the set consisting of last night's thunderstorm and today's gusting of the wind could not pre-exist those events is simple: those events are essential *constituents* of the set (sets have their members essentially). But it is far from obvious that impure properties have constituents in an analogous way. *Being a son of Abraham Lincoln*, for example, is a condition which something has to meet in order to be a token of a certain type: namely, a son of Abraham Lincoln. What is obscure is why we should regard this condition as a complex entity that has the man himself as a part. I shall return to this in a while. For now, however, let us delve a little deeper into why Howell believes that *being a son of Abraham Lincoln* did not exist until Lincoln himself existed. I think that there are two reasons why Howell takes this line, neither of which is convincing.

The first such reason is not explicitly formulated in Howell's article, but its role in his thinking swiftly becomes evident, once a little philosophical excavation has been undertaken.[9] To begin with, it is undeniable that *being a son of Abraham Lincoln* exists at *t* only if, at *t*, there is a fact of the matter as to what it would be for something to be a son of Lincoln: what I shall term *objective satisfaction conditions* for whether something is a son of Lincoln or not. Only then can it be true or false whether something meets these conditions or fails to meet them. But, according to Howell, it is precisely these satisfaction conditions that are lacking before Lincoln's birth. For in Howell's view, before Lincoln was born, Lincoln's identity was not

---

[9] The quotations referred to in this paragraph were provided by Howell in e-mailed correspondence. I thank him for his help.

'available in the actual world'. As Howell himself puts it, 'unless we adopt some sort of quasi-Meinongian view in which Abraham Lincoln is, so to speak, always around within the world even though Abraham Lincoln is not always existent within the world, I don't think that Abraham Lincoln's identity is made available in the world until Abraham Lincoln actually exists in the world.' And what Howell means by this remark is, I think, that before Lincoln existed *there could have been no question* of whether or not something was Lincoln, or indeed a son of Lincoln. These questions could have had no content at this time. But, given the fact that a property F can exist at t only if there exist at t objective satisfaction conditions for being F, and given that the existence of Lincoln is required for there to be such satisfaction conditions, *being a son of Abraham Lincoln* (and the other impure properties concerning Lincoln) could not have existed before Lincoln himself did.

In my view, however, Howell's line of argument here erroneously blurs the distinction between metaphysical and epistemological concerns. At first blush, *availability* looks like an epistemological notion—'Availability *to whom?*', we might ask—and appearances are not deceptive in this instance. It is, no doubt, true that before Lincoln's birth his identity was not made available in the world; but what this means is that it was not available to *us*: that we could have no knowledge of Lincoln. And the reason why this is important is that it entails that, before Lincoln's birth, it was impossible for anyone to *refer to,* or otherwise *have a singular thought about,* Lincoln. But it does not follow from this, as Howell seems to think it does, that at this time there was no fact of the matter as to whether an entity was Lincoln or not. For in 1066 it was a fact, albeit an ungraspable fact at that time, that no entity was Lincoln, and hence that no entity was Lincoln's son.

Howell has thus misinterpreted what is really an important fact concerning the possibility of *reference* and *singular thought*: we can only refer to, or have a singular thought about, things that are available in the world for us. We cannot refer to, or entertain singular thoughts about, things of which we know nothing. True enough, the question of whether an entity is Lincoln's son or not could not have *arisen* for anyone before Lincoln's birth: in 1066 'Abraham Lincoln' could not have been used to refer to the man who eventually became US President. But admitting this is not to deny that properties such as *being Abraham Lincoln* and *being a son of Abraham Lincoln* existed before Lincoln did. The existence conditions of properties and the conditions necessary for reference and singular thought to be possible are distinct matters.

So much for the first reason for denying that impure properties pre-exist the particulars they involve. The second such reason is, like the first, not explicitly acknowledged, but differs from it in being driven by a claim about the ontological nature of impure properties. Let us focus once more on Howell's rhetorical question. Speaking of an impure property, Howell asks: 'How can it already have existed in, say, 1600—or at the moment of the Big Bang—when the specific, concrete entities to which it essentially relates had not yet themselves come into existence?' (2002: 112–13). We may notice immediately that Howell takes *impure properties themselves* to be essentially related to concrete entities (in the present example, to Abraham Lincoln). The 'it' in 'to which it essentially relates' refers to the same thing as the first occurrence of 'it': the property. So what is the essential relation between *being a son of Abraham Lincoln* and Lincoln himself supposed to be? Just how does the property 'involve' the man?[10] Howell's answer is that which I expressed a certain scepticism about earlier: the relation holding between *being a son of Abraham Lincoln* and Lincoln himself is taken by Howell to be that which obtains between a complex object and one of its constituents. The property 'involves' the concrete particular in the sense that the latter is an essential part of the former, a conception demonstrated by Howell's explanation of how *being a son of Abraham Lincoln* comes into existence:

[T]he wholly general, relational property *being a son of someone* already exists (and, for all I know to the contrary, is eternal). When Lincoln comes into existence, he automatically fills the open, 'someone' slot in this property. In consequence, the monadic property *being a son of Lincoln*…automatically comes to be. (2002: 115)

So now we have an answer to the question of why impure properties can only come into existence when the particulars they involve do. This conclusion is entailed by Howell's account of the nature of impure properties: the thesis that impure properties are complex objects that have the particulars they involve as constituents. Such properties cannot exist until all of their constituents exist.

But in my view, the conception of the structure of impure properties that underlies this account is itself inadequately motivated. A property, we saw

---

[10] This talk of properties 'involving' concrete particulars is Howell's own (2002: 126).

in §3.2, is nothing but a condition that something meets, or would have to meet, in order to be of a certain kind. As I noted in §2.4, such properties may vary in complexity in the sense that a particular's having a certain property may or may not consist in its entering into relations with other particulars. *Being a son of Abraham Lincoln* is one such example. But what I fail to see is why such complexity should be *ontologized*: why, in other words, we should read the complexity into *the structure of the property itself* by having the entities to which a particular must be related in order to have the property as very constituents of that property. It can only be a mistake to think that *the property itself*—that entity—is essentially related to Lincoln (in the sense that Lincoln is an essential *part* of it). The thing that must bear a certain relation to Abraham Lincoln (if it is to have the property in question) is the *concrete particular*. To specify a property is to specify what is required for a particular to be a certain way. And to have the property *being a son of Abraham Lincoln*, a particular must instantiate a certain relation to Lincoln. The thing that must be related to Lincoln is a particular that has the property, not the property itself. The property is not complex in an ontological sense. Howell is sliding from a thesis concerning the instantiation of impure properties to a thesis concerning their ontological nature.

My charge could, perhaps, be put another way. In specifying an impure property, we refer to concrete particulars; but we make such reference only to spell out the nature of the condition that must be met by something if it is to have the property in question. It does not follow that we should regard the concrete particulars themselves as parts of the property. Hence, since Howell's second objection to the eternal existence of properties rests upon just this assumption, the objection is toothless.

Needless to say, this is not yet to explain *how* an impure property can exist at a time before the concrete entity that it involves exists. But this, it appears to me, is a philosophical problem more manufactured than real. Once more we need to distinguish carefully the question of whether the property exists at *t* from the issue of whether it can be instantiated at *t*. It would indeed be crazy to suppose that *being a son of Abraham Lincoln* is a property that could have been *possessed by anything* before there was such a person as Abraham Lincoln. But it does not follow from this that the *property itself* did not exist then. It is, of course, true that in 1600, for example, no one would have been able to *express* the property of being a son of Abraham Lincoln, because no one would have been able to refer to

Lincoln. But, as I noted earlier, this is a point about reference, not about the metaphysics of properties. The property existed then, even though it could not have been introduced into a language.

At this juncture, Howell might seek to reply by claiming my account of properties to be obscure. Just what *are* these abstract, yet ontologically simple, entities? To which I can make three replies. First, properties, as I have said, are conditions that particulars may meet. The mistake, in my view, is to assume that properties must have a structure isomorphic to the predicates that express them. This assumption that language mirrors the structure of the world, though beloved by the logical atomists, is little more than a dogma. Second, if Howell were to charge me with obscurity, I could reply with ' tu quoque'. The claim that Abraham Lincoln fills a 'slot' in *being a son of someone* is a metaphor as uncashable as the Fregean declaration that properties are 'unsaturated' things that may be completed by 'saturated' objects. In *what sense* does an abstract entity have a *slot*? How could a concrete particular *fill* such a slot in what is an abstract entity? And why not think of *particulars* as having the slots (to be filled by properties)? I remain to be convinced that these questions are anything but unanswerable. But, finally, I would dispute that my remarks about properties are obscure. They only seem so if one presumes both that properties must be complex objects and that the philosopher's task is to analyse this ontological complexity. Properties are *sui generis* abstract entities that cannot be assimilated to complex objects such as facts or states of affairs. This view may be favourably contrasted with Howell's position on impure properties. Presuming them to be structured entities, he says nothing non-metaphorical about the nature of their structure. I dispute the need for the kind of theory that, in the end, even its most faithful supporter cannot deliver.

3.4 Types and Patterns

So much for Howell's objection to (29): the claim that properties exist eternally. This thesis applies across the board, even to the property-associates of indicated types. Howell's suggestion that impure properties are a counter-example to it is based upon a misconceived way of thinking about such things. But, crucially, this rejoinder is insufficient to silence Howell's concerns. For Howell also denies (28). That is, he denies that the existence of a property at a time guarantees the existence of its type-associate at that time. Consequently, even if he were to grant that all properties exist eternally, he takes himself to be in a position to deny that types are eternal existents. Once again, however, I believe his reasoning to be flawed, and this section is dedicated to explaining why this is so.

Howell's objection to (28) rides on the back of his invocation, and motivation, of an unfamiliar ontological framework. So it would be as well to begin with a brief outline of Howell's ontology of properties, patterns, and types. According to Howell, the existence of *being a k* does indeed entail the existence of an abstract entity, but this is the *K-pattern*, not the *type K* (2002: 116). The pattern, explains Howell, is the mere 'arrangement of parts or features that is possessed by anything having the associated property' (2002: 116). The associated type, meanwhile, is not a simple arrangement of parts; it is this arrangement once it plays an 'important role in nature or human life' (2002: 116). So even if we presume that the properties underlying types are eternal, it does not follow that all types are eternal too. We may say that patterns are eternal existents, but the same is not true of every type. Indeed, Howell argues that indicated types (such as word-types, games, and The Ford Thunderbird) come into being only once a network of human practices has come into existence, and hence are the literal products of the relevant practices. Howell thus takes himself to have shown that indicated types are not eternal.

Let us put to one side our inevitable reservations about regarding patterns and types as 'arrangements of elements'. What, precisely, does Howell have to say about such types seemingly bound up with human practices? According to Howell, the relation between human practices and a type of this kind is one of *production*. Types such as these, says Howell, 'are all initiated. They exist only once the practices in question do. All these practice-related types are themselves to be distinguished from mere patterns that are not currently involved in practices' (2002: 124). So Howell's thought is this: a word-type, such as 'dine', only exists once there is a communal practice of using tokens in accordance with its semantic and syntactic rules. Before this communal practice existed (indeed, even before there were any English-speakers) there existed the property *being a/dine/phonemic sequence used in English to mean dine*,[11] and hence there existed the corresponding pattern;

---

[11] Here I follow Howell's own notation (2002: 117).

but it would be absurd, supposes Howell, to think that the word-type *itself* existed in the Jurassic Age. There were no words before there were any people, and this is because a word only comes into being once 'some community establishes a practice of producing (and recognizing) concrete sound and visual items … that instantiate the relevant pattern and so have the property that underlies it' (2002: 118). Howell then delivers the *coup de grâce* with what he considers to be a *reductio* of his opponent:

> Words do not exist in a natural language merely because properties exist that specify sound-and-meaning patterns that are admissible in that language. 'Glank' does not exist as an actual word (type) in English, meaning *joyful jeep*, simply because there exists, uninstantiated, the property *being a/glank/phonemic sequence in English to mean joyful jeep.* … '[G]lank' was not, before I wrote this paper, an uninstantiated but existent word in English. It was no such word at all, and it remains no word now. (2002: 117)

A word-type, so Howell suggests, only comes to exist once a practice of using the word with a particular meaning and syntactic role is established. To Howell, it is absurd to suppose that a word-type could pre-exist such practices.

But such a thesis is eminently resistible. Indeed, in my view, Howell is wrong about word-types, and is thus unentitled to regard them as a case-study demonstrating how and why indicated types are created by human practices. To see this, we should first of all note that, although the word-type 'glank' does not presently exist *in English*, it does not follow that it does not exist at all. I take it that for a word to exist *in a language L* at *t* is for it actually to have been used in some linguistic practice by speakers of *L* at *t* or some time before *t*. Only word-types that have actually been tokened by speakers of *L* at *t* count as being words of *L* at *t*. A word only enters into a language once a practice of producing tokens of it in accordance with semantic and syntactic rules has been established. Communal practices, then, bring word-types into languages. So it is, indeed, absurd to suggest that 'glank' is presently an actual word-type of English.

But having located the source of the absurdity in the picture to which Howell objects, we are now able to distinguish the truly absurd from the harmless. For although Howell has demonstrated that 'glank' is not presently a word-type in English, he has not shown that the word-type does not exist. The Platonist's point is not, as Howell would have him say, that 'glank' is an uninstantiated but existent word *in English*: a word-type currently present in English but which no one has yet used. It is that 'glank' is an existent word-type that has not entered into English (or any other language). The type lays down a condition for its correct use—that is, that it be used as a noun, that it should be applied to joyful jeeps, that it should be spelt and pronounced in a certain way or ways—even though the word has not entered any language.[12] If a practice of actually using the word were to become established, it would thereby become a part of English. But this has not yet happened and, I dare say, never will. For the Platonist, human practices *are* crucial to understanding language-use, but their function is not that of bringing word-types into existence; it is that of bringing (eternally existent) word-types into languages. Howell's example has not, of itself, subverted this idea.

Nevertheless, Howell might respond by claiming that his distinction between patterns and types enables us to give the best explanation of what happens when, for example, a word-type first enters the language. As Howell sees it, what happens is this: when, through the coming into existence of communal practices, the word-type enters the language, 'the pattern becomes a *type*' (2002: 119). And we have no choice but to regard the type as a new entity, distinct from the pattern, because the type has a property essentially which the mere pattern does not have essentially: namely, the 'property of actually being used in the community in order to carry those qualities' (2002: 119), or, as Howell also describes it, 'the property of being used in the way specified by the practice' (2002: 120). Howell's thought is this: a word-type such as 'dine', unlike the pattern, would not be *that* entity unless it was used in *that* way (and thus had *that* meaning). The same goes, Howell claims, for the hooked cross used in pre-Columbian Amerindian cultures used to signify, amongst other things, fire. Although it shares a geometric pattern with the Nazi swastika, it is not identical with it because the two symbols have distinct uses, and hence differ in meaning (2002: 119–20).

---

[12] One might question the very idea that there can be word-types that are not assigned to a particular language, on the grounds that a word's syntactic role can only be specified by specifying a particular language in terms of which its syntactic properties can be understood. I disagree. One can simply state, e.g., that a word is a name or adjective without having to specify such a language, once it is accepted that a given word may vary in its spelling and in the precise details of its syntactic make-up. One and the same word may thus enter different languages *in different ways*.

In any case, the idea that all existent word-types must be assigned to particular languages is itself counter-intuitive. The same word, we want to say, may occur in more than one language. 'Schadenfreude', e.g., entered English after first being found in German, whilst 'chic' is a word that was once only found in French but is now found in English.

But once more, Howell's discussion of examples, interesting as it is, does not succeed in making his case. According to Howell, the hooked cross and the swastika share a common (eternal) geometrical pattern, but the types themselves, with their different meanings, only came into existence when their respective communities established their distinct meaning-determining practices. But if Howell supposes that we can *only* explain the difference between two symbol-types in this way, he is mistaken. For here is another explanation. Let us call the eternal geometrical pattern shared by the hooked cross and the swastika 'θ'. The two symbol-types have the following distinct property-associates: *being a θ mark used to signify fire* and *being a θ mark used to signify the German Nazi Party*. The condition that a particular must meet to be a token of one is distinct from the condition that must be met by a particular if it is to be a token of the other. Consequently, since the properties that underlie the respective types are different, so are the types themselves. Now, on my view, both of these properties are eternal, and, as we saw in §3.3 above, Howell does not succeed in refuting this view. As a result, given (28)—that is, that a type exists at a time, if its property-associate exists at that time—it follows that both types are eternal too. Naturally, the Nazi swastika is individuated in such a way that it could not have been *tokened* before the Nazi Party existed, but to suppose that this entails that the *type itself* did not exist before this time is to confuse the existence conditions of a type with those of its tokens. Of course, Howell disputes (28), but if his reason for doing so is that the Platonist cannot adequately make out the difference between the hooked cross and the swastika, he is wrong. The hooked cross and the swastika are distinct indicated types, but this difference is not located in the putative fact that respective communities produced them. They differ because the properties underlying them are distinct properties.

This is not to deny that types such as words and symbols are in some sense bound up with human practices. Our specification of the swastika *just is* a specification of a way of using the geometrical pattern. This symbol-type is nothing more nor less than a kind of use that the pattern can be put to in a certain kind of practice. But the establishment of the practice is not required for the symbol-type to *exist*, only for the already existent symbol-type to be *discovered and tokened*. Actual communal practices are the means by which we come across indicated types like these.

This is unlikely to convince Howell, however. As we have seen, he regards a symbol-type as possessing a property essentially which it could only come to have had once the relevant communal practice was in place. This property, 'the pattern's property of *actually being used in the community*' (2002: 119; my italics) to carry semantic or expressive qualities, is what supposedly distinguishes the type from its mere pattern, and which entails that the type only exists once the practice exists. But, once more, there is no need to interpret the place of communal practices in this way. According to the view I favour, it is not an essential property of the swastika—the type—that it *actually be used* to symbolize the Nazi Party. For this type might never have been tokened. *Being actually used to symbolize the Nazi Party*, rather than being a property essentially possessed by the swastika, is a property that must be possessed by any *token*, if it is to count as a token of the swastika. The type merely has the following property essentially: *being such that its correct use is to symbolize the Nazi Party*. But a type can have this property without actually being so used, or even being in a position to be so used. So it follows that the type was not brought into existence once the practice of using it to symbolize the Nazi Party was set up. To my mind, in taking the property of actually being used in a certain way by the community to be an essential property of a symbol-type, Howell once again confuses types with tokens.

We should agree with Howell that cultural, technological, and linguistic types are distinct from what he terms their corresponding 'patterns'. Such patterns are pure types, whereas their corresponding types are items specified by making reference to communal practices.[13] But it does not follow that such types only come to exist once the relevant practices are in place. Types—*all* types—are eternal existents, and Howell has said nothing to undermine this claim.

3.5 Conclusion

Types, I have established, are abstract, unstructured, unchanging, and eternally existent entities. So we now have a clear idea of the commitments involved in the type/token theory. Crucially, these features are shared by *all* types. So even if works of music turned out to be indicated types—which, I shall argue in Chapters 8 and 9, they are not—it would not follow, for

---

[13] Since talk of 'patterns' might encourage the mistaken thought that such pure types are structured, it is probably best to abandon such talk and use the less misleading 'pure type' instead.

example, that they were the sorts of things that could be brought into being by their composers. If *In This House, On This Morning* is a type whose tokens are sound-sequence-events, Marsalis's compositional act could not have involved the literal creation of the piece.

At this point, however, two questions need to be addressed. First, given what we now know about types, *should* we really think of works of music as the type/token theory would have it: that is, as abstract, unstructured, fixed, unchanging, and, above all, eternally existent entities? Second, if musical works *are* types, how are they individuated? The responses I shall make are, respectively, that the type/token theory is the best available answer to the categorical question in the ontology of music, and that (a version of) sonicism is correct in taking such works to be individuated purely in terms of how they sound. The task of making good the first of these claims begins in Chapter 4.

4

Defending the Type/Token Theory I

4.1 Introduction

Our type ontology is now in place. Types are abstract, eternally existent entities that are unstructured and both modally and temporally inflexible. Consequently, we now know that the type/token theory brings with it a commitment to viewing works of music in just this way: that is, as eternal existents that have neither spatial location nor structure, and which are fixed and unchanging with respect to their intrinsic properties.

Of course, we established in §§1.2−1.4 that the type/token theory is the face-value answer to the categorial question. Construing works of music as types of sound-event offers a natural and intuitive explanation of their repeatability, and does so without compromising either our modal intuitions concerning works' occurrences or our presumption that such works are entities in their own right. Nonetheless, a critic might counter that these benefits of the type/token theory are outweighed by objections that emerge now that the ontological nature of types has been clarified. It is to objections of this kind that this chapter and the next are dedicated. Chapter 5 is devoted to defending a conception of works of music, *qua* types, as eternally existent items discovered, rather than brought into being, by their composers. The present chapter, meanwhile, sets out to disarm objections to viewing musical works as abstract, unstructured, fixed, and unchanging. By the end of Chapter 5 we shall see that what might, at first blush, appear to be deeply troubling objections to the type/token theory can, in fact, be countered with relative ease.

4.2 Unstructuredness and Analogical Predication

Let us begin the project of defending the type/token theory by refocusing on the key claim made in §2.4: namely, that types, by their very nature, are unstructured items. To recap, the word-type 'cat', for instance, is not itself *ontologically* complex; on the contrary, it is an item that, though unstructured in itself, binds tokens together according to whether they—the tokens—are structured in the correct way. The word-type itself is an ontologically thin entity; the complexity lies in the condition that something must meet to be a properly formed token of the word.

Given that types have no parts themselves, and that the type/token theory takes musical works to be types of a certain kind, it follows, of course, that the type/token theorist must deny that works of music have parts too. In particular, it follows that musical works—like other event-types, such as The Tango and The F.A. Cup Final—do not themselves have temporal parts. As we noted in §2.4, whilst events are things that take place through time, and hence are temporally divisible, the same cannot be said of types of event. By contrast, although types of event *exist at* times—indeed, exist at all times—they are not *extended* in time. Types, even types of event, are in this respect more like substances than events.

But is such a conception of works of music defensible? An obvious objection to it is that our talk of works of music, if taken at face value, straightforwardly commits us to such works having temporal parts. For example, the following claims would seem to be true:

(32) Bach's Violin Concerto BWV 1041 ends with an A minor chord,
(33) Handel's First Sonata has a trill in its fourth measure,
(34) 'Take Five' is in 5/4 time;

and the truth of each of (32)–(34) would seem to require that the works in question have a temporal extent and, hence, are temporally divisible. A work can only end on an A minor chord, or have a trill in its fourth measure, or be in 5/4 time, if it is something that is itself *spread out* in time.

Presumably, it is the fact that musical works are susceptible to such description that provides a major motivation for the conception of such works as—or as having as constituents—*sound structures*, where a sound structure is taken to be a type that comprises ' "this complex sound [-type] followed by this one, followed by this one," with all audible characteristics comprised' (Levinson 1980b: 88).[1] However, enough has been said already to prove that this idea is an ontological dead end. Bach's Violin Concerto BWV 1041, *qua* type of sound-sequence-event, is not something that has a temporal extent: whilst its occurrences all have temporal parts, the work itself—the thing these occurrences are *of*—does not. Consequently, we can make no sense of the claim that it consists of one sound *following* another. *Following* in this sense is a temporal relation that has application only to things that occur: things extended in time. We have just seen that works of music—in contrast to their occurrences—are not like this.

So how can a type/token theorist reconcile her theory concerning the ontological nature of works of music with our intuition that sentences such as (32)–(34) are genuinely true? One thing is for sure: she cannot treat the sentences' respective predicates as having their usual meanings. If the predicates in (32)–(34) mean what they mean when they are truly applied to performances or playings, then (32)–(34) cannot be anything other than false. As Wolterstorff has remarked (1980: 61), to predicate 'ends with an A minor chord' of a performance is to say that it ends with an *occurrence* of an A minor chord; and this is plainly not what we are attributing to the work itself. Works do not themselves consist of passages of token sounds. Furthermore, if, as we have noted, works are not themselves things that are extended in time, it cannot be true that they begin or end in time, or can be temporally divided in any way.

All of this indicates that a type/token theorist looking to satisfy our intuitions about the truth-values of (32)–(34) should revisit the doctrine of analogical predication introduced in §2.3. Applying this doctrine to predications concerning works of music, and factoring in §1.5's conclusion that works of music are norm-types, a type/token theorist can say this: an utterance of (32), for instance, is indeed true, but only because its predicate, when applied to the work, changes its usual meaning: rather than expressing the property of *ending with an occurrence of an A minor chord* (as it does when it

---

[1] Such is the way that the type/token theory is usually elucidated. A work, on such a construal, is a sound structure or, if we take such works to be indicated types, a type that has a sound structure as one of its elements. One of the morals to be drawn from the discussion of types in Ch. 2 is that type/token theorists have tended to misconstrue the nature of their own claim: works, if types, cannot be structured in this way.

is applied to a work's performances and playings), when applied to a work, the predicate expresses the property of *being such that something cannot be a properly formed token of it unless it ends with an occurrence of an A minor chord.* Likewise, (33) sees the predicate 'has a trill in its fourth measure' express the property of *being such that something cannot be a properly formed token of it unless a trill occurs in its fourth measure,* whilst (34) is true because the property ascribed to the work is that of *being such that something cannot be a properly formed token of it unless it is in 5/4 time.*

The benefit of such an approach is obvious: it enables us to account for the phenomenon of widespread shared predication between works and their occurrences, yet does so without compromising the insights provided by the type/token theory. In other words, the type/token theorist can acknowledge that works are not themselves sound structures, yet explain away the fact that we speak of them *as if* they were. Our theory allows us to assent to all of the sentences that our pre-theoretical intuition would have us assent to; yet it does this without forcing us to treat works of music as themselves temporally structured.

Now, in §1.2 we saw that our description of works of music as objects of hearing can be taken at face value. Works of music, even though abstract types, are audible in a derivative sense, just as material objects are. But having put this case to one side, I would like to suggest that the doctrine of analogy be applied to all other cases in which a predicate used to express a property is transmitted from a token to a type. To reiterate a point made in §2.3, once it is granted that works of music are types, it follows that any predicate true of a performance of a work W in virtue of its being a token of W is thereby true of W itself. As we now know, what does *not* follow from this is that works and their performances share the same properties: works of music, unlike their token performances, are things lacking both temporal parts and spatial location; so Wollheim is wrong to suppose that musical works may have what he terms 'physical properties' (1968: 98). Although it is tempting to suppose that the phenomenon of the transmission of predicates from performances to works is mirrored by the transmission of identical properties, this is not, in fact, generally the case. That a work of music and its performances and playings can share such a wide range of predicates is to be explained, not by taking the work and its performances to share the same properties, but by taking the properties had by works and those had by their tokens to be distinct but systematically related in the way recommended by Wolterstorff.

4.3 Musical Works as Fixed and Unchanging

So much for the thought that works of music, unlike types, are structured. It turns out to be a case in which our pre-theoretic intuitions are trumped, yet accounted for, by mature philosophical theory. The fact that works have no temporal extent means that they cannot have temporal parts; and any tendency to resist such a view can be explained away as the result of a failure to see that our talk of works themselves as being structured can be analysed according to the doctrine of analogy.

But, as I noted in §4.1, the type/token theorist is not merely committed to viewing works of music as abstract, unstructured entities; she must also treat them as fixed and unchanging. Section 2.5 established that types are both modally and temporally inflexible: they cannot have different intrinsic properties to those they have actually; and they are incapable of changing in their intrinsic properties over time. Consequently, musical works, if types, must be fixed and unchanging in just the same sense. Such a claim about works of music is, however, controversial. Indeed, it has been argued—notably by Rohrbaugh (2003)—that the type/token theory ultimately fails because musical works and types differ with respect to their modal and temporal properties. I shall spend this section replying to his fascinating, yet flawed, arguments.

Rohrbaugh trusts that a consideration of examples will demonstrate our intuitions to point in the same direction as his: namely, towards the thesis that musical works could have been otherwise and are capable of genuine change. Thus, in defence of the thesis that musical works are modally flexible, Rohrbaugh claims that Bruckner's Ninth Symphony might have been finished had Bruckner lived longer, and that we can all imagine cases in which a piece could have differed slightly, if its composer had been of a mind to have altered things (Rohrbaugh 2003: 182).

Having said this, Rohrbaugh admits that the case for musical works being temporally flexible is harder to make. Such works are not physical objects, after all, so it is tempting to think that their properties are fixed for all time. Furthermore, one tempting avenue of reply to this observation, seemingly available to the philosopher attracted to the thought that artworks such as photographs admit of temporal flexibility, would seem to be closed off to the defender of a similar thesis in the philosophy of music. To be sure, it could be argued that if a photograph's negative deteriorates, then we are prevented from seeing how the photograph—the abstract object—once was; which, in turn, might be taken as evidence that the photograph itself has changed. But the crucial difference between a photograph and a musical work is that the latter has no physical object analogous to a photograph's negative that may serve as the locus of change (Rohrbaugh 2003: 188). Nonetheless, Rohrbaugh appeals to examples in order to persuade us that musical works *are* temporally flexible. Composers, he says, may *revise* their works after they first compose them (2003: 189); and he also claims it to be tempting to describe a folk-song as having changed, if it is sung differently as time passes. 'How', asks Rohrbaugh (2003: 188), 'are we to describe the fact that a song or story is sung or told differently as it is passed down from person to person if not as change in its structure?'.

Of course, someone may grant that Rohrbaugh is correct about works from the folk tradition, yet nonetheless view scored works as unchanging. That is, it might be countered that a work's score fixes its properties for all time. In response to this kind of reply, Rohrbaugh appeals to theoretical unity. Whilst accepting that 'there are strong intuitions that Austen's *Emma* and Beethoven's Tempest Sonata are not changing' (2003: 188), he claims that 'a general framework which allows for the possibility of change in all artworks is the more powerful one' (2003: 188). Given that sculptures and paintings may change, and that (arguably) folk-songs may change too, any lingering intuitions that scored musical works lack temporal flexibility should be regarded as errant.

To my mind, however, Rohrbaugh's examples of putative temporal flexibility in works can be explained away by employing the strategy outlined in §2.5: namely, that of redescribing the putative cases in which works change as cases in which there really exist a *series* of (inflexible) works that differ in their intrinsic properties. It is quite true, for example, that we commonly *describe* works as being 'revised', but such talk is quite unreflective, and, in any case, it is not obvious that we should regard a 'revised' work as a work that has changed, as opposed to being a distinct work whose composition was based upon an appreciation of the original one. Imagine, for example, that in 1920, some ten years after the composition of the *Fantasia on a Theme by Thomas Tallis*, Vaughan Williams returns to the score and, as perhaps he would put it, decides to make some revisions. To this effect, he produces a new score differing from his 1910 score in several significant respects. Would we say that the work had been *changed* by Vaughan Williams's actions in 1920? I don't think so. What we *would* say, I contend, is that Vaughan Williams had composed a new *version* of the piece; and what we would mean by this is that the two works are distinct, yet belong to the same *broader* type by virtue of sharing much of the same tonal structure (Levinson 1990c: 234).[2]

Rohrbaugh's claim that revisions change works is also subject to a worry of a more theoretical nature. When an object changes, it no longer exists in its previous state. If a painting, for example, suffers discolouration at *t*, then it no longer exists in its pre-discoloured condition at *t*. But now look again at the imagined case in which Vaughan Williams's *Fantasia* is revised in 1920. It would be a mistake to deny that the piece-as-indicated-by-the-1910-score continued to exist after Vaughan Williams's revisions. Indeed, given that the original score would still be recoverable, the original version could continue to be performed alongside the 1920 version. This being so, it is *ontologically on a par* with the piece scored in 1920, rather than being an earlier stage in a single piece's life. If the piece *had* changed, its pre-1920 state would no longer exist post-1920. But, since it is still performable from this time, it plainly *does* exist. Consequently, it is not that Vaughan Williams's imagined revisions change the work; it is that the new score represents a distinct piece based upon the work composed in 1910.

Needless to say, these considerations apply to the example that Rohrbaugh describes as a single song's changing its lyrics though time. Again, Rohrbaugh has said nothing that prevents us from describing this case as one in which distinct *versions*—based upon the original—are sung down the years. And, besides this, the worry about the very idea of a musical work changing recurs. It makes little sense to say that a song has changed with respect to its lyrics at *t*, if it could still be sung with the original lyrics after *t*, as would evidently be possible. In such a case, the original version unquestionably still exists after *t*, and so there is no sense in which it is a mere temporal stage in something that has since changed.

At this point, Rohrbaugh might object that his account of how musical works change is, in fact, simple and unproblematic: '*what it is* for a work to change its structural features', he says, 'is for later occurrences to differ

---

[2] Naturally, this claim and others like it need to be interpreted according to the doctrine of analogy set out in §§2.3 and 4.3.

in their structural features from earlier occurrences' (Rohrbaugh 2003: 189; my emphasis). But for one thing, this remark, once again, presumes that the earlier and later occurrences are occurrences of the same work: something the type/token theorist will dispute. And furthermore, this account of how a work can change fails to speak to the objection raised in the previous paragraph. For a work to have undergone genuine change, it must no longer exist in its pre-change state. Given that works of music are repeatable entities—that is, items that have performances, playings, and other sound-events as occurrences—this means that for a work to change, it must no longer be possible for it to be performed or otherwise tokened in its pre-change state. However, the kinds of cases to which Rohrbaugh draws our attention plainly do not meet this condition. The earlier and later versions of the work or song can both be tokened after the putative change has taken place, thereby revealing that they both exist at the later time, and hence cannot be different temporal stages of one and the same entity.

These considerations, it seems to me, are sufficient to undermine the examples that Rohrbaugh himself takes to demonstrate that musical works are temporally flexible. And in the wake of such objections, it would be a mistake to think that an appeal to theoretical unity could salvage matters. In particular, Rohrbaugh is mistaken in thinking that 'a general framework which allows for the possibility of change in all artworks is the more powerful one' (2003: 188). It is doubtless true that those works of art that are concrete particulars can change: it does not come as news to be told that a sculpture can become more weather-beaten over time. But it is misguided to suppose that an acceptance that sculptures and paintings admit of genuine change puts pressure on us to regard works of music as similarly temporally flexible. To put it bluntly, no theoretical unity should be expected here because, whilst sculptures and paintings are physical particulars, works of music are not. Given that works of music fall into an ontological category distinct from sculptures and paintings, there is no reason to expect that they too should be capable of change, especially since our original concern consisted precisely in wondering how a musical work could change without there being a physical object to act as the locus of such change.

In my view, then, to claim that a work can change through time is unwarranted, and perhaps even incoherent. Despite this, though, an opponent transfixed by the thought that musical works are temporally flexible might yet remain unconvinced that *all* cases of apparent temporal flexibility can be explained away in the style recommended up to now. To adapt our previous thought-experiment, imagine, for instance, that the revisions which Vaughan Williams makes to the score of the *Fantasia* in 1920 are minor, footling even. Perhaps just a note is changed here and there. In a situation such as this it might be tempting to think that the work scored in 1920 is the same as the work scored in 1910, and hence that the work has undergone some intrinsic change. Furthermore, our opponent might also allege that the type/token theorist's strategy for dealing with apparent cases of temporal flexibility does not admit of application to the *modal* case. *Couldn't* Bruckner have completed his Ninth Symphony? *Couldn't* Beethoven have composed the Tempest Sonata—that very same work—with just a few different notes (Rohrbaugh 2003: 184)? The idea that Bruckner, had he completed his Ninth Symphony, would have composed a different piece altogether has a paradoxical ring to it.

So how should a type/token theorist respond to such challenges? One thing is for sure: she cannot allow the *extent* of the differences between an earlier and a later score to determine whether or not the scores count as scores of the same, changing work. As we noted in §2.5, if a later score deviates from an earlier score in *any* way that is not explicitly allowed for in the original, then the new score represents a distinct type. Two scores that specify even marginally variant conditions for a properly formed performance to meet can only count as scores of distinct works.

This being so, the type/token theorist should stand firm and explain why the consequences of taking such a stance cause us no serious problems. Indeed, when it comes to the putative temporal flexibility of works of music, she should point out that what is a relatively minor conflict between the type/token theory and our ordinary thought and talk about works is a small price to pay for avoiding the problems that Rohrbaugh faces in trying to explain how such change in works is possible. True, we might be tempted to regard a composer's very minor revision of a score as a case in which the composer changes the work: but nothing of any great importance seems to hang on describing such cases in this way, rather than as cases in which a composer composes a second work that differs very slightly from the original; and in any case, we have seen that the very idea of such change is philosophically problematic.

Much the same moral also applies to the sorts of examples intended to show that works of music are modally flexible. We do, indeed, say things like 'Bruckner might have completed his Ninth Symphony': a claim that cannot be literally true, if Bruckner's Ninth Symphony is a type. If Bruckner *had* scored an additional fourth movement, his score would have specified a condition for a performance's being well formed that differed (considerably) from that specified by his actual score for the piece. A possible world in which Bruckner 'completes' the Ninth Symphony can only be a world in which he composes a work distinct from the actual Ninth Symphony, but one that shares the actual work's first three movements.[3]

But once again, I see little in this conclusion that need trouble us. Yes, the type/token theorist has no choice but to say that Bruckner's Ninth Symphony could not have differed with respect to its intrinsic properties: had he done what we would describe as 'completing the work', he would, in fact, have composed a work distinct from the work that exists actually. But none of this is *so* counter-intuitive as to undo all the good work that the type/token theory has done up to now. All we need do is to make an adjustment to the way in which we understand our talk of 'completing a work'. As we have seen, if two scores lay down differing respective conditions for a properly formed performance, they thereby represent distinct works. That such a difference may be extremely slight is beside the point. Consequently, since the compositional process inevitably involves the making of additions and changes to a score, this process can only be one in which a composer progressively composes different, but related, items until, with the final such act, a state of resolution is reached, and he takes himself to have finished. 'Completing a work', then, is not a matter of bringing to an end a process of *moulding* a single thing; it consists in arriving at a work by means of successively indicating other entities on the way. Any development of the score, however minor, amounts to the indication of a distinct object. The 'finished work' is the final item composed in this process: the work represented by the score at the point at which the composer regards his aims to have been met, or to have been as well met as he can manage.

---

[3] Naturally, given the unstructuredness of works of music, such talk of works 'sharing' movements must be interpreted according to the doctrine of analogy introduced in §§2.3 and 4.2.

No doubt, many people will find this conception of composition odd. But it is quite coherent and, what is more, cannot be defeated by a mere incredulous stare.[4] It is the tiniest wrinkle in our *prima facie* answer to the categorial question: an answer that we have seen accord with our intuitions on, and explain the nature of, musical works' repeatability and audibility.

4.4 Abstractness and Audibility (Again)

Having defended the theses that works of music, *qua* types, are unstructured, temporally inflexible, and modally inflexible, let us return to issue by their relation to space. Types, we noted in §2.3, are, by their very nature, abstract entities (i.e. things lacking spatial location). Consequently, if the type/token theory is to be believed, works of music must be *abstracta* too. Clearly, such a claim has plenty going for it. At the very least, musical works have—to borrow a phrase of Armstrong's—a 'strange and ambiguous' spatial location (1991: 194). The question 'Where is Beethoven's Fifth Symphony?' has a curious ring to it: its occurrences take place in concert-halls and living rooms, but we do not describe the work itself as inhabiting such spaces. Furthermore, a nominalist's insistence that the work is, nevertheless, concrete is stymied by the available substantive explanations of such a claim. Leaving aside the obviously implausible attempts to identify works with scores or performances, the options would seem to be these: either the work is a scattered object, partially present wherever its performances and other occurrences take place; or else it is a concrete type somehow wholly present wherever its instances are located. Both of these alternatives were raised, only to be dismissed, in §§1.3 and 2.3 respectively. If a work is a scattered object, it follows that an audience in a concert-hall cannot listen to it *in toto*; whilst a conception of types as concrete entities wholly present wherever their tokens are found is (at best) elusive. All in all, it seems best to regard works of music, by contrast with their occurrences, as abstract objects: things located *nowhere*.

As I noted in §1.2, a conception of musical works as abstract entities is likely to prompt the objection that only their concrete performances and playings, rather than the works themselves, are capable of being heard.

---

[4] This phrase is, of course, Lewis's (1973: 86).

Perception, it will be claimed, is a causal process, and abstract entities have no causal powers. But, as it happens, and as I argued in the earlier discussion of this matter, the type/token theory does not so much preclude a musical work's being perceptible as explain what this perceptibility consists in. It is a familiar point that we talk of hearing a work *by* hearing a performance of it, and the type/token theory nicely explains how such talk can be true.

To recap, events are the primary bearers of the causal relation. An object other than an event counts as a cause or effect in a derivative sense if it participates causally in an event that figures in a causal process: if, that is, the object participates in events in an appropriate way. My claim in §1.2 was that there is no principled way of determining what 'appropriate' means here: all we can say is that an object participates in an event in such a way just in case it bears a suitable relation to the said event. One such suitable relation, I maintained, is the relation that stands between an event-type and a token of that type: a type may be counted as participating in an event in a causally active way if the causally efficacious event in question is one of its tokens. Once this point is granted, there is no obstacle to a type/token theorist's regarding a work of music as an object of hearing in this derivative sense: a work counts as such if one of its token sound-events is causally productive of an auditory experience. One's hearing a work by hearing one of its perform-ances adds up to this: a sound-event is causally productive of an auditory experience; and the work of which the said sound-event is a token appropri-ately participates in the event by virtue of the obtaining of this type/token relation. That the type that is the work is abstract is of no consequence.

So far, so good. But perhaps a determined objector will not be finished quite yet. In §4.2 we saw that works of music bear their acoustic properties only analogically: unlike their token sound-sequence-occurrences, works of music, although existent in time, are not temporally extended, so do not themselves begin or end in time, or possess acoustic properties such as *ending with an A minor chord*. Such properties are had by concrete patterns of sounds—tokens of works—but not by works themselves. Indeed, works, by contrast with their tokens, are not *composed* of sounds—the things we hear when we listen to a performance—at all.

This being so, our determined objector is likely to protest that the audibility of a work of music can be no less analogical than its possession of acoustic properties. Perhaps, she will concede, the arguments of §1.2 are sufficient to persuade us that there is *some kind* of derivative sense in which we can be said to hear works in addition to their performances, but this derivative sense can only be an *analogical* sense: were the type/token theory correct, the audibility of a work of music would be nothing over and above the fact that its tokens are audible. The type/token theorist is free to *say* that a work of music is audible, but 'audible' here cannot mean what it means when we describe material objects in this way.

But in my view, this objection moves far too quickly. To be sure, a sound-event-type is audible in a derivative sense only: whilst we hear a performance of a work (that is, a sound-event) directly, we hear the work itself only derivatively. But we must not forget that this derivative sense in which a type of sound-event can be heard is the same sense in which *any* entity other than an event can be causally responsible for an auditory experience. Even material objects such as sticks, stones, and people can be counted as causes only by virtue of being related appropriately to the events that actually *do* the causing. This is not to deny, of course, that there exists an important disanalogy between works of music, *qua* types, and sticks, stones, and people: works of music, unlike these other paradigms of causally efficacious entities, are *abstracta*. But, as we saw in §4.2, there is no convincing rationale for denying that abstract types can similarly participate causally in events. Indeed, the idea that a type may so participate in an event by virtue of the said event's being one of the type's tokens has an intuitive ring to it. So, since there is no good reason to deny that types may be causally active within events, there is, similarly, no good reason to deny that the causal chain leading to an auditory experience may begin with an event in which a type participates causally. And what this means is that a type/token theorist need not deny that works of music are audible in the same sense in which other objects are. When a type/token theorist applies 'is audible' to a work of music, the predicate expresses the same sense as it does when it is applied to material objects.

4.5 Works and Interpretations

A conception of works of music as abstract, unstructured, and dually inflexible is thus eminently defensible. Any conflict with our intuitions can either be explained away or else regarded as a small price to pay for a categorial theory that so neatly explains musical works' repeatability. However, even if all this is granted, one might nonetheless wonder whether it is right to view such works as types whose tokens include performances. Indeed, according to Sharpe (1979), it is *interpretations* of works of music, rather than those works themselves, that are types of performance.[5] In the remainder of this chapter I shall explain why I think Sharpe's argument against the type/token theory is unsound.

Sharpe's argument (1979: 438–9) goes as follows:

(35) A part of a token of a type K can always be replaced by a corresponding part of another token of K and yet remain a token of K.

(36) But two performances of a work of music W may cease to count as performances of W, if they exchange some of their corresponding parts.

So (37) Works of music are not types.

(38) Exchange of corresponding parts between performances of W is permissible only when the performances interpret the work in the same way.

So (39) The type of which performances are tokens is an interpretation of W, not W itself.

We should not quarrel with Sharpe's first premiss. As he himself puts it,

I could cut off part of a linen red flag and replace the missing part with the corresponding part of a plastic red flag of the same size. It is still a red flag, a token of that type. I could replace the pages containing Molly Bloom's monologue from my Penguin copy of *Ulysses* with the corresponding passage from the Bodley Head edition and it remains a copy of Ulysses, a token of that type. (Sharpe 1979: 438)

Sharpe has, indeed, hit upon an important fact about types and tokens here. However, when discussing the case of switching corresponding parts of tokens of the same novel, Sharpe appears to come out with a *non sequitur* that, ultimately, reveals why premises (36) and (38)—once the latter is appropriately disambiguated—are both false. Let us delve further.

After having set up the case in which tokens of *Ulysses* have corresponding parts exchanged, Sharpe goes on to claim that 'crucially, the operation makes no aesthetic difference' (1979: 438). This remark, though,

---

[5] Here Sharpe presupposes that the type/token theorist will formulate her thesis as the claim that works of music are types of performance. For our present purpose, nothing important hangs on this. His argument, and my reply, are unaffected if we treat the type/token theorist's doctrine to be that such works are types of sound-sequence-occurrence.

is more than a little puzzling. For why should whether any *aesthetic* difference results be relevant to the point at issue? For that point concerns only whether the tokens remain tokens of the type in question, not their resultant aesthetic merit. Sharpe's first premiss, remember—that is, (35)—states merely that both tokens will continue to exist as tokens of K, not that their aesthetic properties will remain unaltered. A linen red flag, after all, is an uglier flag, if part of it is replaced by a corresponding part from a plastic token.

Why does this *non sequitur* matter, though? It matters because, once uncovered, it explains Sharpe's erroneous commitment to (36) and, as we shall see, a fatal lack of clarity when it comes to (38). For why does Sharpe think that two performances may cease to count as performances of a given work, if they undergo an exchange of parts. His answer is clear: it is because the result may not be interpretationally coherent:

[I]f I remove the last movement of Walter's performance of Mahler's *Das Lied* and replace it with the last movement of Bernstein's my action does have aesthetic repercussions. For one thing we expect a conductor to present in performance a unified view of a work. If he believes that the last movement is the climax of the work and that the tempi, phrasing and dynamics of all the other movements must be calculated accordingly then his conception of the work will be lost by making such drastic alterations. (Sharpe 1979: 438)

Interpretational unity demands that substitutions only be made between performances according to the same interpretation. But now the chickens have come home to roost. For, as I noted a moment ago, the fact that such an exchange of parts results in the production of a performance lacking such interpretational unity does not entail that it fails to qualify as a token of the work. Indeed, as Stephen Davies has urged (2001: 184), such a performance will surely qualify as a rendition of the work, if it obeys the score. Such a performance would, no doubt, be aesthetically unsatisfactory, but there is no reason to suppose that we would deny that it was a performance of the work at all.

What this indicates is that Sharpe has given no good reason for supposing (36) to be true. He commits himself to (36) as a result of conflating the question of what is required for a performance to count as a performance of a given work with the wholly separate question of what makes such a performance aesthetically satisfying.

When it comes to (38), we can see how this same confusion causes Sharpe to inadvertently trade on an ambiguity. In defence of (38), Sharpe says that '[i]t is permissible to substitute a section from a different performance if it is by the same artist but if the artist's interpretation has changed in the interim then it is not allowable. In other words a performance must be throughout a performance of a single interpretation' (Sharpe 1979: 438). But what does 'permissible' mean here? Premiss (38) gains its intuitive ring by our taking 'permissible' to mean *aesthetically acceptable*. Performances that lack interpretational unity are, after all, confusing and chaotic. But, crucially, this cannot be the sense that attaches to 'permissible' in (38) if Sharpe is to derive his conclusion. For, if the intended disanalogy with the case of the red flag is to make sense, he must claim that exchanging parts of performances that differ in their respective interpretations results in the performances *ceasing to be tokens of the work*. In other words, a 'permissible' substitution must mean a substitution that preserves the tokens' status as tokens of the work in question. However, (38)—once it is disambiguated in this way—is false. Sharpe, as we saw earlier, has given no adequate reason for supposing that such substitutions are only permissible in this sense if both tokens share the same interpretation. Once we distinguish these two kinds of permissible substitutions, Sharpe's case against my face-value theory crumbles. He has said nothing to undermine my conviction that the relation obtaining between a work and one of its performances is the type/token relation.

4.6 Conclusion and Resumé

According to the type/token theory, a work of music is a norm-type whose tokens are sound-sequence-events. As such, it is the natural resting-place for a would-be ontologist of music since, in stark contrast to those of its competitors examined in Chapter 1, it explains musical works' repeatability in familiar terms whilst allowing for the fact that such works can be heard in their entirety. Furthermore, we have seen in the present chapter that several of the type/token theory's controversial commitments—namely, that such works are abstract, unstructured, and both modally and temporally inflexible—are, in fact, insufficiently disruptive of our intuitions to justify our giving up what is the face-value answer to the categorial question. Of course, the type/token theory's Platonism—its commitment to the idea that works of music exist at all times—has not yet been defended; and it is to this task that I now turn. But, as we shall see, sacrificing the idea that musical works can either be created or destroyed turns out to be a small price to pay for a convincing account of such works' ontological nature.

5

Defending the Type/Token Theory II: Musical Platonism

5.1 Introduction

As I noted in §3.2, types exist eternally. They exist at all times. The reason why is this: a type exists at a time if the property of which it is the associate exists at that time; and properties—all properties—are eternal existents. According to the type/token theory I recommend, *In This House, On This Morning* is a norm-type: specifically, a type of sound-sequence-event, ψ, whose tokens, if they are to be properly formed, must have all of the set Σ of properties normative within ψ.[1] Since this type's property-associate—*being a properly formed instance of* ψ[2]—exists eternally, so does the type: the musical work. Musical Platonism results.

Three significant things follow from the fact that musical works exist eternally: they are not dependent for their existence upon being performed, played, or otherwise tokened; they cannot be brought into being by their composers; and they cannot be destroyed. As one might expect, each of these consequences—although particularly the second—has attracted a good deal of criticism;[3] and it is widely assumed that the Platonist position is unsustainable.[4] However, in this chapter I shall argue both that it is much less counter-intuitive than might be supposed, and that the arguments

---

[1] Just what kinds of properties these are has, as yet, not been specified. In Chs. 8 and 9 I will argue for (timbral) *sonicism*. This view has it that only *acoustic* properties are members of Σ. All that matters, for whether a sound-sequence-event is a properly formed token of *In This House, On This Morning* is how it sounds.

[2] i.e., the property of instantiating every member of Σ.

[3] e.g., from Cox (1985), Fisher (1991), Howell (2002), Levinson (1980b, 1990c); Margolis (1980), Predelli (1995, 2001), Sharpe (1995, 2001), Trivedi (2002), and Zemach (1986).

[4] Stephen Davies, for one, claims that, when it comes to Platonism, 'critics of this line clearly win the day' (2001: 38).

against it are unsuccessful. The fact that musical Platonism is a consequence of the type/token theory should not be held against it.

5.2 Platonism it is: Replies to Anderson and Levinson

If musical works are types, then they exist at all times. However, before this Platonist consequence is defended, it is worth considering two attempts to reconcile the type/token theory with the thesis that composers bring their works into being: one inspired by Wolterstorff (1980: 88–9) and elaborated by James Anderson (1985); the other proposed by Levinson (1980b: 78–82). In this section I shall argue that any appearance of such a reconciliation is illusory. Platonism is the position where any type/token theorist inevitably ends up, and we had better just get used to this fact.

As most readers will have gathered by now, the type/token theory I recommend is greatly influenced by Wolterstorff's work (1980: pt. 2). Although I depart from his view in allowing that a work can have occurrences that are neither performances nor playings, this departure concerns a mere point of detail: we agree that musical works are norm-types whose tokens are sound-sequence-events, and I second his doctrine of analogical predication. I also agree with his claim that '[t]o compose is not to bring into existence what one composes' (1980: 88). Musical works do, indeed, 'exist everlastingly' (1980: 88), and so cannot be brought into being by their composers. Where we differ is in our respective attitudes to the Platonism that inevitably ensues. Seemingly troubled by its apparent counter-intuitiveness, and keen to assuage the intuition that composers bring their works into being, Wolterstorff seeks to draw a subtle distinction between the entity that is the work and the entity *qua* work. Attempting to sweeten the Platonist pill, Wolterstorff claims that whilst a piece's composer does not bring the entity that is the work into existence, he nonetheless turns this entity into a work:

What the composer does must be understood as consisting in bringing it about that a preexistent kind becomes *a work*—specifically, *a work of his*. It is to bring it about that something becomes a work. And the composer does that by selecting properties as criteria for correctness in occurrence. (Wolterstorff 1980: 88–9)

Wolterstorff's idea would seem to be this: in composing a work, a composer selects some of the eternally existent type's properties as normative, thus transforming a merely descriptive type into a norm-type: a type that can have well-formed and malformed tokens.

As we shall see presently, the idea that composition involves the composer's selecting as normative certain properties of a descriptive sound-event-type is an important insight into the nature of musical composition (as long as it is recognized that the summation of such a process is the discovery of a norm-type). However, there are two reasons why Wolterstorff's particular spin on this proposal—that a composer transforms a descriptive type into a norm-type—is incoherent. First, as Anderson has noted (1985: 43), if it is the case, as Wolterstorff claims (1980: 88), that musical *works* exist eternally, it is plain that a descriptive type cannot be transformed into a work of music by its composer. Nothing can become what it is already. Second, it was established in §2.4 that types are both modally and temporally inflexible: so, given that a norm-type's normativity is an intrinsic feature of it, it is impossible for a type to be transformed in this way. Types are fixed and unchanging. If works are norm-types, they have eternal existence as such. Wolterstorff cannot take the edge off the Platonism that ensues from his own theory of types.

Having said this, Anderson adapts Wolterstorff's position in a way that both avoids these problems and, so he claims, rescues Wolterstorff from the clutches of Platonism. Anderson's idea is that the eternally existent descriptive type of sound-sequence-event and its corresponding norm-type—the descriptive type with certain properties selected as normative by its composer—are distinct entities. The composer *discovers* the descriptive type; but once he stipulates that certain of its properties are to be regarded as normative, he thereby brings into being a new entity: the work of music. 'It is', he says, 'in virtue of this activity that the norm-kinds that are musical works come into existence' (1985: 47). Whilst a work of music's corresponding descriptive type is a natural kind, the work of music itself—the norm-type—is not (1985: 48).

But although Anderson avoids the two troubles facing Wolterstorff's original position, he cannot evade a third. A work of music is, it is true, distinct from its corresponding purely descriptive sound-event-type: the work, but not the descriptive type, is a type of sound-event that has certain properties as normative. But the crucial point is that even this norm-type exists everlastingly. For *all* properties are eternal existents: even the properties associated with norm-types. *In This House, On This Morning*, I have said, is the norm-type ψ, whose normative properties make up the set Σ; the property of which this type is the associate is *being a properly formed instance of* ψ. But this property, no less than any other, exists eternally; which means, by (28)—the thesis that a property exists at t only if its type-associate exists at t—that the norm-type is an eternal existent too. Composition does indeed involve the selection of certain properties as normative, but the summation of this selection is a kind of *finding*: the selection of something that is already there. Since Anderson questions neither Wolterstorff's assumption that properties exist eternally, nor his commitment to (28), there is no way in which Anderson's adaptation of Wolterstorff's framework can avoid Platonism.[5]

So much for Wolterstorff's own views on composition and Anderson's development of them. Wolterstorff's and Anderson's remarks yield some insights into the nature of composition, but cannot deflect the type/token theory from fully-fledged Platonism. Levinson, by contrast, seeks to avoid the conclusion that musical works, *qua* types, exist at all times by very different means: namely, by construing works of music as *indicated types*: types that Levinson has described as 'contextually qualified, person-and-time-tethered abstract object[s]' (1990c: 216). Such items are, supposedly, structures in which contextual features figure ineliminably (1980b: 82). Thus *In This House, On This Morning* is not, according to Levinson, the pure sound-event-type ψ, but the indicated type ψ-*as-indicated-by-Marsalis-in-1992-in-musico-historical-context-C*,[6] in which *indication* typically (as in this case) involves the writing of a score.[7] Why does Levinson believe that

---

[5] As Zemach puts it, 'since all properties and all kinds exist for all eternity, so does, in particular, that kind which has the following property: having those, and not others, of its properties as criteria for correctness. The everlasting existence of that Platonic object is *logically guaranteed* by the system which Wolterstorff adopted' (1986: 250).

[6] This is a simplification of Levinson's position but, for my present purposes, a forgivable one. Actually, Levinson believes the instrumentation specified in a work's score to be essential to it (1980b: 73–8), which leads him to view ψ as not simply a type of sound-event, but as a '*performed-sound structure*' (1990c: 261). I shall challenge this view—a version of what I call *instrumentalism*— in Ch. 8.

[7] Levinson's original proposal (1980b: 79) does not include explicit reference to a musico-historical context, his presumption being that tethering a pure type of sound-sequence-event to a person and a time is sufficient to capture *contextualist* intuitions: intuitions that rule out the possibility that composers working in distinct musico-historical contexts can compose the same work, even if their respective scores are indistinguishable. As Currie has noted (1989: 59–60), however, this assumption is not justified. Self-styled contextualists will hold that if Marsalis had composed a work sonically indistinguishable from *In This House, On This Morning* in 1992, he nonetheless would not have composed the very same work, had the whole of musical history up to 1992 been different. Being a card-carrying contextualist, Levinson takes Currie's point to indicate that the performed-sound structure must be tethered to the creative context as well as to the composer and time of composition (1992a: 219–20).

such a view enables such items to satisfy what he terms 'the creatability requirement' (1980b: 67)? Because, he believes, indicated types are thereby 'initiated types': types brought into being by the act of indication to which they are tethered:

When a composer θ composes a piece of music, he indicates a ... structure ψ, but he does not bring ψ into being. However, through the act of indicating ψ, he does bring into being something that did not previously exist—namely, ψ-as-indicated-by-θ-at-t_1 [-in-musico-historical-context-C]. Before the compositional act at t_1 no relation obtains between θ and ψ. Composition establishes the relation of indication between θ and ψ. As a result of the compositional act, I suggest, the world contains a new entity, ψ-as-indicated-by-θ-at-t_1 [-in-musico-historical-context-C]. (Levinson 1980b: 79)[8]

As we shall see in Chapter 8, the putative creatability of indicated types is not the sole motive for Levinson's construal of musical works as such entities: he also believes that a conception of such works as indicated types allows us to do justice to what he takes to be the truth in contextualism, as well as to his intuition that a work's instrumentation is integral to it. I dispute both of these claims, preferring a sonicist conception of the types that are works of music. However, for the time being, it suffices to make the following point: indicated types can no more satisfy the creatability requirement than can pure types. Given my discussion of Wolterstorff's position, the reasons for this may seem obvious, but they are, nonetheless, well worth spelling out.

As with norm-types, indicated types cannot be a counter-example to the thinking which led us in Chapter 3 to regard types as eternal existents. For we can just apply the same argument to Levinson's favoured candidate for *In This House, On This Morning*: ψ-as-indicated-by-Marsalis-in-1992-in-musico-historical-context-C. This type's property-associate is *having the sonic structure determined by ψ, and also being produced in a way that is properly connected to Marsalis's 1992 act of indication:*[9] an entity, which—by (29)—exists eternally. Consequently, by (28), the type itself is an eternal

---

[8] See n.7 for an explanation of the matter added in square brackets.

[9] Someone who holds musical works to be indicated types believes that a performance counts as a performance of a certain work only, if it is linked via an intentional-causal relation to the dated compositional act that actually occurred (Levinson 1980a: 98–100): e.g., had Marsalis composed a sonically indistinguishable work a year later, a performance of it would not have been a performance of *In This House, On This Morning*, since such a performance would have been intentionally-causally linked to a different compositional act. Here, at the level of the relation between a performance and a work, we have the indicated type-theorist's commitment to contextualism.

existent. To be sure, the indicated type with which Levinson identifies *In This House, On This Morning could not have had any instances* before Marsalis composed it in 1992; but the point is that whether a type exists at a time is determined, not by whether it can have any instances at that time, but by whether the property of which it is the associate exists at that time. And the property-associate in question—*having the sonic structure determined by ψ, and also being produced in a way that is properly connected to Marsalis's 1992 act of indication*—exists at all times.

What, then, explains Levinson's failure to see that indicated types exist eternally? To my mind, the major cause of his error is evident in his early discussion of why non-indicated sound-event-types are eternal existents. Levinson says that the eternal existence of pure types of sound-event is 'apparent from the fact that they—and the individual component sound types that they comprise—can always have had instances. ... Sound structures predate their first instantiation or conception because they are possible of exemplification *before* that point' (Levinson 1980b: 65). So the suggestion being made is that such pure types exist at all times because they can have instances at all times. More precisely, Levinson seems to think that a type K exists at t if and only if it is possible for K to have instances at t, and hence that if it is impossible for K to have instances at t, then K does not exist at t.

Of course, it is easy to see how this proposed explanation of why non-indicated types are eternal invites Levinson's suggested emendation of the type/token theory. If Levinson's explanation of why such types exist at all times is correct, then, if we wish to allow for the fact that a musical work was created by its composer, we need to identify the work with a type which could only have had tokens from the time t of its composition. And the most obvious way of generating the sort of type which we need would seem to be by tethering the type to t: that is, by treating the work as the (performed) sound-event-type-as-indicated-by-X-at-t (in-musico-historical-context-C).

Having said this, Levinson's claim that pure sound-event-types exist at all times *because they can have instances at all times* is a *non sequitur*. For, as we saw in Chapter 3, a type exists at t if the property of which it is the associate exists at t; and properties (if they exist at all) exist at all times, since a property exists at t just in case there is some time (before, after, or simultaneous with t) at which it is possible for it to be instantiated. Given that this is so, a type that cannot be tokened at t nonetheless exists at t as long as there is some time or other at which it is possible for it to be tokened. And there is something intrinsically plausible about this. Consider, for simplicity's sake, a non-norm-type K. Even if it is impossible for K to be tokened at t, it is still plain what condition a token would have to meet at t in order to be a token of K: it would have to be a k. It is just that it is impossible for there to be anything of this type at t. A concrete example may help matters. Consider the type: child born in 2007. Clearly, this type could have had no tokens in 1066; but the point, surely, is not that the *type* did not exist in 1066, but that the condition something must meet in order to be a token of that type—namely, be a child born in 2007—could not have been met by anything in 1066. The condition something has to meet in order to be a token of the type was the same in 1066 as it is today; it is just that in 1066 nothing could meet it, and hence that there could be nothing of that type at that time.

This same error re-emerges in the context of Levinson's discussion of what he takes to be further examples of indicated types.[10] The Ford Thunderbird, according to Levinson, is a metal/glass/plastic structure: ψ-as-indicated-by-the Ford Motor Company-in-1957 (1980b: 81). And Levinson holds that it follows from this conception of the Ford Thunderbird that it is an initiated type: '[i]t beg[an] to exist', Levinson claims, as a result of an act of human indication or determination (1980b: 81). But when it comes to the question of why we should therefore suppose that this type did not exist in, say, 1900, Levinson only says, once more, that 'there could not have been instances of the Thunderbird in 1900' (1980b: 81). In other words, the reason why The Ford Thunderbird (the type) did not exist in 1900 is, he thinks, that it was impossible for there to have been any tokens of it in 1900. But we have just met this view, and we can make the same reply to it now that we made before. Whether a type can have any tokens at t does not determine whether the *type* exists at t. The type exists at t if there exists at t the property that a token must have in order to be a token of that type: that is, *having the physical structure determined by* ψ, *and also being produced in a way that is properly connected to the act of indication by the Ford Motor Company in 1957*. This property is an eternal existent. Hence, the type is an eternal existent too. This being so, it is better all round simply to say this: in 1900 the type which is the Ford Thunderbird—the abstract entity—existed,

---

[10] For argument's sake, I will not question Levinson's claim that The Ford Thunderbird is an indicated type.

but could not have had any tokens at this time. And if this is so for this time-tethered type, then it is the same for any other. Our conclusion stands: if musical works are time-tethered types, they too exist eternally, and hence cannot be initiated (i.e., brought into being by an act of indication).

All in all, Levinson's suggestion for avoiding Platonism is a failure based upon a misunderstanding. If a work of music is a type—*any kind* of type—it exists at all times. In my view, though, this is a consequence worth living with, especially so given the type/token theory's naturalness and intuitiveness. In what follows I shall defend the three striking consequences of this Platonism: that works of music do not depend for their existence upon having occurrences; that such works are discovered, rather than brought into existence, by their composers; and that works of music cannot be destroyed.

5.3 The Existence Conditions of Works of Music

Clearly, a major source of objections to musical Platonism will be a dissatisfaction with one particular *consequence* of this doctrine: namely, that works of music are not created by their composers. As we shall see in §§5.4–5.7, it is my view that, once a sophisticated Platonist account of the nature of musical composition is constructed, such objections wither away. For the time being, however, it would be as well to appreciate that a critic's strategy for dealing with musical Platonism may take a more direct form than this. That is, it might be argued that, even if we put to one side the question of the validity of *the creatability requirement*, the Platonist offers an account of the existence conditions of works of music that is questionable *in itself*. It is such a direct attack on Platonism that I shall consider in the present section.

Musical Platonism holds that any work of music exists at all times (if it exists at all): even at times at which no performances, playings, or other occurrences of the work exist, and even at times when there are no copies of the score and no memory traces of the work. Such a view will, no doubt, be claimed by some to offer a metaphysical picture that is unsatisfyingly austere. If works are to this extent independent of the mental states and actions of those occupying the material world, does this not place them in a distinct realm, thereby immediately ruling out the possibility of there being an account of how composers and performers can get their minds round them?

A Platonist, though, should not be swayed by such complaints. Given that types are intrinsically *of* their tokens in the sense set out in §3.2, it follows that works are *essentially instantiable* even though they exist when uninstantiated. A work, *qua* type of sound-event, is an entity conceptually tied to the possibility of concrete occurrence. It is a kind of concrete occurrence (i.e. a kind of sound-sequence-event), not the inhabitant of a strange realm.

Nonetheless, our objector may try a different tack, claiming that it is more plausible to view a work of music as dependent for its existence upon a historical flow of concrete particulars: the sorts of entity that Rohrbaugh—a leading defender of this alternative conception—calls a work's *embodiments* (Rohrbaugh 2003: 191). According to such a position, a work comes into existence only with its first embodiment (a run-through in the composer's head or a first performance, presumably), and is destroyed once no such embodiments (such as performances, playings, copies of the score, or memory-traces thereof) exist. As yet, however, we have little more than a sketch of a position hostile to musical Platonism. Why should the Platonist be threatened by it? Rohrbaugh appears to offer two reasons, each of which may be approached by considering the very idea of an embodiment of a work of music.

An embodiment, according to Rohrbaugh, is anything that 'preserves what [the work] is like and leads to new performances' (2003: 191). So, one reason why one might think that such works depend for their existence upon having embodiments is this: that there can only exist facts about a work's individuation if there exist embodiments of it; or, as Rohrbaugh himself puts it, a work's embodiments 'preserve what it is like' and, in so doing, 'ground the facts about what [the work] is like' (Rohrbaugh 2003: 191). The idea would seem to be that, without the existence of some such embodiment, there would be no fact of the matter as to the work's nature, and, hence, the work would cease to be.[11]

But to the Platonist's way of thinking, the idea that a work of music's nature is grounded in the historical flow of its embodiments is just false. For, as I noted in §1.2, a work of music, *qua* type of sound-sequence-event, is individuated according to the *condition* it lays down for something to be

---

[11] This, according to Rohrbaugh, is why the continued existence of a photograph requires at least one of its prints, or its negative, to exist. '[T]hese possibilities', he says, 'count as evidence of a photograph's existence because they indicate that there is still a way the photograph is, one determined by the continuing arrangement of silver-grains on a negative or print' (2003: 191).

one of its (properly formed) tokens; and this in no sense requires that such tokens (or other embodiments) actually exist. What makes a musical work *that* work is that a correctly formed token must sound like *that*; but it does not follow from this that for there to be facts about what the work is like at *t*, there must exist such tokens at *t*.

So, as it has been formulated up to now, Rohrbaugh's thinking is eminently resistible. But, as it happens, there is another species of anti-Platonist argument present in Rohrbaugh's text, a line of thought suggested by his second explanation of the notion of an embodiment: that is, his claim that an embodiment of a work 'leads to new performances' (2003: 191). For if the important feature of a work's embodiments is that they enable us to produce further performances, and if *this* is why the work depends ontologically on there being such embodiments, then the leading idea would seem to be this: there exist no facts about what a work is like unless there is *available to us*, in the form of an embodiment, a template for producing new tokens. According to this second suggestion, a work depends for its existence upon a historical flow of embodiments because, without such a flow, we would be unable to produce new performances of the work. In other words, what Rohrbaugh terms a 'lack of access' (2003: 191) to a work ensures the work's destruction.

But this, it seems to me, is even less convincing than our first anti-Platonist argument. For it would seem to have merely introduced an unargued anti-realism into the proceedings. The claim that a work's existence depends upon our 'access' to it can only be the product of an unjustified commitment to the thesis that facts about what works are like cannot outstrip our ability to recognize them. And it is such a picture that the Platonist sets her face against from the very beginning. For a Platonist, a work of music is a mind-independent, eternally existent object. To simply assume that the individuation of such works is dependent upon our having access to them is to beg the question.

Once we see the flaw in Rohrbaugh's reasoning, the claim that works of music *cannot* pre-exist their composition and *must* be capable of being destroyed looks increasingly undermotivated. Indeed, when it comes to the first half of this claim, direct *arguments* that do not rely on the idea that composition necessarily involves creation are hard to come by. True enough, Rohrbaugh presents us with examples designed to demonstrate that works come into existence with their first embodiment; but, as we shall now see, such cases can be redescribed in a way congenial to Platonism.

Focusing primarily on the case of photographs, but taking his findings to be straightforwardly applicable to all of the repeatable art-forms, Rohrbaugh (2003: 177) claims that a photograph comes into existence at the moment of the film's exposure. Photographs, he explains,

> come into existence when they are taken. At the moment the button is pressed, the shutter opens and closes, exposing the film, and we say that we have 'taken a photograph'. The phrase has what is called 'success grammar'. If I forget to load the film and blithely snap away at your birthday party, then I should correct my claim to have taken photographs of it; without exposed negatives, no such photographs exist. What is so important about the moment at which the film is exposed? This event determines certain crucial facts about what the photograph is like, in particular, structural facts. (Rohrbaugh 2003: 190)

But let us suppose for a moment that we take the repeatability of photographs—that is, the fact that they admit of multiple copies (in the form of prints)—to indicate that photographs are types.[12] Given this assumption, together with the argument of §3.2, it follows that photographs (by contrast with their token prints) exist eternally: if photographs are types, Platonism about photographs follows. So, if Rohrbaugh's reasoning were correct, one would expect such Platonism about photographs to be untenable. But is it? Does the linguistic data appealed to by Rohrbaugh really undermine such a Platonist position?

The answer to this question is surely 'No'. For Rohrbaugh's data need not be explained by taking photographs to be brought into existence at the push of a button. Admittedly, if a camera contains no film, then no photograph can be taken. But this does not entail that *the photograph itself* only comes into existence once the film has been exposed, only that *the taking of a photograph*—a certain event—requires the exposure of film and

---

[12] This is a big supposition, of course, and one to which I do not wish to commit myself. After all, it is possible that the kinds of arguments that lead us to view works of music as types do not apply to the case of photographs, or that there are special reasons why the repeatability of photographs is best explained by a rival to the type/token theory. Nonetheless, examining how a Platonist about photographs may respond to Rohrbaugh's arguments enables us to appreciate how a Platonist about works of music can do the same.

the production of a negative. The Platonist is free to regard the taking of the photograph as the creation of a negative that thereby enables the eternally existent type to be first tokened.[13]

Along the same lines, and in light of the reply to Rohrbaugh's reasoning made a moment ago, a Platonist will not accept that the taking of a photograph 'determines certain crucial facts about what the photograph is like' (Rohrbaugh 2003: 190), if this is supposed to mean that the event in question brings it about that the photograph is a certain way. What *is* thus determined by the photographer's point of view, his equipment, and the process of exposure is the nature of the negative and, hence, of which eternal type (i.e. photograph) any future prints will count as tokens. Rohrbaugh's talk of the moment of exposure bringing a photograph into existence can simply be reformulated as a matter of this moment's determining which eternally existent photograph is tokened.

At this point, I should make it clear that it is not my job to defend the thesis that photographs are (eternally existent) types. But what I *do* wish to point out is this: given that the Platonist about photographs can reply in the way suggested, it is plain that such a reply is also available to the defender of the position that I *do* wish to defend: *musical* Platonism. To see this, first of all note that a Platonist about music will simply deny that the production of the score for *In This House, On This Morning* brought the work itself into existence. On the contrary, she will insist that this act of composition (just like the photographer's production of a negative) was the specification of a recipe for the production of its tokens. Marsalis's indication of the work did not determine the work's nature; it determined which (eternal) work he composed (i.e. creatively discovered). At this stage, of course, our account of composition as creative discovery has been neither introduced nor defended: this is the task of §§5.4–5.7. My present point stands, however: we have yet to be presented with a telling objection to the idea that works pre-exist their composition.

The same goes for the thesis that works of music cannot be destroyed. In fact, there is something deeply *im*plausible about the idea that a work is destroyed once it ceases to have any embodiments. *Even if* we were to accept that works of music *come into* being, it would be hard to resist what Levinson calls 'the residual pull' (1990c: 263) of the idea that works

---

[13] In this respect, a negative has a function analogous to that of musical score.

of music, once created, last for all time. Such a work might, he says, 'just inhabit the abstract realm of the universe ... forever. Why should it lapse into non-existence, just because we do?' (1990c: 263).

This last question is a deep one. Given that works of music are not physical entities, just what *would* constitute their destruction? The mystery remains as to why we should think that the existence of a work is sustained by a historical flow of performances, playings, memories, and the like. Levinson himself finds himself pulled in opposite directions, on the one hand tentatively suggesting that the elimination of all records and memories of a piece would suffice to destroy it (1990c: 262); but, on the other hand, finding himself unable to justify this suggestion, and finding comfort in the idea that works of music are destined to outlast us (1990b: 263).

To my mind, Levinson's predicament illustrates just how flimsy the thesis that musical works can be destroyed really is. Indeed, the only *argument* for it would seem to be this:

(40) Musical works are created by human actions.

(41) Symmetry dictates that musical works can be destroyed in the same way.

So (42) Musical works can be destroyed by human actions.

As Levinson himself puts it, 'If musical works can be created, and by human agency, it stands to reason—or at least recommends itself on grounds of symmetry—that they could be destroyed, possibly in the same way' (1990c: 262).[14] However, this is an argument whose premises are both false. It is quite unclear, to me at least, why the (presumed) fact that musical works are created should demand that one view them as destructible. Levinson himself explores the possibility that a work of music could be brought into being by its composer and yet, once composed, exist for ever; and there is nothing incoherent about this. It is, perhaps, one more unfortunate fact of life that the world is not in every respect symmetrical. To argue soundly from the thesis that works of music are created to the conclusion that they can cease to exist, one must come up with a *reason* why such works are created if and only if they can be destroyed. In the light of my discussion of Rohrbaugh's arguments, I dare to predict that no such argument will be forthcoming. Certainly, a mere appeal to 'symmetry' will not do the job.

---

[14] Trivedi (2002: 77) argues similarly.

(41) is thus false. But, as we shall see in the remainder of this chapter, we should insist that (40) is false also. Musical works are best viewed as types; types exist eternally, so musical works exist eternally. We should only be deflected from this conclusion, and from the type/token theory that entails it, if the Platonist is unable to set out and defend an account of composition as a species of discovery. But this, as we shall now see, is far from true.

5.4 Composition as Creative Discovery

If *In This House, On This Morning* has always existed, what did Marsalis's composing of it consist in? Given the truth in Platonism, Marsalis did not create the piece; he could only have discovered it. The work existed already. Having said this, a fully satisfying Platonist account of composition must meet the following *desiderata*: it must explain the nature of the process of selection made by the composer; it must allow that this process is often highly creative; and, finally, it must provide a plausible epistemology of discovery: that is, explain how a composer can get his mind round an eternally existent, abstract type.

Let us start by outlining the nature of the composer's selection in composition. As I noted in §5.2, the compositional process involves selection in the following way. The composer considers various descriptive sound-sequence-types, something he does by imagining how tokens of these types would sound and (typically) by producing such tokens on a musical instrument. All the while, he selects certain properties of these descriptive sound-events as criteria for correctness in performance of his composition, a process whose summation (once criteria for correct performance have been selected) is the representation of an eternally existent norm-type by a score.[15] In composing the conclusion of his Violin Concerto BWV 1041, for example, Bach imagined sound-events of various descriptive types, and, on the basis of this, in the end decided that his piece should end with an A minor chord. That is to say, in imagining various endings for the work, Bach probably considered numerous descriptive sound-event-types but selected the one whose tokens end with an A

---

[15] Or something which the plays the role of a score, such as a paradigmatic performance.

minor chord. In doing so, and thereby setting a standard for correct performance, Bach represented, in his score, a norm-type, λ—distinct from its corresponding descriptive type—one of whose normative properties is *being such that something cannot be a properly formed token of λ unless it ends with an A minor chord.*

The moral to be drawn from this is that the composer's exercise of choice can be explained nicely in Platonistic terms. The composer selects certain properties of a descriptive sound-event type as normative, and, in so doing, thereby selects an eternally existent norm-type. The composer unearths something that was already there: he *discovers* criteria for correct performance. A critic hostile to Platonism will, no doubt, suspect that to omit an element of literal creation from the compositional process is to falsify it. But as Peter Kivy has explained (1983: 113), what is essential to our concept of musical composition is that its *creativity* be recognized, not that composers be conceived as people who bring things into being. And at this point we can draw an analogy between musical composition and the kinds of creative discoveries made in mathematics and theoretical science. Andrew Wiles's discovery of a proof of Fermat's Last Theorem was one such act of creative finding; Einstein's discovery of the facts constituting the Special Theory of Relativity was another. In both cases, it took paradigmatically creative thinking to conceive of, and then uncover, things such as these. In my view, something similar goes for the composition of *In This House, On This Morning.* This (norm-) type of sound-sequence-event has always existed, but it took a composer with a huge musical imagination, coupled with a sensitive feel for the history of jazz, to discover it and score it. *Creativity* can coexist with Platonism: we can acknowledge a composer's originality and creative brilliance in seeing what is beyond the ken of the rest of us. It is only the *creation* of musical works that is ruled out.

Appealing to the analogy between musical composition and scientific theorizing also helps us to understand how the Platonist may do justice to the esteem in which we hold the composer's achievement. Einstein discovered the facts that constitute the Special Theory of Relativity; he did not bring them into existence. This, however, does nothing to undermine our sense of Einstein's peerless brilliance and creative thought: only someone very much like Einstein could have uncovered such facts. The Platonist, it seems to me, should say exactly analogous things about musical composition. It is no insult to Marsalis to compare his discoveries with the mould-breaking discoveries of Einstein.[16]

Without doubt, the idea that musical works are discovered by their composers tends to attract a disbelieving stare. But to my mind, this kind of response reveals not so much that such a position is genuinely unnatural or counter-intuitive, but that people have swallowed, and failed to digest, a folk *theory* about the nature of composition. For one thing is clear: the phenomenology of composition points in neither one way nor the other. As Kivy reminds us (1987: 248), there is nothing about the phenomenology of the compositional process that determines that we should regard it as one of creation rather than discovery. A composer typically works away—imagining and reimagining sequences of sounds, playing and amending sequences on an instrument—until he reaches some kind of resolution. Alternatively, an idea for a phrase or theme may just pop into his head. But nothing demands that we treat the object of either the hard-earned musical achievement or the 'popping' (Kivy 1987: 249) as literally brought into existence by the composer. For discoveries can be made in both of these ways too. A mathematician can—if he is lucky—have a 'Eureka' moment, though he is more likely to uncover a proof or fugitive fact by dint of a mixture of creative thinking and doggedness.

An objector is unlikely to be assuaged, however. Indeed she may be spooked by the way in which the Platonist position generalizes. If musical works, *qua* types, exist eternally, it follows that all types are likewise eternal and that nobody can create anything (Sharpe 1995: 38). But, as I noted in §3.2, this conclusion only has the *appearance* of a *reductio*. For our talk of people 'inventing' types can be reinterpreted along Platonist lines. In short, to count as 'the inventor' of K is to be the person who is ultimately responsible for K's first tokening. Looking at it this way does nothing to lessen the esteem in which we hold an inventor; on the contrary, it enables us to do justice to his achievement without ascribing to him the mythical ability to bring a type into existence.

Nonetheless, the thought that Platonism inevitably downplays the composer's creative achievement is hard to dislodge. Sharpe, for one, claims that '[i]f a work of music is an abstract entity, a sound pattern that exists

---

[16] Or, indeed, Newton. As Kivy puts it, with characteristic wit and elegance, '[i]n the company of Newton, after all, one is hardly slumming' (1983: 113–14).

independently of the composer, then, instead of creating it, he merely selects it' (1995: 39). And it is clear what Sharpe has in mind by 'mere' selection. If what a composer does is just to select one of the available types of sound-sequence-event, then it might seem that all he is really doing is unimaginatively lifting a work of music off the ontological shelf; and one can do this, supposes Sharpe, without dint of creativity or imagination.

However, such a criticism seems to me to be wholly misconceived. For the moral to be drawn from thinking about cases of creative discovery in mathematics and theoretical science is precisely that the great discoveries in these areas required their discoverers to exercise a special level of creative thinking. Wiles's proof is the kind of thing that could only be discovered by—dare one say it?—a mathematician of genius. His selection of strategies for proving the theorem was selection all right; but it was the kind of selection that could have been made only by the most creative of mathematical minds. His knowing where to look for the proof in conceptual space, and knowing how to go about uncovering it, could not have been more imaginative. The same goes for the great musical discoveries.

A further analogy may help the point to stick. As I noted in §3.2, Frege regarded propositions as eternal entities: 'the thinker does not create them,' Frege says, 'but must take them as they are' (1918: 51). Naturally, there is plenty wrong with the details of Frege's exposition, but, to my knowledge, no one has seriously suggested that the eternal existence of propositions is incompatible with the truism that we may think and speak creatively. The fact that we do not literally create the entities that we think and say does not entail that we are mere dullards. And the reason why this is so is that whether one thinks creatively is determined, not by whether one brings any propositions into existence, but by the nature of the propositions one thinks. To think creatively is to grasp propositions that few others can grasp, and to be able to see connections between propositions that others cannot see. Something similar goes for creativity in the field of musical composition. A composer is creative, not through bringing works into existence, but by exercising creativity and imagination in composing the works she does. A creative thinker is someone who has the imagination to entertain thoughts that are beyond the reach of most people. A creative composer is someone who has the imagination to compose works of music that others do not have the capacity to compose. Composition is, indeed, a form of discovery involving a process of selection; but such a process can most certainly be creative.

Nonetheless, Sharpe is quite right to point out that the Platonist must come up with an epistemology; in particular, he must provide 'an account of how the abstract entity enters into a causal relationship with the composing mind' (1995: 39). Selection, after all, is a causal relation, so we had better be able to explain how a composer can come into causal contact with an abstract type. However, this demand—in what amounts to a statement of the final *desideratum* of a Platonist account of composition—can, I think, be met. Given the details of my defence of the claim that musical works, *qua* types, may be heard,[17] it should come as no surprise to the reader to be told that a composer enters into a causal relationship with an abstract type by virtue of coming into contact with one or more of its tokens.

Before we get on to this, though, we should prepare the ground by removing any trumped-up obstacles from our path towards a satisfying Platonist epistemology. It may be tempting, for example, to think of works, *qua* types, as denizens of Platonic heaven: items occupying an ontological realm distinct from that occupied by composers. Obviously, such a construal could only compromise our attempt to explain how the composing mind could grasp such things: the suggestion that there could be a causal relation uniting items from such disparate realms looks more like magic than philosophy. But, as we saw in §3.2, and as I reiterated in §5.3, there is no need to resort to such a myth because the kind of Platonism about types I recommend—a Platonism that insists on their being eternal existents—stops short of placing them in their own ontological realm. Types, as we have seen, are not self-subsistent in Dummett's sense, but items conceptually tied to their tokens: although there can be untokened types, a type is essentially *of* its tokens in the sense that we can only think of it as being a kind of concrete particular. A work of music, on this view, is not a weird inhabitant of a ghostly realm, but a sound-event-type. As such, it is conceptually rooted in the physical world.

Having removed this misconception about the nature of types, it nonetheless remains for us to explain exactly how, in composition, a human mind can come into contact with an abstract type. However, the answer to this question is, ultimately, quite simple: a composer gets his mind round a sound-event-type *by* imagining and, usually, performing one of its tokens.

---

[17] See §§1.2 and 4.4.

Once more, the conceptual apparatus of the type/token distinction enables us to provide a down-to-earth explanation of what might seem to be a peculiar phenomenon. We saw in §§1.2 and 4.4 that we can dissolve the puzzle of how a work of music, *qua* abstract type, can be listened to by pointing out that such listening is *indirect*. One listens to the type *by* listening to one of its tokens: the abstract type counts as an object of hearing because one of its tokens—a sound-event—is the event at the beginning of the causal chain that leads to an auditory experience. That this sound-event is one of the type's tokens ensures that the type participates in the event in the right kind of way to count as causally relevant and, hence, as a thing heard.

A similar kind of puzzle confronts our account of composition, and it invites a similar solution. Rather than having to posit what might seem to be a strange causal process in which an abstract object somehow floats before or enters a human mind, we can just say this: a composer composes a work of music—that is, a normative type of sound-event—by imagining and performing tokens of descriptive sound-event-types, all the while selecting certain properties as normative. That is, he considers possible and actual sound-sequences—respectively, by fancying himself listening to such extracts (Ryle 1949: 256), and by playing such extracts on an instrument—and, in doing so, decides upon criteria for correct performance of his composition. The end result of this process of selection is the 'creative' discovery of a norm-type which, since its property-associate exists eternally, exists at all times. With this account of composition in place, it is clear that the causal relation obtaining between a composer's mind and his work is not occult; it obtains by virtue of the obtaining of the causal process that is the imagining or producing of sound-event-tokens, and which results (typically) in the production of a score. Once more, the abstract entity itself counts as causally related to a human mind by virtue of one of its tokens—a concrete sound-event—being so related.

The three *desiderata* of a Platonist account of composition can thus be met; and, as we have seen, a crucial part is played in this account of composition by the analogy between discoveries in music and discoveries in mathematics and theoretical science. Having said this, such an analogy should be viewed soberly. For it is important to note two equally important *disanalogies* between a composer's creative discovery of a work of music and a mathematician's discovery. First, as John Andrew Fisher has noted (1991: 133), the discoveries of mathematics and the theoretical sciences tend to be propositional: they are discoveries of *facts* rather than discoveries of *things*. Although we describe Pythagoras as having discovered the theorem that has come to bear his name, what he actually discovered was *the fact that* the square on the hypotenuse of a right-angled triangle is equal to the sum of the squares on the other two sides. Now, Fisher himself presents this as a problem for the Platonist: whilst the analogy between composition and mathematical discovery looks to be the most promising avenue for the Platonist to explore (since the discoveries made by mathematicians are abstract and eternal), it is clear that the composition of a work of music is the composition of a thing, not a fact (Fisher 1991: 133). What the analogy with mathematics gives with one hand, it appears to take away with the other.

But the Platonist need not become too down-hearted at this point. For the analogy with mathematical discoveries was intended only to be taken *so far*. The analogy's success consists in its enabling us to see that a discovery may yet be original, imaginative, and creative. It should not overly concern us that the analogy does not extend to the respective natures of the things discovered. When it comes to this latter question, it is an analogy with more everyday discoveries that is more enlightening. Columbus's discovery of the Americas was not the uncovering of a fact; it was the finding of a thing, a place in this instance. In the light of the fact that *some* discoveries are of objects rather than facts, the Platonist, it seems to me, should simply say this: composition is a kind of discovery that has aspects in common with *both* discoveries in mathematics *and* discoveries of a more common-or-garden kind. As with Pythagoras's discovery, a composer's process of composition is a creative one whose object is an eternal existent. But, as with the case of the discovery of a concrete entity, the thing discovered by a composer is not propositional in nature. Composition is a form of discovery that is unique, combining elements from the kinds of discoveries of Columbus and Pythagoras. Pointing this out would only count as identifying a weakness in the Platonist's position if one were to take an unnecessarily reductionist approach to the concept of discovery.

The second disanalogy between musical composition and mathematical discoveries is, potentially more damaging, however, since it seems to point to a feature shared by *all* cases of discovery that is absent from musical composition. The Platonist cannot in this case reply by observing that empirical discoveries lack this feature also. So what is this supposed respect in which musical composition is unlike paradigmatic cases of discovery?

It is this, according to Fisher and Sharpe: whilst, in a genuine case of discovery, the discoverer might have been mistaken in thinking that she had uncovered her quarry, it makes no sense to say that a composer might have got it wrong in an analogous way (Fisher 1991: 133). Wiles might have been mistaken in thinking that he had proved Fermat's Last Theorem, and Columbus could have got it wrong in supposing that he had discovered the Americas. Beethoven, on the other hand, could have made no such mistake in the compositional process that led to his composing the Archduke Trio (Sharpe 2001: 326). Of course, Beethoven's compositional process could have gone differently; he could have ended up composing a work other than the Archduke Trio (although he might have given it the same name). But in such a possible world Beethoven would not have *made a mistake* in failing to compose the Archduke Trio. He would not have *got things wrong*; he would just have composed a different work.

Put more formally, the objection we are at present considering takes the form of the following argument:

(43) For a person A to discover an entity o, it must be possible for A to have been mistaken.

So (44) For Beethoven's composition of the Archduke Trio to have been a discovery of the work, it must have been possible for Beethoven to have been mistaken.

(45) But Beethoven could not have been so mistaken.

So (46) Beethoven's composition of the Archduke Trio was not a discovery of the work.

What are we to make of this? I do not wish to question (45) here: my quarrel is with (43). For (43) sees an observation concerning *certain cases* of discovery presented as a conceptual truth. And it is nothing of the kind, as I shall now explain.

In fact, counter-examples to (43) are easily constructed. Let us consider a case in which someone discovers something by, as it were, stumbling across it. So imagine that my daughter comes across a coin whilst pottering in the flower-beds, picks it up, and says 'Look what I've discovered!' Now it is clear that she might not have found the coin. But it is also clear that it would be senseless to say that she might have been *mistaken*: for what could such a mistake have consisted in? Since she did not set out to find such a thing, merely coming across it by accident, there are no criteria of correctness here that she could have failed to meet. Nonetheless, it would be equally implausible to deny that my daughter had indeed discovered the coin. (One would not 'correct' her by saying, 'No, Eleanor, you didn't discover the coin; you see, you couldn't have made a mistake.') This being so, we have a clear counter-example to (43). *Pace* Sharpe and Fisher, an agent may discover an entity and yet it be inappropriate to describe the situation as one in which she might have been mistaken.

To explain the nature of Sharpe's and Fisher's mistake, we must return to the cases of discovery with which we started: those of Columbus and Wiles. Why does it make sense to say that Columbus and Wiles might have got things wrong? Fisher says little on this topic, but Sharpe's answer to this question would seem to be this: the possibility of being mistaken is a corollary of the fact that what is discovered is a genuinely mind-independent entity. As Sharpe himself puts it, 'what we discover exists and with that goes the possibility of being mistaken' (2001: 326). But this is not quite right, as our counter-example illustrates. The point is not that *discovery* is conceptually linked to the possibility of making a mistake; it is that in *certain cases* of discovery the agent's project of *enquiry* is constrained by criteria of success, criteria that, as we shall see, are not present when a discovery is made which is something other than the end product of a process of enquiry.

When it comes to Columbus's discovery of the Americas and Wiles's discovery of his mathematical proof, the existence of criteria of success is a corollary of the fact that both agents were engaged in a *search* for a particular thing: both Columbus and Wiles were trying to find something fitting a certain description; and hence, each might have failed to find what they were looking for. In both cases, the language of possible error is applicable because what would count as a mistake is determined by the point of the search. Consequently, the moral to take from our counter-example to (43) is that it is only a *subspecies* of discovery—what we might call *discovery by enquiry*—that has a conceptual connection to the possibility of being mistaken. When a discovery is something other than the culmination of an enquiry—when the purpose of the agent's activity is something other than that of uncovering some entity or some fact—there is no such conceptual connection.

Having made this point, the consequences for the case of musical composition should be obvious. To be sure, composers do not stumble across their compositions like happy-go-lucky gardeners, but Beethoven's composition of the Archduke Trio has at least this much in common with my daughter's discovery of the coin: although he came across something that existed prior to his compositional act, he did not set out to uncover an entity fitting a certain description. The piece was there *anyway*, but Beethoven did not form a conception of it and then compose it. Indeed, to view Beethoven's achievement in this way would be to misrepresent the nature of composition. Beethoven's coming to form a clear conception of the Archduke Trio *just was* his compositional act, so there existed no gap between conception and search, as there was for Columbus and Wiles.

It is thus fair to say that Sharpe and Fisher mistake norms of enquiry for norms of discovery. The fact that Beethoven, when composing what turned out to be the Archduke Trio, could not have been mistaken illustrates not that he did not discover it, but that his discovery was not the consummation of an enquiry. And I take it that this conclusion coheres with the way in which we ordinarily think about the purpose of composition. Clearly, whilst Einstein was aiming to *find things out*, Beethoven was not. Beethoven's aim, by contrast, was (roughly) that of expressing himself musically (and thereby adding value to his life and the lives of others). It is for this reason, and not because Beethoven's composition of the Archduke Trio was not a discovery at all, that it makes no sense to say that Beethoven might have been mistaken. Composition is a species of creative, but not inquisitive, discovery.

5.5 The Nature of the Compositional Process: Replies to Objections

We now have, in outline, a Platonist account of the nature of musical composition. It is a creative process in which descriptive sound-event-types are evaluated, certain of their properties selected as criteria of correct performance, and which ends with the discovery of a norm-type. Such discovery, however, is not the summation of a project of enquiry, and it is this, and this alone, that explains why it makes no sense to describe a composer as having been mistaken in his compositional act.

It would be naïve, though, to suppose that what I have said up to now would be sufficient to convince the sceptic. Indeed, the usual response is to regard such an account of composition as a *reductio* of the Platonist's claim that musical works are eternally existent entities. Specifically, objections to the view of composition as creative discovery tend to fall into one of two categories: either they allege that Platonism misrepresents the compositional process; or else they charge Platonism with a view of composition that foists unacceptable commitments upon us concerning either the nature of our aesthetic appraisal of music or our concept of art more generally. The following three sections are devoted to replying to objections of both kinds.

Two objections of the first sort can be disposed of reasonably quickly. Both concern the fact that composition involves *choice*. Cox argues that the fact that a composer's choices are infinite entails that the composed work could not have pre-existed its composition. Music, she points out, is not a closed system: there are an infinite number of possible elements for a composer to choose from and, what is more, musical styles and guidelines change through time (1985: 371). Her creationist conclusion follows, she believes, because 'it seems we are likely to refer to a work as a "creation" rather than as a discovery, selection, or arrangement, when there is a seemingly infinite array of possible choices involved in the compositional process' (1985: 370). A Platonist will be unmoved by such an objection, however, since the supposed connection between infinite choice and creation has been stated rather than argued for. Platonism does not deny that a composer's choice is infinite, and that new musical styles may become apparent to us through time. But, crucially, the point at issue is not whether this is so, but whether the *objects* of such choices made by composers pre-exist their first tokenings. The Platonist thinks that they do—because they are types of sound-sequence-event, and because types exist eternally—whilst Cox simply denies this. As it stands, her claim that the infinite nature of the choices facing a composer entails that he creates his works is a *non sequitur*. Metaphysical space is infinite, so it has room for an infinity of eternally existent musical works (Kivy 1983: 119).

Fisher too focuses on the choices facing a composer in composition, but, for him, the telling feature is a composer's freedom of choice to change his composition at will. As he himself explains:

Composers can change their minds. They can decide, as well, to change their music. How is this compatible with the idea that they discover the music? The piece of music is a free choice of the composer who can change it at will. But any object that can be changed at will doesn't have an independent character to discover. (Fisher 1991: 133)

But, once more, the Platonist can reply to this relatively simply. It is true that an object that can be changed at will (i.e. by dint of thinking alone) is not sufficiently mind-independent to admit of being genuinely discovered. But, contrary to what Fisher supposes, musical works are not malleable in this way. As we saw in §4.4, the Platonist simply refuses to accept that works of music are temporally flexible. Cases of apparent temporal flexibility—such as Vaughan Williams's imagined 'rewriting' in 1920 of the *Fantasia on a Theme by Thomas Tallis*—can be relatively easily explained away: such cases do not see changes wrought in a single work, but the composition of a new (and unchanging) work that is based upon an (unchanging) original. Where there is apparent change, there is, in reality, an additional work. And, as I noted in §4.4, there is no principled reason for rejecting this alternative way of describing things in favour of the supposition that works of music are temporally flexible. Nothing of great import hangs on works being capable of undergoing genuine change. Fisher's presumption that the Platonist must accept that a composer can bring about changes in his compositions is simply unargued.

With these relatively untroubling objections out of the way, we are free to consider what is, perhaps, the greatest threat to the idea that composers discover their works. In miniature, the worry is this. A discovered entity could have been discovered by other people, and at any time at which the entity in question existed. That is, the following principle holds good:

(47) *o* could only have been discovered at *t* if *o* could have been discovered at any time *o* existed, and by other individuals. (Fisher 1991: 130)

Musical works, however, 'are so tied to their composers and historical contexts that it makes little sense to imagine that the works could have been composed in very different times and contexts' (Fisher 1991: 130). Consequently, given the existence of such a tie, the truth of (47) can only mean that works of music cannot be objects of discovery (and, by implication, types of sound-event).

Indeed, to return to what is now a familiar case, it is undeniable that Marsalis's composition of *In This House, On This Morning* was the outcome of his occupancy of a particular position in history: he was influenced by the work of Ellington and, like Ellington in *Black, Brown and Beige*, sought to do justice to the Afro-American experience in music. Equally,

Marsalis's composition of the piece reflected his musical personality: it is a development of his *œuvre*, and has a distinctive style and sound. Facts such as these serve to suggest that only he could have composed the work and hence, by (47), that his composition of the work could not have consisted in his discovering it. What all this shows, it could be alleged,[18] is that the piece is essentially a *product* of the unique musico-historical context in which Marsalis found himself.

What we have here, then, is an apparent conflict between the contextually conditioned nature of composition and the concept of discovery. For, as has been suggested already, whilst the former would seem to indicate that a work could not have been composed by another composer at another time, the latter is subject to (47). So how should the Platonist reply? One option would be to deny (47): to follow Kivy in arguing that musical discoveries *just are* essentially tied to a time and a person. According to Kivy,[19] even scientific discoveries are time-bound. Considering, first, a case in which we are invited to suppose that a scientific discovery could have been made at a much earlier time than it actually was, Kivy claims that 'it is as flat out impossible for a contemporary of Plato's to have discovered (say) Kepler's laws of planetary motion, or Newton's gravitational laws as to have composed—*i.e.* discovered—the sound structure of Beethoven's 7th, and for the very same reasons' (1987: 250). In this kind of case, an example of scientific discovery supposedly refutes (47), so there is no harm in viewing the case of musical discovery as providing just one more counter-example to it.

Things get more difficult for Kivy, though, when he considers the question of whether it is possible for two people simultaneously to discover the same thing. For here a serious disanalogy reappears for him. Notably, such cases have actually occurred in mathematics and science, Newton's and Leibniz's discovery of the calculus being the most famous example; so the case of scientific and mathematical discovery provides no grounds for supposing musical discovery to be person-bound in the way in which Kivy supposes. This being so, when presented with cases such as these, Kivy has little choice but to simply hold the line when it comes to music. Musical composition (i.e. discovery), he claims, is unlike mathematical or scientific discovery in that the discoveries of music are not shareable. We just have

---

[18] This style of objection is also made by Cox (1985: 371).

[19] Sharpe, erroneously as we shall see, presumes that I would take this line too (2001: 327).

to accept that 'certain objects are so unique as to be discoverable only by a single individual' (1987: 251). It took *Marsalis* to compose *In This House, On This Morning*. No one else could have composed it, even in 1992.

In my opinion, however, Kivy's position is too extreme. First of all, the thinking behind (47) is clear and, it seems to me, persuasive. For *o* to have been genuinely discovered, it must be mind-independent: it was not brought into being by the act of discovery; it was there *anyway*.[20] But if this is right—if *o* has a mind-independent existence—then it is possible for someone else, at another time, to have come across it. Authentic objects of discovery are analytically tied neither to the people who actually discovered them, nor to the actual time at which they were discovered. Furthermore, and to consider one of Kivy's own examples, I can only disagree with his claim that it is 'flat out impossible' for Archimedes to have discovered Newton's gravitational laws. Kivy claims that such laws were 'not only undiscoverable but unthinkable' (1987: 250) to the ancient Greeks, since, to be understood, they would have required the internalization of a conceptual scheme completely alien at that time. But what follows from this? Not that such a discovery was 'flat out impossible'. All that follows is that, *for Archimedes to have discovered Newton's gravitational laws, the history of science up until the time of his discovery would have to have been different.* What this means, to be sure, is that possible worlds in which Archimedes discovers Newton's gravitational laws are *distant*: in such worlds the history of science is a far cry from how it is actually. But there is no sound reason to suppose that such worlds do not exist. Levinson is surely correct in pointing out that 'Kivy's "flat out" would appear have more than a few hills and bumps in it' (1990c: 225). If Kivy supposes his examples to tell against (47), he can only be mistaken.

Having internalized this diagnosis of Kivy's mistake, an alternative way out for the Platonist begins to emerge. Rather than denying the conceptual truth that is (47), we should exploit the notion of metaphysical possibility to drive a wedge between the fact that the compositional process is contextually conditioned and the thesis that a work could only have been composed by its actual composer and at its actual time of composition. In other words, the right way to reply to our objector is to acknowledge

---

[20] This use of 'anyway'—minus the particular philosophical spin he places on it—is borrowed from Bernard Williams (1978: 64).

the bare metaphysical possibility of *In This House, On This Morning* being composed by someone else at some other time—thereby denying that works are 'tied' to their composers and the musico-historical contexts in which they were composed—and yet insist that Marsalis's musico-historical situation played a part in *his coming to compose* the work.

Musical works are not composed in a vacuum. Marsalis came to compose *In This House, On This Morning* as a result of his having been immersed in a particular musico-historical context: his composition of the work was the product of his location at a set of co-ordinates in musico-historical space. But in saying this, we need not commit ourselves to the thesis that the context of composition is essential to the *work*, and hence to the view that it is impossible for a given work to have been composed by someone else at some other time. Contextual factors (such as Marsalis's desire to emulate Ellington, or his wish to put the experience of Black Americans to music) partially explain why he composed the work that he did. But though such contextual features are—as a matter of contingent fact—causally relevant to the composer's *discovery* of the work, they are not integral to the work itself.

Ultimately, then, the Platonist should stick out his chin and grant that *In This House, On This Morning* might have been composed in the sixteenth century. But, of course, a possible world in which this occurred is a very distant world. And the reason why this is so is that it is the composer's position in musico-historical space that enables him to discover the works that he does. The fact that Marsalis had internalized much of the history of jazz up until that point, and was part of a social and artistic milieu, inevitably determined his compositional output. Consequently, for someone else to have composed the work in the sixteenth century, without the input of the musico-historical context that enabled Marsalis to compose it, something anomalous and astounding (though not impossible) would have to have happened. Such a composer's genius and originality would have to have been peerless; most likely, he would have to have somehow broken out of the epoch in which he was working. There would have to have been a huge imaginative leap: an occurrence that somehow skipped chapters in musical history. But notice that this appeal to the part played by context in musical composition falls short of tying the work to Marsalis's compositional act. We appeal to context in order to shed light on how composers come to creatively discover the works they do; but this is compatible with acknowledging that anomalous compositional acts—acts such as the counterfactual one that we have just been imagining—are metaphysically possible.

The moral is this: to admit the bare metaphysical possibility that a work could have been composed at a different time, and by a different person, is not to deny that composition is contextually conditioned. Marsalis composes the works that he does because he occupies the position in musico-historical space that he does. This does *not* mean, however, that such works are *tied* to their composers and to musico-historical contexts. Such a thesis is an unwarranted gloss applied to the truism that the nature of a composer's work is in part explained by his occupancy of a musico-historical context.

An appeal to the notion of metaphysical possibility is thus sufficient to undermine the force of the original objection. Armed with a grasp of this concept, we can acknowledge the truth in (47), yet do justice to the contextualist intuitions that lead people to suppose (wrongly, as we shall see in Chapter 9) that contextual features enter into the identity conditions of works. Having said this, I do not, at this stage, pretend to have put the matter to bed. For, to quote Levinson, it might yet be supposed that 'a musical work, stripped of its contextual co-ordinates in musico-historical space ... is incapable of bearing many of the aesthetic properties that we ascribe to it' (1990c: 222). Let us call this view *contextualism*. The committed contextualist will argue, for example, that *In This House, On This Morning* is *conservative, influenced by Ellington*, and *expressive of pride in the Black Americans of the Deep South*: properties that an imagined sonically indistinguishable piece composed in the sixteenth century would not have. True enough, it could be said, there is a (very distant) possible world in which *In This House, On This Morning* is joined by a sonically indistinguishable piece composed by a sixteenth-century composer; but this would not be a world in which one and the same work was composed by another composer at another time. The sixteenth-century sonic replica of *In This House, On This Morning*—lacking some of the contextually determined properties possessed by Marsalis's piece—would, by Leibniz's Law, be a distinct work.

I will not respond to this position right now. The contextualism that it champions is used by Levinson in an influential argument against the second constitutive thesis of the simple view: sonicism. Having made a case for contextualism, Levinson goes on to argue against it by *reductio*, pointing out that sonicism entails contextualism's falsehood (1980b: 68–73).

It suffices for me to say this: in Chapter 9 we shall see that it is contextualism that is, in fact, false. The supposed contextually determined properties of a work of music are either not genuinely contextually determined, or else properties of composers and their actions, rather than of the works themselves.

5.6 Composition and Aesthetic Appraisal: A Reply to Levinson

The conclusion to be drawn from the previous section is that a properly formulated and elaborated account of composition as creative discovery does nothing to misrepresent the nature of this process. However, philosophers hostile to Platonism have also alleged that it would disfigure our concept of art and, especially, misrepresent our practice of appraising both works of music and their composers. The next two sections reply to concerns along these lines.

Without doubt, it is Levinson who has provided the Platonist with the most well-known challenges of this kind. Tellingly, Levinson grants that discoveries may be creative, yet insists that it is creat*ability*, not simply creat*ivity*, that is required for a satisfying account of the nature of composition (1990c: 228). Why is this? In Levinson's view, it is central to our concept of art that we regard artists as bringing their works into the world:

The whole tradition of art assumes art is creative in the strict sense, that it is a godlike activity in which the artist brings into being what did not exist beforehand—much as a demiurge forms a world out of inchoate matter. The notion that artists truly *add* to the world, in company with cake-bakers, house builders, lawmakers, and theory constructors, is surely a deep-rooted idea that merits preservation if at all possible. (Levinson 1980b: 66–7)

Levinson seems to offer three reasons why our concept of art is as he describes it. First, he suggests that we take there to obtain what he terms an 'I–Thou' relation between an artist and her work: 'a relation of unique possession' in which a work belongs to an artist 'in no uncertain terms'. This intuition, he argues, can only be captured if the work an artist possesses is literally created by her (1990c: 218). Second, he claims that the status we attach to musical composition is dependent upon works being created by their composers. 'If', he says, 'we conceive of Beethoven's Fifth Symphony as existing sempiternally, before Beethoven's compositional act, a small part of the glory that surrounds Beethoven's composition of the piece seems to be removed' (1980b: 67). Finally, he suggests that theoretical unity demands that we view composers as creating their works. We have, he thinks, a unitary notion of creativity in the arts that determines that we view musical composition, like sculpture and painting, as involving the literal creation of an entity.[21]

But what are we to make of these putative explanations of the putative fact that the thesis that composers create their works is so central to our concept of musical composition? In my view, the aspects of our thought and talk that Levinson takes to embody a clear intuition that musical works are created are, in fact, susceptible of alternative explanation. So, whilst it is indeed true that people commonly *believe* works of music to be brought into being by their composers, this belief is, I contend, a product of a naïve philosophical theory rather than an account demanded by the linguistic and conceptual data. For example, when it comes to the claim that we hold composers to 'truly *add* to the world, in company with cake-bakers, house builders, law makers, and theory constructors' (1980b: 67), I feel that Levinson is moving a little too quickly. For the things that cake-bakers and house builders undeniably create are not types, but *tokens*: token cakes and token houses, respectively. Of course, there may be a person whom we may wish to call 'the inventor of the chocolate éclair', but our use of this definite description does not conflict with the type/token theory's denial that a type can be created. For, as I explained in §3.2, our everyday use of 'the inventor of ψ' does not embody the thesis that the people we describe as 'inventors' bring types into existence. 'The inventor of the chocolate éclair' actually refers to the person whose act of conceiving of such a confection was responsible for the type's first being tokened. The type has always existed; the person we call its 'inventor' was the (ingenious) individual who first had the idea of such a thing and whose imaginative act started the process which led to the creation of the type's first token.

Here, then, our talk of people 'adding something to the world', or even of their 'inventing' things, turns out not to involve us in any anti-Platonistic commitments. But let us return to the case of musical composition. When

---

[21] 'Shall paintings, drawings, etchings, sculptures, palaces, dances, films and so on all be truly creatable, in the full sense of the word, and only symphonies and novels denied this possibility? There would be little profit, and false economy, in that' (1990c: 220).

we talk of composers as having 'added something to the world', this too does not thereby commit us to the idea that an entity—namely, a musical work—has been literally created. True enough, speakers may *take* it to involve such a commitment, but this is an unwarranted gloss placed on the facts. For let us consider what 'addition' really means in this context. A composer of a great work adds *value* to our lives. This she does by giving us the chance to enrich our experience in some way by listening to the work; and she gives us this chance by discovering the work, (typically) scoring it and thereby making it possible for us to listen to it and get something from it. No assumption of creation need be made. Indeed, the discovery of the Victoria Falls, or the tomb of Tutankhamen, 'added something to the world' in a similar sense. Such discoveries made it possible for us to appreciate the things discovered.

The fact that our talk of composers 'adding something to the world' does not imply that their works are created by them is further evidenced when we attend to what 'the world' means in this setting. To say that a composer has added something *to the world* is to say that she has added something *to our culture*; and this latter way of talking does not (although, to the untutored eye, it might seem to) embody the doctrine that her composition has literally been brought into existence by her. In composing *In This House, On This Morning*, Marsalis certainly added the work to our culture, but adding a work to our culture is a matter of introducing it into our cultural life, of placing it within our culture and opening it up to appreciation. And Marsalis did this, not by bringing the work into existence, but by first scoring it, first tokening it, and thereby bringing it to the notice of the jazz world. To do this, he need not have actually created the piece. Adding something *to our culture* is not a matter of creating something that did not exist before; it is placing something within our culture that was not there before.[22] This, I contend, is what our talk of composers 'adding something

---

[22] Saam Trivedi objects to my analogy between the respective ways in which the discovery of the Victoria Falls and the composition of a work of music may 'add something to world', claiming that 'this analogy fails. For unlike in the musical case, the Victoria Falls clearly pre-existed out there in the *external* world independently of us and our minds, and the discovery of the Victoria Falls merely added something to *our knowledge* of the external world, not to the external world itself, as newly created musical works do, if I am right' (Trivedi 2002: 78–9). But such a move is question-begging. I have offered an account of what it is for something to 'add something to the world' with a view to defending the thesis that a musical work may *both* be discovered (i.e. be a part of the 'external' world in one sense of this word) *and* its discovery 'add something to world'. Such discoveries do this by adding something

to the world' actually amounts to, even if the man or woman in the street fails to see this.

At this point, however, Levinson would, no doubt, argue that other 'creation' locutions are central to our thinking about music. Indeed, he draws our attention to the fact that we speak of musicians 'making', not 'finding', music; that we talk of pieces being 'composed', not 'described' or 'registered'; and that musical works are commissioned 'on the understanding', Levinson claims, 'that something will be brought into existence as fulfilling the commission' (1990c: 219). But, once more, these locutions do not make an unambiguous commitment to the thesis that musical works are created. To begin with, the fact that we speak of *musicians* making music is irrelevant to the question of whether *composers* bring their compositions into existence. When musicians make music by performing a work, what is brought into existence is a *performance* of the work, not the work itself. Furthermore, Levinson makes a huge, and unjustified, leap from the fact that composers are commissioned to compose works to the conclusion that we need regard such works as brought into existence by their composers. For it is composers, not works, who are, strictly speaking, commissioned; and they are commissioned to compose works. No particular account of the nature of composition is presupposed.

Yet, Levinson is quite correct to say that we speak of works being 'composed' rather than 'described' or 'registered'. But this fact about our discourse does not tell against the idea that works of music pre-date their composition. For, as we noted earlier, the Platonist need not suppose the composition of a musical work to be a matter of mere *description*. The fact that composition is a process of discovery does not entail that the composer has no need to think creatively. A composer does not apprehend the abstract type and just, so to speak, transcribe it. Such 'apprehension' is nothing but a myth. Composition, by contrast, is a process of selection in which various sound-event-types are evaluated and, on the basis of this, criteria for correct performance formulated. The composer evaluates which kind of sound-sequence-event, once tokened, will achieve the effect he wants

to our *culture* (which is what 'the world' means in this context). In response to this, it is no use denying that musical works pre-existed their discovery, since it is precisely this claim that is moot. Additionally, my view is not that the discovery of *either* the Victoria Falls *or* a work of music solely adds to our 'knowledge' of the world: my claim is that these discoveries add something to our culture by enriching and adding value to our lives.

to achieve and, as a result, comes to creatively discover a normative type of sound-sequence-event. Of course, the end result of this evaluative process is that the composer scores (or otherwise indicates) something that already exists: he lights upon just one of the infinite number of such (normative) types of sound-event that there are. But this process is nonetheless both creative and evaluative. The creative act *is* the discovery of the work.

In the wake of this, it is of no use for Levinson to claim, as we have seen him do, that '[i]f works are to *belong* to artists in the full sense—to be theirs in no uncertain terms—then creation rather than discovery seems to be called for' (1990c: 218). And, what is more, we are entitled to probe what this 'full sense' of belonging could be. Levinson would appear to be confronted with a dilemma. If a work belongs to an artist in this sense only if the artist has created it, then we have turned in a very small circle indeed, and the proponent of the simple view will just *deny* that works belong to artists in this way. If, on the other hand, Levinson tries to resist characterizing the 'full sense' in which a work belongs to an artist in question-begging terms, he runs the risk of prompting an obvious reply. For, as Levinson himself recognizes (1990c: 218), it looks as if an intimate relationship can likewise exist between a discoverer and the thing she discovers. Just such an 'essential intimacy' exists between, say, Pythagoras and the theorem which bears his name. The theorem is *Pythagoras's*: he was the creative genius who first discovered it, and it will always be associated with him.

To a case such as this, Levinson can only say the following:

Of course, the *discovery* is theirs—their act—if that is all that is going on, but what is *discovered* in not in the same way theirs. Columbus's America wasn't in this sense logically his in virtue of his discovering it. But Ives's symphonic essay *The Fourth of July* is irrevocably and exclusively his, precisely in virtue of his composing it. (Levinson 1990c: 218)

But this move does not get Levinson anywhere, since it sees him returning to the dilemma's other horn. For what else can it be for Ives's work to be 'logically his' other than for it to have been created by him? If, as seems to be the case, this is the only content which can be assigned to a work's being 'logically' that of a composer, the supposed fact that musical works logically belong to their composers cannot provide an independent reason for supposing that composers are the creators of their works. The putative 'logical' sense in which a work of music belongs to its composer is what Simon Blackburn would call a piece of 'Pentagonese' (1984: 225): nothing but an important-sounding way of formulating the very claim that Levinson is supposed to be arguing for.[23]

So much for the supposedly distinctive 'I–Thou' relationship existing between composers and their works. What of Levinson's second reason for taking the idea that musical works are created to be so well entrenched? Is it really the case that the status we assign to composition is dependent upon compositions being literally created? The answer to this question, as one would suspect, given this chapter's arguments up to now, is 'No'. The status and value of composition would, indeed, be undermined if composition were a Gradgrindian matter of pure description. But this is not the view that I am recommending. Platonism, as we have noted, is compatible with recognizing that composition is a creative, imaginative act. Consequently, it is easy to see that it matters not one jot whether or not the composer is credited with bringing an abstract entity into being. As we saw in §5.4, our opinion of Wiles's achievement would not be any greater if we were to regard his proof of Fermat's Last Theorem as having been created, rather than discovered, by him. What staggers us is how someone could have the creativity, rigour, and imagination to make such a discovery. And the same can be said for the composition of great works of music. We may marvel at a great piece of music, according to Platonism, not (as Levinson supposes (1980b: 67)) because its composer brought it into existence, but because it took such brilliance to come across it. Great composers are, indeed, enveloped by a 'special aura' (1980b: 67), but we need not read an anti-Platonic message into this. For the aura exists, not because great composers are 'true creators' (1980b: 67), but because they are truly creative. What matters, when it comes to the question of judging the status of a scientist, writer, or composer, is the originality, importance, and value of their work; and this is an evaluative question, not an ontological one.

---

[23] Another reading of what it is for Ives's piece to be 'logically his' is this: the identity of the work turns on that of the composer (because the work is an indicated type that has the composer as one of its elements). But such a position—besides relying on the controversial claim that works of music are indicated types—cannot form part of an argument against the thesis that composition is a form of discovery. As I noted in §5.2, even indicated types exist eternally, so even if works were indicated types, they could not be created.

But what of Levinson's claim that theoretical unity demands that we regard musical works as being, like paintings and sculptures, created entities? As I argued in §4.3, when discussing Rohrbaugh's claim that we should treat musical works as temporally flexible, I dispute that any such theoretical unity need be acknowledged. Given that the artworks produced by painting and sculpture are concrete, physical particulars, it is by no means obvious that the level of theoretical unity that Levinson craves is necessary. For if there really is such a great difference between a symphony and a painting (the former being a type, the latter a concrete particular), it is far from clear that we should expect features we associate with one kind of entity to be instantiated by the other. Indeed, given that types are, by their very nature, eternal entities, we cannot expect the types that are symphonies to be akin to paintings and etchings in actually being brought into existence by an artist.

Trivedi, however, is unhappy with such a response, and he makes two kinds of reply to the position I now take.[24] First, he claims that the fact 'that musical works and paintings are ontologically different in some ways (in that the former are types and the latter concrete particulars) does not preclude their being similar with respect to being created' (2002: 75). Second, he takes the question of *how* and *where* supposedly eternal types exist to be unanswerable (2002: 76–7). In my view, though, these replies fall some way short of their intended target, as we shall now see.

To begin with, Trivedi begs the question in stating that a conception of works of music as types does not preclude their being created. The argument of Chapter 3—the conclusion of which is that types exist eternally—is an argument for the negation of just this claim. Trivedi can only earn the right to say that types are creatable by demonstrating my argument to the contrary to be unsound, and this is a challenge that, thus far, he has failed to take up.

Of Trivedi's objections to my attempt to explain away the supposed 'false divide' between music and the other arts, this just leaves us with his claim that I cannot explain *how* and *where* eternal types exist. But, given the account of types offered in Chapters 2 and 3, these questions look either malformed or else harmless. For to ask *where* such entities exist is to presume

---

[24] I say 'now take' because in my 2000 and 2002 I remain agnostic about whether paintings, sculptures, and the like are concrete particulars or abstract types. Trivedi's article is a response to my 2000, and includes objections to treating such artworks as types that I have no need to discuss here.

that they must exist *somewhere*, which they do not. Types do not exist in Platonic heaven or any*where* else; in common with sets, numbers, propositions, and facts, types have no spatial location. And to ask, as Trivedi does, 'how did these allegedly pre-existent musical works exist eternally... *before* the advent of humans and the human activity of music making? (2002: 76–7) is to ask a question that the type ontology offered in this book can answer relatively easily. Types pre-exist their first tokening because, although intrinsically *of* tokens, they are not dependent for their existence upon actually being tokened. The case for such a position was been made for word-types in §3.2; and the same considerations apply to sound-event-types. Naturally, viewing musical works as eternally existent types means that composition sees people discover, rather than create, works of music. But I take myself to have shown that this conclusion, far from distorting our folk concept of composition, sits comfortably with those features of it worth preserving.

5.7 Composition and Aesthetic Appraisal: Understanding, Interpretation, and Correctness

Let us now move on to consider objections to Platonism that charge it with distorting the nature of our aesthetic response to works of music. In this section I shall reply to the following objections: that Platonism is incompatible with the nature of our *understanding* of musical works; that it does not leave sufficient room for varying *interpretations* of such works; and that it cannot explain the fact that what counts as *correctness in performance* may, in part, be determined by the cultural context in which performers find themselves. We shall see that the kind of Platonism I have elaborated has the conceptual resources to rebut these three charges.

It is Michael Morris (forthcoming) who raises the first objection. In Morris's view, once we have appreciated what it is for an auditor to understand a piece of music, we see at once that the understood work must have been created. What we have here is a kind of transcendental argument (Morris forthcoming, MS 17 n. 13): an argument that, if sound, takes us from a premiss concerning our experience of music to a conclusion concerning its origin.

To begin with, though, do we really want to say that works of music can be *understood*? In my view, Morris is quite right to point out that we do. As he explains, what seems to be distinctive about works of art in general—what gives them a distinctive importance—is 'that there is such a thing as doing justice' to them (forthcoming, MS 13). Artworks merit our attention; they demand that we appreciate them. What, then, *is it* to do justice to a work of art? In Morris's opinion—and I do not wish to quibble with this—doing justice to a work of art involves understanding it (forthcoming, MS 14–15). To appreciate a work of music is to respond to it in the kinds of way that it merits, and this is best seen as a kind of understanding. For example, someone who finds the Adagio in Mahler's Fifth Symphony comic, or chirpy, has failed to understand it.

Clearly, as Morris points out, we should not assimilate such understanding to the understanding of a sentence (forthcoming, MS 7–8). If understanding a piece of music were like 'grasping' the proposition expressed by an utterance of a sentence, an absurd conclusion would follow: namely, that people could truly claim to have *completely* understood Mahler's Fifth Symphony. People who make such claims have ass's ears:[25] a symphony, like a photograph, does not have a finitely statable propositional content. It provokes a persistent interest, and no interpretation (i.e. paraphrase) of it does justice to it completely. So, rather than one's understanding of a piece of music consisting in propositional knowledge, it is preferable to view such understanding as manifest in a whole range of responses, including those of the emotions. It may be appropriate, truly manifesting one's understanding of Mahler's Fifth Symphony, for example, that one feels swelled with melancholy as one hears its Adagio; and that one should be uplifted by Ellington's 'Take the "A" Train'. These are the responses merited by the music, and one's having them shows one to have understood it, however incompletely or imperfectly.

At this point, however, Morris introduces a teleological element into his account of understanding, an element of which, he claims, the Platonist cannot explain. Works of music, he suggests, are not just *capable* of being understood in the sense that we have just explicated; they are *there to be understood* (Morris forthcoming, MS 12). A work of music has, as its *purpose*, that it be done justice to: that is *why* it exists in the world. From which it follows, argues Morris, that the work must have been created (forthcoming, MS 17). That works of music (and works of art generally) have the teleological purpose that they do entails that they were brought into being by an artist.

---

[25] I learned this satisfyingly abusive phrase from Kivy (1983: 123).

In other words, Morris seems to be offering the following argument:

(48) The purpose of a work of music, W, is that it be understood.

(49) W could not have had this purpose unless W's composer had created W for that purpose.

So (50) W's composer created W.

But once the argument is set out like this, it becomes apparent that a Platonist will deny (48), resisting all talk of a work having such a purpose *in itself*. A musical work, a Platonist will insist, is not in itself *for* anything: it is an eternally existent type of sound-sequence-event. Understanding such a work is not a matter of grasping the reason *why it is there*; it is to *appreciate the work's nature* by responding in the right kind of way to occurrences of it.

This, it seems to me, is much more than merely an *ad hoc* escape. It is not being denied that considering a composer's reasons for composing the work he has will shed light upon the work's nature. In this sense, the intervention of the composer opens up the work to aesthetic understanding. Finding out, for example, the nature of the response that the composer wishes to prompt in the audience may well render members of the audience susceptible to responding in precisely that way to the work itself. But the crucial point is that one's understanding of a work consists in one's responding correctly to it, not fathoming what it is there for.

An analogy might help. Works of music, according to the Platonist, are akin to works of found art. It takes a creative imagination to see a piece of driftwood as a work of art: to appreciate, for example, its shape, colour, and grain. Choosing one piece of driftwood rather than another—on the basis of aesthetic criteria—requires the artist to make aesthetically replete choices. Now, in the case of a work of found art, the mere fact that the artist makes choices in selecting it does not entail that it is created by her. Such things existed already. So it no more follows in the case of works of music either. The composer's choices lead him to uncover a pre-existent work; and these choices are relevant to our evaluation of it only inasmuch as they enable us to respond fittingly to the work discovered.

Another way of putting the Platonist's reply is this: understanding a work of music requires us only to view it as *composed* by someone, not as *created* by someone. Inasmuch as we have seen that the intervention of an artist opens up works for aesthetic understanding, it follows that the object of our aesthetic understanding is a composed piece. But it does not follow from this that composition involves literally bringing the piece into being. Understanding a work involves us in considering why its composer, in composing the piece, made the choices she did: with such knowledge, we are better placed to appreciate features of the work that would otherwise pass us by. But it is quite compatible with this fact to view the composer's aesthetic choices as prompting the (creative) discovery, rather than creation, of a work.

Having said this, Morris considers the kind of reply just given but, nonetheless, finds it lacking. In Morris's view, such a position fails to take account of the fact that works of music are '*essentially* meaningful' (forthcoming, MS 20), by which he means that musical works are not simply there to be understood, but essentially so. According to Morris, 'those things which are in fact works of art could not exist without being meaningful' (forthcoming, MS 8). Consequently, if Morris is right, composing a work cannot be discovering a sound-sequence-event because 'we could not have had the very same thing before the intervention of the artist' (forthcoming, MS 20): the artist's intervention—the process of presenting the item as an object of aesthetic understanding—automatically brings forth a new entity.

But this latter claim, it seems to me, is both undermotivated and counter-intuitive in its consequences. It is undermotivated because it is unclear what is so objectionable about denying that musical works are essentially meaningful in Morris's sense. As we have noted, the Platonist holds that the meanings of works only become apparent to us once the works have been composed (i.e. creatively discovered). Interpretation is only called for once a work has been discovered; before this time, it is just one more undiscovered item in the world. Furthermore, the idea that any intervention by an artist thereby brings a new entity into existence is hard to swallow, as is evident from a consideration of found art. The idea that placing a piece of driftwood in an art gallery thereby brings a new entity into existence, though claimed by Morris to be 'hardly a counterintuitive claim' (forthcoming, MS 20) is, in fact, deeply puzzling. Putting a piece of driftwood in a gallery does not cause *something else* to pop into existence in addition to the 'mere piece of driftwood'; it just enables us to classify the existing piece of driftwood *as* an artwork. Indeed, the very idea of found art militates against Morris's account of what goes on. The point of found art, surely, is that *a thing found by an artist*, and not made by her, can count as an artwork. This idea would not be well served if the item found turned out to be, not the work of art itself, but merely the item whose placement in an art gallery brought the true artwork into being.

Ultimately, then, Morris's objection to Platonism founders. The Platonist has a perfectly acceptable account of aesthetic understanding. Predelli, however, offers a different, but equally challenging, criticism of the Platonist's position: to his mind, the Platonist cannot account for the way in which the criteria for correct performance are culturally determined (1995: 346–7). As he explains, differing interpretations of a work of music—perhaps relating to its tempo or rhythmic pattern—may yield widely differing performances; and performances, what is more, that may go in and out of fashion:

Our pre-theoretical decisions on what counts as a correct performance of a piece are based on transient aesthetical and cultural criteria, and do not appear to be constrained by an immutable set of prescriptions associated with an everlasting abstract entity. ... Standards of correctness shift according to the interpreter's skills, and do not conform to the Platonist picture. (Predelli 1995: 347)

Such an objection, however, seems to me to misunderstand the nature of the relation obtaining between a type and its tokens. Predelli seems to assume that the correctness condition laid down by a type is determinate in all respects, so that there is no possibility of there being two tokens that differ structurally, whilst both counting as properly formed tokens of the type. On such a reading of the type/token theory, a score that does not specify exhaustively and determinately such a correctness condition reveals the composer to have had a 'lack of care for the details of her work' (Predelli 1995: 346). Such a score, rather than specifying the sound-event-type accurately, is a mere approximation of the fully determinate type intended.

But, as we saw in §2.5, such a conception of types is hugely uncompulsory, for types may be indeterminate in two distinct ways. First of all, the correctness condition laid down by a type may be such that whether a well-formed token need have a certain feature is simply left unspecified; and second, this condition may be such that it specifies a certain feature in a fuzzy way. Clearly, the type/token theorist should point out that the types that are musical works are susceptible to both kinds of indeterminacy. Bach's *The Art of Fugue*, for example, offers us an extreme case of indeterminacy of the first kind, inasmuch as its score is silent on the question of its instrumentation. And when it comes to the second kind of indeterminacy, we would do well to remember that the conventional ways of specifying tempo, articulation, dynamics, pitch, and even note-length are vague.[26] Furthermore, the fact that composers do not artificially precisify their scores need not be seen by the type/token theorist as a dereliction of compositional duty: the type/token theorist can (and should) insist that the works represented by scores are *just like that*: fuzzy in certain respects.

Given that this is so, it is evident that there is no conflict between a Platonist type/token theory and the fact that standards of correctness in performance may vary through time. The fact that works of music are indeterminate in the two senses just set out leaves play for the possibility of such culturally determined variance in opinion over what constitutes a correct performance. Such difference in opinion is the product of the composer's laying down a correctness condition that does not specify in all respects how a performance should sound, or else makes a fuzzy such specification. The work is such that it does not precisely determine how it should be realized in performance in all respects.

As it happens, an appreciation of the same phenomenon—the inde-terminate nature of works of music—enables the Platonist to reply to the final objection that I shall consider in this section. This objection has it that a Platonist account of composition is untenable because it is incompatible with the role of *interpretation* in performance. Musical works, the objector charges, are essentially subject to interpretation: their nature is such that they invite differing interpretations; and much of our interest as listeners comes from comparing and evaluating distinct interpretations, and considering which, if any, reveals a greater understanding of the piece. But, our objector claims, works could not, in this way, essentially invite interpretation if Platonism were true. If a work were an eternally existent, unchanging type, its normative properties would be laid down in advance, and so the performer's views as to the nature of these normative properties would count for nothing. Predelli puts the accusation nicely:

[T]he existence of interesting options left to the performer would turn out to be the result of accidental customs, and it would always be at least *possible* that a musical work be carefully defined in its minutest significant details, so that little choice beyond that of her clothing would be left to the performer. It is, however,

---

[26] When it comes to pitch, a note played at 440 Hz and a note played at 441 Hz both count as examples of an A. Likewise, any performer who has been told, for example, to sustain a dotted quaver for 'a smidgen longer' is aware that musical notation is vague, even in the case of note-length.

a fundamental tenet in our understanding of performing arts that a composition is *essentially* subject to interpretation. A picture of the relationship between a work and its performances which reduces the role of the performer to the choice of features disregarded by the composer as unimportant or conventionally sanctioned as non-normative, misses a crucial characteristic of that relationship. (Predelli 1995: 346)

Platonism would indeed be undermined if it were committed to the downplaying of interpretation in this way. A performance of a piece of music is, most certainly, the result of a two-way relation between the performer and the work. A performer does not merely seek to obey the composer's instructions; she necessarily brings something of herself to the piece. Crucially, however, the Platonist can allow for all of this. As we have just noted, the tempo of a performance, the dynamics with which a piece is played, the timbre of its instrumentation,[27] and even aspects of its rhythmic pattern, are usually not precisely determined by the work itself. The gaps left are to be filled by the performer's interpretation, and, I stress, these gaps are sufficiently large to render the resulting interpretations 'interesting' (Predelli 1995: 346). The performer's activity is certainly *not* reduced to that of filling in those gaps that the composer has simply *neglected* to fill in, or else deemed to be trivial. Works are—by their very nature—fuzzy.

At this point, however, Predelli might press his point by asking the Platonist to imagine a case in which every aspect of the sounds to be made by a performer are determined precisely by the performed work's score. Must not a Platonist admit that there can be such works? And would not the Platonist have to say that such works were *not* essentially open to interpretation, thereby falsifying the relationship between a work and its performances? Well, the answer to the first question is 'Yes', for sure. But the crucial point here is that such fully determinate works would only have limited interest for us and would, at best, be regarded as interesting academic exercises. Listening to works in performance grips us precisely because such works invite interpretation in the way Predelli describes. We listen, not merely to gain a conduit to the work performed, but to consider the performer's take on it. Given that this is so, the Platonist should admit

---

[27] Famously, Duke Ellington composed 'Cottontail' with the sturdy, gruff tenor saxophone of Ben Webster in mind. But the work itself does not determine that the tenor saxophone part should be played in this way. An interpretation by Stan Getz, whose own tone was smoother and lighter than Webster's, may well have been an enlightening and valuable one.

the possibility of compositions that are carefully defined in their minutest details, yet insist that he can grant the *spirit* of Predelli's claim by saying that works *typically* invite interpretation. The works of music central to 'our understanding of the performing arts' *are* essentially open to interpretation; but it does no harm to admit that there could be other, peripheral works for which interpretation is ruled out.

5.8 Conclusion

The type/token theory, it is true, entails that works of music are eternal existents. Ultimately, however, this is a conclusion that should not trouble us unduly. There is no good reason for supposing musical works to depend for their existence upon performances, playings, or other claimed 'embodiments'; and there are certainly no convincing grounds for supposing that such works can be destroyed. Finally, and most importantly, the idea that musical works must be created by their composers has been revealed to be a piece of philosophical myth-making. A conception of composition as a kind of creative discovery is defensible in itself, and has no troubling consequences for our concept of music, the esteem in which we hold composers, or the way in which we think about our aesthetic engagement with music.

This concludes my defence of the type/token theory against objections. Despite this, the case for accepting the theory has not yet been completed. For although certain of the type/token theory's rivals have been shown to be either incapable of accounting for musical works' repeatability or else beset by objections (or both), two of the type/token theory's most significant competitors have not yet been called to account. Specifically, we have not yet considered the claims made by those who take musical works to be continuants (i.e. particulars that are susceptible to change through time), and those who suppose such works to be compositional actions (whether such actions are to be understood as types or tokens). It is to such theories that I turn in the next two chapters.

6
Musical Works as Continuants: A Theory Rejected

6.1 Introduction

The type/token theory neatly explains what the repeatability of works of music consists in, and it does so by assigning such works to a familiar ontological category. Musical works are inherently multiple by virtue of being types (of sound-sequence-event): items that have multiple instantiability built into them. As we saw in §§1.2–1.4, the perennial alternatives to the type/token theory do not fare so well: they either fail to explain the repeatability of works of music, fail to explain how a (whole) work can be heard, or else fall victim to ontological naïvety. It is for this reason that we have come to regard the type/token theory as the face-value answer to the categorial question in the ontology of music.

In matters metaphysical, however, time marches on; and in recent years the type/token theory has come to be challenged by two fascinating alternative approaches. One such approach, whose leading proponents are Gregory Currie (1989) and David Davies (2004), has it that works of music (and indeed, works of art generally) are *compositional actions*, in which these are construed either as action-types (as Currie thinks) or as action-tokens (as Davies has it). The other significant type of theory to emerge in the past few years takes musical works (and, once more, artworks across the board) to be *continuants*: that is, particulars (i.e. things that do not admit of instances) rather than types. The task of this chapter and the next is to critically examine both of these rival accounts. By the end of Chapter 7, it will be clear that neither of these alternative contemporary accounts matches the type/token theory for explanatory power and ontological clarity; and with this conclusion having been reached, the defence of the type/token theory will be complete.

6.2 A Theory Introduced

The task of the present chapter, then, is to focus on the claim that musical works are continuants, rather than types. But what does this claim mean? What *is it* for something to be a continuant? Before we can evaluate the theory, we need to be clear about the ontological category under which it places works of music.

One way of shedding light initially on the notion of a continuant is to give examples of such things. The items we pre-philosophically label 'things'—entities such as people, planets, trees, and stones—are all continuants; so the claim being made by a propounder of what we may call *the continuant view* is that works of music are, in some respects or other, like these. But in *what* respects exactly? Two apparent differences between works of music and paradigmatic continuants spring to mind at once. First, *In This House, On This Morning*, unlike a tree, a person, or a stone, is not a material object. As we shall see in a while, proponents of the continuant view may differ as to whether musical works occupy space or not (i.e. whether they are abstract or concrete), but one thing is for sure: they are not composed of matter. Second, and even more importantly, *In This House, On This Morning*, unlike a stone, a tree, or a person, has *occurrences*: it is repeatable. Indeed, the repeatability of works of music is the major datum that any answer to the categorial question must explain. Given these differences between works of music and the paradigm examples of continuants, we need to know why such differences do not immediately undermine the suggestion that musical works should be assigned to this ontological category. In other words, what the supporter of the continuant view must provide is an explanation of what it is to be a continuant that does not immediately problematize the continuant view of works of music itself.

With a view to producing such an account, there appear to be four conditions that an entity must meet to be a continuant, at least if Guy Rohrbaugh (2003)—the leading defender of the conception of musical works as continuants—is to be believed.[1] First, and as I have mentioned

---

[1] Rohrbaugh uses 'historical individual' where I use 'continuant', but this difference simply concerns the label used to express the concept.

  Approaches similar to that of Rohrbaugh have been suggested by both Michael Morris (forthcoming) and Stefano Predelli (forthcoming). Notably, both Morris and Predelli deny that works of music are instantiable entities, although they do not accept all of the details of Rohrbaugh's account. However,

already, for an entity to be a genuine continuant, it must be a particular; and what this means is that continuants are not generic entities in the sense explained in §1.2: they are not multiply instantiable. Unlike sets, continuants do not have members; unlike properties, they do not have instances; and unlike types, they do not have tokens. Musical works, if continuants, are repeatable all right (Rohrbaugh 2003: 177): this is taken for granted by the type/token theorist and the supporter of the continuant view alike. The key difference between them, however, is this: according to the continuant view, the repeatability of a work of music has to be explained in some way other than by appeal to such entities being generic. As Predelli explains, the continuant view has it that musical works 'are not themselves instantiables, and... their performances do not bear to them a relation accountable on the model of the exemplifiable-exemplar ontological pattern' (Predelli forthcoming, MS 6). Musical works have *occurrences* but do not have *instances*.

The natures of the second, third, and fourth conditions are familiar from the discussions of §§2.5 and 4.3. For something to be a continuant it must be modally flexible (i.e. capable of having intrinsic properties other than those it has actually), temporally flexible (i.e. susceptible to change in its intrinsic properties over time); and it must both come into and go out of existence. Putting these conditions together, we can say that continuants, unlike types, have a finite 'life-span' and ' "a life story". They are all subject to change over time, and all, had their life stories gone differently, could have been somewhat different than they in fact are' (Rohrbaugh 2003: 199). On this view, works of music—though not themselves material objects—have more in common with such items than with types, properties, or sets.

Having said this, it should be apparent already that, although the continuant view sets out to assign such works to a familiar ontological kind, such an assignment threatens to disrupt this very category. For, since musical works are repeatable—that is, have sound-sequence-events as occurrences—it follows that musical works, if continuants, would have to be continuants of a hitherto undiscovered kind: continuants that, despite being particulars, nonetheless have occurrences. This being so, works of music, on the continuant view, look increasingly like suspiciously cross-categorial entities: on the one

---

Rohrbaugh's conception is certainly the most worked-out version of the thesis available, and hence will form the basis of my discussion.

hand, they are particulars, inasmuch as they do not have *instances*; on the other hand, they are nonetheless capable of having *occurrences*. Such continuants, if they existed, would be ontologically novel: the particulars with which we are familiar—rocks, trees, people, and the like—are incapable of having occurrences. Indeed, the idea that an entity's having occurrences may be explained other than by means of its being a *generic* entity is highly revisionary. As Rohrbaugh himself admits, the kind of analysis he recommends in fact turns out to require 'innovation at the level of metaphysics, the introduction of a new ontological category' (2003: 197).

Naturally, this admission by Rohrbaugh raises the stakes for the continuant view. If the introduction of this new kind of ontological category is not to be seen as merely an *ad hoc* move, its introduction had better both be well motivated and genuinely explain the relevant phenomena (i.e. musical works' repeatability). In what follows, I shall argue that the continuant view can do neither.

6.3 Explicating and Motivating the Continuant View

Clearly, the task facing a supporter of the continuant view is to explain the nature of musical works' repeatability and to demonstrate that the overall merits of her theory outweigh those of the type/token theory. So what form will such an explanation of musical works' repeatability take? What, according to the continuant view, does the repeatability of *In This House, On This Morning* consist in, if not the fact that it is a type that can be repeatedly tokened?

The answer, it seems, will make use of the notions of *ontological dependence* and *embodiment*. Marsalis's work, it will be claimed, is a continuant that depends for its existence, in a generic sense, upon the series of concrete particulars that are its embodiments (Rohrbaugh 2003: 191–2).[2] As I noted in §5.3, an embodiment is anything that 'preserves what [the work] is like and leads to new performances' (2003: 191). Consequently, it is

---

[2] That the supposed ontological dependence of a musical work upon its embodiments is taken to be *generic* amounts to the following claim: a work of music depends for its existence upon there being at least one such embodiment; but there is no embodiment such that the work would go out of existence, were this particular embodiment not to exist. The existential dependence in question is not, in this sense, *de re* (Fine 1995: 287; Lowe 1995: 35).

natural to regard a work's embodiments as including its performances and playings but also, perhaps, copies of the work's score and memory-traces of it. This being so, a plausible way for the continuant theorist to proceed is to seek to explain a work of music's multiplicity in terms of a suitably restricted version of this phenomenon of embodiment. The relation obtaining between *In This House, On This Morning* and its occurrences, it will be claimed, is not that of instantiation, but is just 'a more specific form of the embodiment relation' (Rohrbaugh 2003: 198); one whose second kind of relatum is restricted to items that display the work's qualities and are relevant to appreciation and criticism: that is, sound-sequence-events, rather than copies of the score or memories.

Having made this move, it swiftly becomes apparent that a conception of musical works as continuants may take one of two forms, depending on how this embodiment relation and the notion of ontological dependence are to be understood. Perhaps drawing inspiration from Kaplan's conception of words, the first version of the continuant view treats embodiment as *constitution*: the items upon which a work ontologically depends are said to literally to constitute it. Kaplan has famously suggested that 'utterances and inscriptions are *stages* of words, which are the *continuants* made up of these interpersonal stages' (1990: 98), and our first version of the continuant view thinks of a work of music in the same way: namely, as a continuant that is a fusion of the occurrences which are its temporal parts. On such an account, *In This House, On This Morning* turns out to be a *perduring* entity: an entity whose persistence through time is a matter of the succession of its temporal parts, and for which change consists in the difference in those successive temporal parts.[3]

Equally clearly, such a conception will treat musical works as concrete (i.e. spatially located) entities, because a perduring entity cannot have *concreta* as its temporal parts without itself being concrete. As David Lewis has suggested, a temporal stage of an object must be of the same ontological kind as the object itself.[4] It is at this point that the perdurantist's intended

---

[3] See Sider 2001 for an excellent discussion of perdurantism and endurantism.

[4] Challenged to explain what a person-stage is, Lewis replies by pointing out that nothing could be simpler to do: 'A person-stage is a physical object, just as a person is. (If persons had a ghostly part as well, so would person-stages.) It does many of the same things that a person does: it talks and walks and thinks, it has beliefs and desires, it has a size and shape and location' (Lewis 1983: 76). As for people, so for works of music: an entity's temporal parts cannot be concrete without the entity itself being so.

analogy between persistence through time and extension in space has bite. Time-slicing an object is like space-slicing a piece of salami: one slice is pretty much like any other.

So much for the perdurantist version of the continuant view. Although Rohrbaugh himself appeals to Kaplan's conception of words in his exposition (2003: 204 n. 22), he elaborates his own of musical works as continuants in a way that is crucially different. For, according to Rohrbaugh, such works are ' "higher level" objects, dependent on *but not constituted by* physical or spatial things' (2003: 198–9; my emphasis). The entities upon which a work ontologically depends (in a generic sense)—which include its occurrences—are not its (temporal) parts; the embodiment relation does not admit of mereological explication. On the contrary, Rohrbaugh's claim is simply that a work is embodied in its performances, playings, and other embodiments inasmuch as it depends on them, generically, for its existence.

Rohrbaugh's development of the continuant view differs from the perdurantist version in two significant respects. First of all, since he denies that musical works have their embodiments as temporal parts, Rohrbaugh is free to regard such works as *enduring* (rather than perduring) entities: items wholly present at all times at which they exist, and which change by means of gaining and losing properties through time.[5] Equally, he is free to acknowledge the intuitive pull of the thesis that works of music are abstract. If musical works do not have their concrete occurrences as temporal parts, he can resist the idea that works, like their occurrences, must be located in space.[6] Significantly, though, by virtue of being ontologically dependent upon their concrete embodiments, musical works count as 'real', since their existence is rooted in the physical world (Rohrbaugh 2003: 199–200).

One question sure to be prompted by all this is whether either of these proposed explanations of musical works' repeatability are really convincing, but this is a question whose discussion I shall postpone until §6.4. The remainder of the present section is devoted to examining the continuant view's initial motivation. This latter issue is, of course, of no little import. We need to be assured that there is a clear point to admitting ontologically novel entities—namely, continuants with occurrences—into our ontology.

---

[5] In correspondence Rohrbaugh has pointed out that he favours a conception of musical works as endurants.

[6] This is a consequence which Rohrbaugh embraces happily. As he himself puts it, 'if works of art are in time but not in space, then they are at least in good company' (2003: 200).

In particular, we need to be convinced that there are cogent *prima facie* reasons for preferring the continuant view—in either of its manifestations—to the type/token theory. In my view, no such reasons exist.

The continuant view gains any plausibility it has by virtue of meeting presumed conditions of adequacy that are not met by the type/token theory. Specifically, if musical works are continuants, then they come into and out of existence, and are both modally and temporally flexible. As a consequence, the supporter of the continuant view, unlike the type/token theorist, can, it is claimed (Rohrbaugh 2003: 195), assuage our intuitions that *In This House, On This Morning* was brought into being by Marsalis, could have been different in certain respects, and can undergo change through time. However, as I noted in §4.3, the type/token theorist takes our intuition that works are temporally flexible to be both overruled by philosophical argument and capable of being explained away. Talk of a work's being 'revised' need not commit us to the idea that the work itself has been changed by the composer: a 'revised' piece is typically an alternative version of it, a distinct work that shares much of the original's tonal organization. Furthermore, the idea that a composer's 'revision' of a work changes it is subject to a quick and decisive objection: if a work were to undergo genuine change once it has been 'revised', it would no longer exist in its earlier state, a corollary plainly contradicted by the fact that an earlier version of a work may still be performable (if, for example, the original score is recoverable, or if someone remembers it).

Again, as we saw in §4.3, the kinds of cases taken to illustrate the modal flexibility of works of music, though they have *prima facie* appeal, can be explained away by essentially the same strategy. According to the type/token theorist, a possible world in which it appears that Bruckner's Ninth Symphony has been finished by him is, in reality, a world in which Bruckner composes a distinct work that is, nonetheless, substantially similar to his actual Ninth Symphony. The idea that we should reject this explanation in favour of the thesis that musical works are modally flexible is undermotivated: nothing of independent importance depends upon our doing so. Consequently, the fact that the continuant view, but not the type/token theory, allows for works being modally flexible, offers scant reason for preferring the former to the latter.

Having made these points, it would, nonetheless, be foolish to deny that many people *do* have a strong intuition that works are brought into existence by their composers. And one of the perceived benefits of the continuant view might be that it purports to give an explanation of what this process consists in: since works are dependent upon their embodiments for their existence, they come into existence with their first embodiment (Rohrbaugh 2003: 191). But, be this as it may, there are two problems with the claim that the continuant view trumps the type/token theory by virtue of its satisfying 'the creatability requirement' (Levinson 1980b: 67). First, as the arguments of Chapter 5 demonstrated, although many people have such intuitions, they are more the products of a nascent, and crude, folk philosophical theory than they are evidence for the truth of the thesis that composers literally create their works. It turns out that it is far from obvious *why* we should regard Marsalis as the creator of *In This House, On This Morning*, rather than its (creative) discoverer: certainly, nothing about the compositional process, the regard in which we hold composers, or the nature of our aesthetic experience demands that we hold works to come into being at the time of their composition.

Second, we should be clear from the outset that there is a clear *cost* involved in satisfying the creatability requirement in the way in which the continuant view does. Treating works of music as ontologically dependent upon their embodiments certainly enables us to say that composers create their works; but the problem is that the instrument by which this is achieved—namely, by taking such works to be (generically) dependent for their existence upon their embodiments—is too crude for the theory to be plausible. A consequence of such a thesis of ontological dependence is that a given work exists only if it has at least one embodiment. But, as I noted in §5.3, there are strong intuitions against such a thesis, since it entails that works are destroyed when they are no longer played, performed, or remembered. Works of music, we are inclined to think, are not things that go out of existence when we do; they outlast us. They are works for an audience, but will not cease to exist once there is no audience for them. As a result, *even if* we were to accept that an answer to the categorial question should satisfy the creatability requirement, it would not follow that we should regard works of music as ontologically dependent upon their embodiments in the way in which the continuant view intends.

So, if we can resist the thesis that musical works are temporally and modally flexible, and if we can counter the intuition that such works are brought into being by their composers, how else could a supporter of the

continuant view seek to motivate her position? I can think of three reasons
why the continuant view might yet have some appeal. First, a treatment of
works of music as continuants might be found attractive because it leaves
open the possibility that the category *artwork* is ontologically homogeneous.
Given how natural it is to regard paintings and certain kinds of sculptures
as continuants, it might be supposed a benefit of the continuant view that
it places works of music (and, by analogy, the works of the other repeatable
art forms) in the same ontological boat. By contrast, it might be supposed
that an acceptance of the type/token theory inevitably commits us to the
idea that the concept *artwork* is ontologically disjunctive. If works of music
and, by implication, the works of the other repeatable art-forms are types,
it looks like we have no choice but to accept that there are *two* kinds of
things that works of art are: continuants (such as paintings and sculptures)
and types (such as works of music, novels, plays, and etchings).

Such an argument is weak, however, for two reasons. To begin with, it
is a mistake to think that an adherence to the type/token theory *obliges* us
to treat artworks as ontologically diverse. According to P. F. Strawson, for
example, the only obstacle to our treating all artworks as types is a contingent, *technological* one: the fact that we are unable to make reproductions
of pictures and statues which are completely indistinguishable, by direct
sensory inspection, from the originals (1974: 183–4). In Strawson's view, if
we *were* able to produce indistinguishable copies of paintings and sculptures,
there would be no reason why we should not treat such artworks as types and
their instances (including the original produced by the artist) as their tokens.

Well, this is one possible reply to the claim that the continuant view
is best placed to acknowledge the fact that the concept *artwork* must be
ontologically homogeneous. But I do not wish to commit myself to the
thesis that all artworks are types, and nor need I. For another, altogether
more convincing, and less extravagant, reply is simply to deny the premiss
upon which the continuant theorist's argument is predicated: namely, that
we should regard all artworks as belonging to the same ontological category.
There seems to be no reason why we should expect *artwork* to display any
more ontological unity than those things grouped under a concept such
as *things liked by Eleanor*. Indeed, our ordinary intuitions point in the
opposite direction. We describe certain artworks—items such as works
of music, plays, dances, and novels—as having multiple 'performances'
or 'examples', but regard others—such as paintings and sculptures—as

concrete particulars: things found on art gallery walls and in public spaces. The latter we assume to be physical objects: material, space-occupying things that are produced, for example, by applying paint to canvas or by modifying material objects such as lumps of clay. Being made of matter, they can discolour, or rot, or fall to bits. The idea that works of music, plays, and dances could similarly deteriorate would be greeted by most people with a quizzical stare, as would the suggestion that such artworks themselves (as distinct from their occurrences or examples) have a spatial location. Given these differences, it would come as a great surprise if all artworks turned out to belong to the same ontological category.

So if the quest for an ontologically unified account of artworks is itself poorly motivated, are there other potential ways of motivating the continuant view? Two more spring to mind. First, Rohrbaugh suggests that construing musical works as continuants sits better with both our pre-theoretical conception of the ontological nature of works of music and the way in which we talk and think about them. Noticing that '*In This House, On This Morning*' never functions as a predicate, nor as an abstract singular term standing in a systematic relation to a predicate, Rohrbaugh concludes that our thought and talk of musical works embodies the thesis that they are 'things in their own right' rather than 'property-like entities' (2003: 197), as the type/token theorist would have it.

How should a type/token theorist reply to this point? One response would simply be to endorse an error theory about our thought and talk: it could be claimed that our conceptual scheme embodies a philosophical mistake, and that musical works really are property-like. But, in fact, such a move is unnecessary. For, in the light of the way in which I distinguished types from properties in §1.2, it is a mistake to suppose that a type/token theorist must deny that works, *qua* types, are 'things in their own right'. The significant relation between types and properties concerns their existence conditions: types share their existence conditions with the properties of which they are the associates. But it does not follow from this, nor should it be claimed, that types *are* properties or in any significant sense ontologically akin to them. Properties are expressed by predicates and referred to by abstract singular terms (such as 'redness' and 'being red') formed from predicates; types, by contrast, are referred to by singular terms (often involving the institutional 'the'), and are never expressed by predicates. Given the fact that types are not predicative in the way in which properties are, it is no more true of types than it is of continuants that they are essentially 'gappy'. Types are not properties of their tokens any more than continuants are properties of their embodiments. The tokens of a type are the multiple instances of a thing in its own right.

Be this as it may, the supporter of the continuant view may insist that it offers an explanation of the repeatability of musical works that coheres better with a naturalistic world picture. And this is the final way in which one might try to motivate a conception of works of music as continuants rather than types. For, whether one regards musical works as concrete items that have their embodiments as temporal stages, or whether one agrees with Rohrbaugh that such works are 'higher-level objects' (2003: 199) located in time but not space, 'the existence of all such items is rooted in the physical world' (Rohrbaugh 2003: 199–200). The type/token theorist, it may be alleged, places works of music in Platonic heaven; the continuant view, by virtue of having works of music ontologically dependent upon their concrete embodiments, anchors musical works firmly in the physical world.

But, as I have noted already, such a picture of the type/token theory can only be a pastiche. True enough, the continuant view, but not the type/token theory, has it that works of music are in some sense ontologically dependent upon their actual occurrences; but, as we came to appreciate in §3.2, types need not be exiled to Platonic heaven. According to the conception of types I recommend, although types are in no sense existentially dependent upon being tokened, a type exists at a time t just in case there is some time (identical with, before, or after t) at which it is *possible* for it to be tokened. Types are thus *instantiables*, and it is for this reason that they are *of* their tokens in the following sense: to think of a type is to think of actual or possible tokens of that type. Types thus have a *conceptual*, if not an ontological, dependence on items in the natural world; so identifying works of music with types of sound-event is to anchor them, conceptually, to that world. For the charge of offending against naturalism to stick, therefore, it must be shown that a defensible naturalism must take a work of music to be ontologically dependent upon its embodiments, and not just conceptually tied to the idea of such embodiments. However, I have no idea how such a task could be successfully completed: as we shall see in §6.5, it is unclear why ontological, rather than merely conceptual, dependence should be required. As a result, the only possible reason for adopting either version of the continuant view would it be that it explained musical works' repeatability better than does the type/token theory. But, as we shall see in the next section, this is not true.

6.4 The Continuant View and Repeatability

Let us, then, return to the question of whether either variant of the continuant view can satisfactorily explain what the repeatability of works of music consists in. The key idea, remember, is that the relation obtaining between a work and its occurrences is that of (a specific form of) *embodiment*. The work is embodied in its occurrences in the sense that it depends upon them for its continued existence. At first blush, though, one might wonder why it follows from a thing's being in this sense ontologically dependent upon other entities that these other entities are its occurrences. What, exactly, has ontological dependence to do with repeatability? One has the suspicion that ontological dependence is one thing, repeatability another.

As it turns out, our initial query on this issue is well grounded. For, on either variant of the continuant view, it is far from clear that it is the *repeatability* of works of music that has been explained. According to the perdurantist version, the repeatability of a work consists in its having its embodiments (the concrete items upon which it depends for its existence) as *stages* or temporal parts. However, it is a familiar fact that entities may have temporal parts upon which they ontologically depend, yet whole and part *not* stand in the relation of thing and occurrence. Events are one example of this: the fifth minute of the 1975 Cup Final is a temporal part of the match, but this temporal part is not an occurrence of the match, and the match itself (i.e. the event) is not repeatable. Likewise, if we took people to be fusions of their temporal parts, it would not follow that people were repeatable entities or that their temporal parts were *occurrences* of them. The point is this: since an entity can be composed of stages, yet not be repeatable, merely saying that a work's occurrences are stages of it does not thereby explain what its having occurrences consists in. If we are to accept that works, *qua* continuants, have occurrences, the explanation of this fact must, it seems, come from elsewhere.

Similar considerations apply to the endurantist manifestation of the continuant view. The claim made by Rohrbaugh, to recall, is that a work's being repeatable consists in its being ontologically dependent upon the items he christens its embodiments. But this purported explanation too looks like a *non sequitur*, since an object may be ontologically dependent upon an entity or entities without these entities being occurrences of it. For example, in many cases of what may be termed *singular ontological dependence*—cases in which one object, α, is said to depend ontologically upon another object, β—β is *not* in any sense an occurrence of α. The ontological dependence of Socrates' life upon Socrates is one such example of this, as is the dependence of {Socrates} on Socrates: although the singleton is ontologically dependent upon its member, there is no sense to be made of the claim that Socrates is an *occurrence* of the set. Consequently, since relations of ontological dependence may obtain between things that are not related as thing and occurrence, merely saying that a work of music depends for its existence upon its embodiments cannot be an explanation of such works' repeatability.

By way of reply, it might be alleged that such examples, drawing as they do upon the phenomenon of singular ontological dependence (i.e. the ontological dependence of one object upon another) are not strictly analogous to the case of the claimed dependence of a work upon its multiple occurrences. This latter form of dependence, remember, is generic rather than singular: a work of music, it is insisted, depends for its existence upon there being *at least one* embodiment, but not upon any *particular* embodiment. This being so, if the charge against Rohrbaugh is to stick, it must be shown that the thesis that works, *qua* continuants, *generically* depend for their existence upon their embodiments cannot be an explanation of such works' repeatability.

But to this reply there is a decisive rejoinder. It may be granted that an entity that generically depends for its existence upon other items is repeatable. The problem is that the kinds of things that are generically dependent upon other objects are themselves *generic* entities rather than continuants. It is significant that, when pressed to provide examples of such generic dependence, we can only come up with examples such as the following (Fine 1995: 287–9): the ontological dependence of a set on its members; the (putative) ontological dependence of a property upon its instances; or (still more controversially) the ontological dependence of a type upon its tokens (a thesis which, in my view, is false). The crucial point about these cases, however, is that in each such example the ontologically dependent entity is something that fits the instantiable–instance ontological pattern. Consequently, such examples of generic ontological dependence cannot provide support for the thesis that a work of music's repeatability consists in its being a genuine *continuant*—that is, a particular rather than an instantiable item—that generically depends for its existence upon its embodiments. Generic dependence seems to be limited to instantiables.

The problem facing the endurantist version of the continuant view is thus that we have little idea of how a genuine continuant—as opposed to a set, property, or some other such instantiable entity—could be generically dependent for its existence on another range of objects. And what this means is that an appeal to this idea cannot amount to a genuine *explanation* of musical works' repeatability. Whichever version of the continuant view is preferred, and whichever notion of ontological dependence is taken as the model, no such explanation is forthcoming. Of course, at this point, the supporter of the continuant view could argue that coming up with an explanation of the repeatability of works of music, *qua* continuants, has not been ruled out *in principle*. But, to my mind, we should treat such a response with a healthy scepticism. In §6.1 I noted that the very idea of there being a repeatable continuant works against the grain of our existing ontological categories. In the light of this fact, and of the difficulty involved in finding examples of generic ontological dependence that do not presuppose the instantiable–instance ontological pattern, I dare to predict that no alternative explanation of how a continuant could be repeatable will be forthcoming.

6.5 Further Objections to the Continuant View

Given the difficulties that both of its versions face in trying to account for the repeatability of works of music, it is evident that the continuant view fails to measure up to the type/token theory. But it is important to realize that, even if this were not the case, the continuant view would still come a poor second. For in this section we shall see that both variants of the continuant view, besides being unable to explain the nature of musical works' repeatability, are inherently problematic. The perdurantist version forces its propounder into unacceptable commitments, whilst the endurantist version, though initially more plausible than its cousin, ends up in a cul-de-sac of ontological obscurantism.

The perdurantist version of the doctrine should be rejected because it faces two disabling objections. Although perdurantism about, say, persons is a familiar and, arguably, defensible view, it becomes problematic once applied to the case of musical works. The first such objection to what might be termed *musical perdurantism* is that it entails the absurd thesis that works of music cannot be heard *in toto*. The reason for this is, it seems, both simple and compelling. A given performance is but a temporal part of the piece. Consequently, for an audience member to hear the whole work—that is, to hear *all* of it—she would thereby have to audit all of its constituent temporal parts (i.e. all of its performances and other occurrences). Such a possibility, however, is ruled out by the very nature of the perdurantist thesis: one can only hear a temporal part of a perduring entity, if it is present at *that* time to be heard.

How should a musical perdurantist try to reply to this objection? One option would be to 'bite the bullet' and accept that an audience fails to hear the whole of a work in performance (Caplan and Matheson 2006: 61): it could be claimed, for example, that if an audience member stays for the whole concert, then she hears a whole *performance* of a work, but she does not thereby audit the totality of the work itself. Additionally, a musical perdurantist might seek to make this position more palatable by pointing out that musical perdurantism is no worse off than, say, perdurantism about persons on this score (Caplan and Matheson 2006: 63): analogously, a perdurantist about persons must say that the whole of a person is unavailable at any one time to be perceived.[7] But, to my mind, such bullishness will not do. For it is plainly intuitive to think that an audience hears entire works in performance; and, in addition, we have seen how this intuition can be accommodated by the type/token theory. In the wake of this, a perdurantist's acceptance that she cannot allow for a whole work's being heard in performance amounts to an admission that there is a strong reason for preferring the type/token theory to perdurantism.

Of course, Caplan and Matheson are right to point out that, when it comes to this 'argument from perception' (2006: 61), the musical

---

[7] This much is agreed by perdurantists. Theodore Sider, for example, accepts that his brand of perdurantism about persons entails that it is impossible to touch the whole of a person: 'Even if you could somehow touch all of a person's spatial parts at once, you would still fail to touch all the person, for not all the person is *then* to be touched. To touch all of a person you must hold him in an interpenetrating total embrace from his birth until his death; only thus would you have access to all his past and future temporal parts' (Sider 2001: 2–3).

perdurantist fares no worse than does a perdurantist about persons. But there are two things to say about this observation. First, it might be taken merely to reveal how revisionary *any* form of perdurantism about continuants really is. And second, *even if* one were to accept perdurantism about persons, and thereby acquiesce to the thesis that we cannot perceive whole persons, there seems to be a *special* counter-intuitiveness to the analogous doctrine in the ontology of music. Because persons admit of genuine change, there is, perhaps, some intuitive mileage in the thought that we cannot perceive a whole person in a moment: if one were to think of perceiving a whole person as a matter of *becoming aware of the totality of her perceptual properties*, then one might find it tempting to say that one fails to see her *in toto* at any given time (because some of these properties are only had by her at other times). But, as noted in §4.3, it is far less clear, and perhaps even incoherent, to think of works of music as changing. Consequently, there are no analogous grounds for challenging the intuitive thought that a performance of a work presents that work in its entirety. *Each* performance of a work presents a picture of the complete work: the work itself cannot change in the time between two distinct performances of it.

This being so, the perdurantist's most promising way of dealing with the objection from perception looks to be that of insisting that she *can*, in fact, accommodate the intuition that works are heard in the entirety. To this end, she might well claim that an audience *derivatively* hears the whole work by virtue of *directly* or *fundamentally* hearing one of its temporal parts. And she may argue, further, that she is able to explain how such a phenomenon is possible in exactly the same way as the type/token theorist has been seen to explain the possibility of hearing a work by virtue of hearing one of its tokens. That is, the perdurantist might insist that 'if in cases of deferred perception one can hear a type in virtue of hearing one of its tokens, then in cases of deferred perception one can also hear a whole in virtue of hearing one of its parts' (Caplan and Matheson 2006: 62).

But such a move looks like it misses the point of the original objection. It is quite true that one can hear or see an entity by hearing or seeing a part of it: a perdurantist about persons will point out that I can see Tony Blair by seeing one of his temporal parts; and a perdurantist about musical works will claim, rightly, that if such works have their performances (and other occurrences) as temporal parts, then one can hear *A London Symphony* by virtue of hearing one such temporal part (e.g., a performance). But this fails to address the objection as originally stated: for this objection was *not* that the perdurantist cannot account for how *A London Symphony* can be heard *at all*; it was that she cannot account for how the work *as a whole*—that is, its entirety—can be heard. An analogy between the temporal and spatial cases should help here. It is true that one can see Tony Blair *by* catching sight of his left hand; but we would not want to say that someone had seen Tony Blair *in his entirety* if this was all that she had seen of him. Such a person would have failed to see his head, torso, legs, and the rest. Switching back to the temporal case once more, the objection to perdurantism is this: whilst we suppose a performance of a work to present *the whole work* to an audience, this could not be true if perdurantism about works of music were correct. The work as a whole cannot be presented in performance because the work, if constituted by its performances as temporal stages, would not be wholly present at the time at which the said performance occurs.

At this point, though, the perdurantist might be tempted to counter with a 'tu quoque'. How, she might ask, can one hear a whole type by virtue of hearing one of its tokens if one cannot hear a whole perduring object by virtue of hearing one of its temporal parts? But this question could only be asked by someone who had failed to see the crucial difference between types and perduring entities. Precisely because a type is *wholly* present in time when each of its tokens exists, it follows that perceiving a type by virtue of perceiving one of its tokens cannot be *anything but* the perception of the type in its entirety. Since types do not themselves have temporal parts, it can only be the type *as a whole* that stands behind the token and which, as a result, is perceived derivatively. By contrast, when one sees or hears a temporal part of a perduring entity, it is not the case that the entire perduring entity is available to the perceiver at this time: its past temporal parts no longer exist, and its future temporal parts have yet to be. Not all the entity is *then* to be perceived. As a result, since one cannot perceive the whole of something at t unless it exists as a whole at t,[8] it follows that

---

[8] Caplan and Matheson complain that it is not clear why a perdurantist should accept this principle (2006: 63). But, tellingly, Sider, a card-carrying perdurantist, believes it. Indeed, if Sider did not take the principle to be true, he would not deny, as he does, that perceiving one of x's temporal parts amounts to perceiving all of x (Sider 2001: 3). It is precisely because a perduring entity's temporal parts are not all available *then* to be perceived that the entity as a whole cannot be perceived then. What is

it is impossible for one to perceive a perduring entity as a whole by virtue of perceiving one of its temporal parts. Given our strong intuition that we hear a whole work—that is, all of it—in performance, this strongly counts against the perdurantist version of the continuant view.

My conclusion, then, is that the musical perdurantist cannot accommodate the intuition that one can listen to a whole work in performance. But this is not all. Coupled with this objection is another: namely, that musical perdurantism implies the problematic thesis that the temporal parts of musical works may differ with respect to their ontological nature. Let us now examine this charge in more detail.

To begin with, let us suppose that two performances take place of *In This House, On This Morning*, *e* and *e**, occurring in different places, but starting and ending at the same time. The problem for the perdurantist is this: her doctrine seems to demand that both *e* and *e** be counted as temporal parts of the work, but common sense says that they cannot be. Intuitively, an entity cannot have more than one temporal part beginning and ending at the same time. (There was, for example, only one fifth minute of the 1975 F. A. Cup Final, a part located at Wembley Stadium; it makes no sense to say that there was an additional fifth minute of the match taking place somewhere else.) So how could the apparent commitment to such an absurd consequence be explained away? Only, I suggest, by treating *e* and *e** as two spatial parts of one and the same temporal part. That is, the obvious move to make is to claim that some of the work's temporal parts are—or, at least, could be—scattered objects. And what this means is that *A London Symphony* has ontologically multifarious temporal parts: at times at which one performance is occurring the work's temporal part is a spatially unified object, but at times at which more than one such performance takes place, the temporal part is spatially scattered.

There would seem to be three good reasons for looking askance at such a suggestion. First, if (temporal stages of) works are spatially scattered, then we have one more reason for denying that a perdurantist can explain how a work can be heard in its entirety. If a spatial part of *A London Symphony* is located in a place beyond the reach of their ears, an audience cannot hear

more, Sider's intuitions are surely spot on here. Far from being unmotivated, the thought that one can only perceive the whole of *x* at *t* if the whole of *x* exists at *t*, is as strongly intuitive as philosophical theses get. You cannot perceive the whole of something at a time if some of that thing's parts do not exist to be perceived at that time.

this part of the work. Second, the claim that a musical work's temporal parts may be spatially scattered lacks independent motivation. Scattered objects are quite familiar, of course: we are happy with the idea that a jacket located in London and a pair of trousers found in Sydney may be parts of the same scattered object: my suit. But we certainly do *not* regard two spatially discontinuous performances as parts of the same thing in an analogous way: we do not describe (a temporal stage of) *A London Symphony* as being 'partly in Sydney and partly in London', for example. Given that this is so, we require a good philosophical reason for adopting such an unnatural position, and the problem is that no reason exists bar the fact that it enables us to prop up musical perdurantism.

Third, and finally, the idea that a musical work's temporal parts may be ontologically multifarious—some spatially unified and some spatially scattered—violates the previously introduced principle that all of a perduring entity's temporal parts fall into the same ontological category. An entity's temporal parts are just time slices of that entity, and so they all inherit its ontological nature. Naturally, one reply to this worry would be to deny that the above-mentioned principle is exceptionless. Caplan and Matheson (2006: 64–5), for instance, point out that perdurantists about persons commonly claim that in exceptional cases a person *may* have scattered spatial parts in addition to unified ones: an example of such a case being one in which a person travels back in time to meet her earlier self. Indeed, at this point a perdurantist may attempt to make her case by introducing a distinction between temporal parts of a person and person-stages (Sider 2001: 101). If, the story goes, I travel back in time and come face to face with my 10-year-old self, then we have *two* person-stages—that is, two momentary person-like perduring entities occupying the same stretch of time—but just *one* temporal part: the fusion of these two stages. As Sider explains (2001: 101), a perdurantist is likely to argue that the temporal parts of people are *usually* person-stages, but that in cases of time travel a person's temporal parts are fusions of such stages. So here, it is claimed, we have a recipe for producing counter-examples to the thesis that a perduring entity cannot have ontologically multifarious temporal parts; and hence the objection fails to go through.

But not so fast. The imagined exceptions to the principle that an entity's temporal parts cannot be ontologically divergent—that is, time-travel cases—are too far-fetched to be of much help to the musical perdurantist.

Even if it is granted that time-travel cases make sense (which might be disputed[9]), we have only been shown, at best, that perduring entities have ontologically divergent temporal parts in cases of time travel. We await a reason for supposing that entities that cannot travel in time—notably, works of music—could also be counter-examples to the principle to which I have appealed. It is not enough merely to come up with a counter-example to the said principle; we need to be told why musical works could constitute another such example. Without such a reason, we are free to simply amend the principle by excluding time-travel cases from its intended domain of application, thereby enabling the principle to stand for musical works. And what this means, of course, is that the original objection to musical perdurantism stands.

It is thus my view that the musical perdurantist both lacks independent motivation for his position and finds himself unable to reply convincingly to the two powerful objections facing him. Rohrbaugh, of course, may grant all this: after all, he is no perdurantist. But, as it happens, he is no better off, for the endurantist version of the continuant view is stymied when it comes to the question of how we should characterize the proposed relation of ontological dependence obtaining between a work of music and its embodiments. Rohrbaugh himself says little on this matter, but we can, at least, try to reconstruct his thinking. With this aim in mind, the first thing we should note is this: in supposing the sense in which a musical work depends upon its embodiments to be existential—something with which I have been complicit up to now—the supporter of the endurantist version of the continuant view is taking sides on the question of the nature of ontological dependence. In speaking of a work of music's embodiments as 'those things on which it ontologically depends *for its continued existence*' (2003: 198; my italics), Rohrbaugh, for one, supposes that this notion of ontological dependence should be explained existentially. Putting this together with the insight that any proposed dependence of a musical work upon its embodiments must be generic rather than singular, a first attempt at capturing what Rohrbaugh is looking for would seem to be the following (Lowe 1995: 35):

(DG) x ontologically depends upon objects of kind K = $_{df}$ Necessarily, x exists only if something y exists such that y is of K.

---

[9] I should note at this stage that both Sider (2001: 106) and Caplan and Matheson (2006: 65) have more faith than I do in Lewis's (1976) attempt to explain away the paradoxes of time travel.

However, there are two reasons why (DG) cannot provide the supporter of the endurantist version of the continuant view with the notion he requires. First, if the *definiens'* consequent expresses a necessary truth (as it would, if the objects of kind *K* were the real numbers), then the *definiens* comes out as true whatever entity *x* is taken be. Any entity at all will turn out to be ontologically dependent upon the real numbers, which is absurd. Second, the existential construal of ontological dependence allows for such dependence to be symmetrical. This is especially clear if we consider non-generic dependence, which, on the existential account, would amount to

(DN) *x* ontologically depends upon *y* = $_{df}$ Necessarily, *x* exists only if *y* exists.

According to (DN), the set {The Eiffel Tower} ontologically depends upon The Eiffel Tower, which is the result we expect; but it is also the case that The Eiffel Tower ontologically depends upon the singleton that has it as its member. This, needless to say, offends against the intuition that ontological dependence is asymmetrical: that, in this case, sets depend ontologically upon their members, but that the converse does not hold. For although it is true that neither of The Eiffel Tower and {The Eiffel Tower} can exist without the other existing, devotees of ontological dependence nonetheless regard the singleton as the truly dependent entity: a belief embodied in our inclination to say that the {The Eiffel Tower} exists *because* The Eiffel Tower exists, and not vice versa (Lowe 1995: 39). What this demonstrates is that the existential construal of ontological dependence fails to capture the intuition that motivates the search for an account of ontological dependence in the first place.

Now let us return to (DG). Given that (DN) allows for symmetrical dependence, there is no reason to suppose that (DG) should not. And indeed, the case of works of music looks to be a case in point. Let us assume, for the sake of argument, that *In This House, On This Morning* is, in the generic sense explicated by (DG), existentially dependent upon its embodiments. Is it not equally true that a work's embodiments (whatever these may be) are dependent for their existence upon the work? Any performance of the work is a performance of that work and, as such, could not exist unless the work did. So the dependence would seem to go both ways, and once more the moral can only be that the *definiens* fails to catch hold of the fugitive notion.

In the light of these concerns, it might seem tempting to follow Lowe in reconstruing ontological dependence, not as existential dependence, but as identity-dependence. According to Lowe's alternative account of the non-generic notion (1995: 41), we should replace (DN) with

(DN*) x ontologically depends upon y = $_{df}$ Necessarily, the identity of x depends upon the identity of y,

where, for the identity of x to depend upon the identity of y is for which thing of its kind x is to be (at least, partially) determined by which thing of its kind y is (Lowe 1995: 41). Clearly, this yields the right answers when it comes to the example of The Eiffel Tower and its singleton. Is {The Eiffel Tower} ontologically dependent upon The Eiffel Tower? Yes, since what makes {The Eiffel Tower} *that* set is that it has The Eiffel Tower as its only member: the axiom of extensionality is a criterion of identity for sets. Is The Eiffel Tower ontologically dependent upon {The Eiffel Tower}? No, because the identity of The Eiffel Tower is not to any degree fixed by the identity of {The Eiffel Tower}. What makes The Eiffel Tower that object has nothing to do with the identity of any set.

Presumably, the application of this idea to the notion of generic ontological dependence needed by the endurantist version of the continuant view would see us replace (DG) with something like

(DG*) x ontologically depends upon objects of kind K = $_{df}$ Necessarily, the identity of x depends upon the identity of K.

Unfortunately, though, there is a clear reason why this move will not help. Put bluntly, it is that

(51) Necessarily, the identity of x depends upon the identity of K

does not entail

(52) Necessarily, x exists only if something y exists such that y is of K.

(52), remember, is what the propounder of the continuant view wishes to defend if x is a work of music and K is taken to be the type whose tokens are x's embodiments. The leading idea behind such views is that the repeatability of a musical work consists in its being embodied in, and existentially dependent upon, its performances, playings, and other embodiments. However, secondary qualities, if construed as response-dependent properties of objects, turn out to be a counter-example to the thesis that (51) entails (52). Let us suppose that 'experience enters into the analysis' (McGinn 1983: 8) of redness in the following sense: an object's being red consists in its being such as to look red (to normal observes in standard circumstances). If this is the case, it follows that it is necessary that the identity of the property of redness depends upon the identity of a certain kind of response: namely, the kind whose tokens are experiences as of redness. But it does not follow from this that the property of redness exists only if at least one such experience as of redness exists. For it is quite compatible with the response-dependent view of colour that things keep their colour in the dark and, indeed, that things were coloured before there was any sentient life. Something's being red consists in its possessing a disposition to look red to normal observers in normal circumstances, and it still possesses that dispositional property in the dark, and it had that disposition even before anyone was around to look at it. The claim is just that *if* a normal observer had looked at the object in normal conditions, it *would* have looked red to her. In other words, if x in (51) is a colour-property, and K is the kind of perceptual experience that fixes the colour-property's identity, then (52) does not follow from (51).

Given that secondary qualities provide a counter-example to the thesis that (51) entails (52), there is no reason to suppose that the supposed identity-dependence of a musical work upon its embodiments will entail the thesis that such works 'depend for their existence' (Rohrbaugh 2003: 199) upon their embodiments. In Chapter 5, we doubted whether this thesis accorded with our intuitions; it is now apparent that there is no good reason to believe it. For, on this account, such dependence does not turn out to be *existential* at all.

This, it seems to me, presents Rohrbaugh and like-minded philosophers with a dilemma. Either the sense in which a work of music is supposed to depend ontologically upon its embodiments is obscure; or else, if we accept Lowe's account of the notion, works do not depend for their existence upon their embodiments. Either way, the choice is invidious. If the construal of musical works as continuants is to be defended adequately, then this notion of dependence cannot be left unexplained. But, equally, if it is accepted that such dependence is not existential—that it amounts to no more than identity-dependence in Lowe's sense—then the continuant view begins increasingly to look like nothing but a badly formulated version of the type/token theory. For, as we noted earlier, the type/token theorist can acknowledge that musical works—*qua* types—are intrinsically *of* their occurrences in a strikingly similar way. Specifically, works, if types of sound-event, are instantiables and, as a result, are things that can be thought about only by means of thinking about actual or possible tokens. Works, thus construed, are not self-subsistent, yet exist when untokened.

But of course, whereas the type/token view can nicely explain the nature of musical works' repeatability, the same cannot be said for the continuant view. On the one hand, we have an account of musical works that places them in a familiar ontological category and which nicely explains the fact that musical works have occurrences; on the other, we have a theory that requires us to introduce 'new kinds of objects' into our ontology (Rohrbaugh 2003: 197) and which, as we saw in §6.3, fails to deliver an account of the 'occurrence of' relation. Rohrbaugh himself admits that we should introduce such new kinds of objects only if they 'can be understood to serve some widespread systematic and philosophical need' (2003: 197). No such need exists. Indeed, in order to provide a convincing answer to the categorial question, we should give the continuant view a wide berth.

7

Musical Works as Compositional Actions: A Critique

7.1 Introduction

The conclusion of the previous chapter was that works of music are better viewed as types of sound-event than as continuants. The type/token theory nicely explains the nature of a work's repeatability; by contrast, the thesis that a work's repeatability consists in the obtaining of a specific form of the relation of *embodiment* prompts more questions than it answers. But ontologists of music, and ontologists of art quite generally, are ingenious people; and in recent years, another approach to the ontology of art has emerged, an approach that treats an artwork, not as the thing created or (if the artwork is a type) discovered by the artist, but as the artist's action of creating—or discovering—this thing. In this chapter I shall explain why such an approach cannot yield a satisfactory ontology of music.[1] In so doing, I shall complete the task of motivating the type/token theory.

The central plank of the kind of view I shall discuss in this chapter has it that a work of music is the composer's compositional action. But, of course, 'action' here exhibits a type/token ambiguity, so there are, in fact, two versions of the view to be considered. According to the first version, defended impressively by Gregory Currie (1989), a musical work is an action-*type*: it is a type of which the composer's datable, locatable compositional action (or series of actions) was a token. According to the second version of the view, defended equally impressively by David Davies (2004), the work is the unrepeatable compositional action itself. A musical

---

[1] My conclusions have straightforward application to the ontology of the repeatable arts quite generally.

work, according to Davies, is an action-*token*: a species of event. In my view, however, neither version of the idea that musical works are (compositional) process-like is defensible. In what follows I shall explain why not.

7.2 Currie's *Action-type Hypothesis*

Like the type/token theorist, Currie (1989: ch. 3) agrees that works of music are types. The distinctive feature of Currie's view lies in his denial that performances, playings, and the like can be the tokens of such works. For, as Currie sees it, *In This House, On This Morning* is not a type of sound-sequence-event, but a type of *action*. Specifically, the work is a type of *composing*: the type of which Marsalis's composition of the piece is a token. Such acts of composition—and not sound-events such as performances and playings—are the work's tokens (Currie 1989: 76).

Such is the theory in outline, and even at this early stage one might be struck by its iconoclasm. For although Currie agrees with the type/token theorist (and, indeed, the holder of the continuant view) that works of music are repeatable, he locates a work's repeatability in a relationship between the work (*qua* type of composing) and compositional action-tokens rather than in a relationship between the work and concrete patterns of sounds. For Currie, a work has occurrences all right, but these occurrences are not the things that pre-theoretical intuition would have us believe. Given that this is so, one is entitled to wonder what the performability of a work consists in, if not the fact that its performances are its tokens. Furthermore, given that the type/token theory nicely explains how a work is audible in its performances precisely by taking such performances to be amongst the work's tokens, one is as entitled to question whether the action-type hypothesis is as well-equipped to explain this most quotidian of phenomena.

We shall return to these questions presently. For now, let us focus on the nature of Currie's answer to the categorial question. What, exactly, would Currie say about the ontological nature of *In This House, On This Morning*? He would start by giving an account of the nature of the action-token—that is, the event—that is Marsalis's compositional action (1989: 69). This, he would claim, is an event which has five constituents: Marsalis himself (C); the work's sound structure (S); the 'heuristic path' (H) by which Marsalis came to discover the sound structure;[2] the three-place relation *x discovers y by heuristic path z* (D); and the time of composition (*t*). Marsalis's datable, locatable, compositional action-token can thus be represented as: [*C, S, H, D, t*]. Thinking, *pace* Levinson (1980*b*: 68–73), that it is counter-intuitive to regard either a work's composer or its time of composition as constitutive of it, Currie concludes that the work itself is the action-type which has two open places for a composer and a time: something that can be represented as: [*x, S, H, D,τ*] (1989: 70). The first half of this chapter is devoted to arguing that this view is both inadequately motivated and beset by compelling objections.

7.2.1 Motivating the Action-type Hypothesis

Let us begin by examining the rationale behind Currie's treatment of musical works as types of composing. As he himself explains (1989: 11), this ontological claim is supposed to be strongly suggested by an independently argued aesthetic theory: a theory that explains the nature of aesthetic appreciation. The thesis that works of music are types of composing is, claims Currie (1989: 12), the account that best coheres with this overall theory.

What, then, is Currie's overarching aesthetic theory? Crucially, the starting-point of Currie's discussion sees him use aesthetic empiricism as a stalking horse. The intuition behind aesthetic empiricism, when applied to the case of music, is that only a work of music's acoustic properties—that is, its manifest, perceptible qualities—are relevant to its aesthetic appreciation. Formulated more precisely, in order to deal with various problem cases, the claim is that a work of music's aesthetic properties—those that determine its aesthetic value—supervene upon its acoustic properties together with the category of art to which it belongs.[3] In other words, the empiricist claims that there can be no aesthetic difference between works of music without a corresponding acoustic difference (or else, without the works differing in the artistic categories to which they belong).

---

[2] As Currie would have it, Marsalis's heuristic path includes all of those factors which led him to select the work's sound structure (1989: 71). In the course of elaborating this notion, Currie claims that an element of a composer's heuristic path need not have been known to him at the time (1989: 72). As Levinson notes (1992*a*: 216), this move means that Currie's notion differs little from the familiar concept of the musico-historical context of composition.

[3] A discussion of such cases, and a defence of this version of musical empiricism, will be undertaken in Ch. 8 below.

So what, if anything, is wrong with aesthetic empiricism? In Currie's view, the idea that a musical work's aesthetic value can be detected merely by listening to it (and being aware of what category of art it falls under) is nothing but a myth-eaten piece of philosophical dogma. For what the empiricist fails to recognize is that 'aesthetic judgements are, in part, judgements about the artist's achievement in producing the work' (1989: 38–9). A work's aesthetic merit, Currie thinks, is partly determined by its 'achievement properties':[4] properties that pertain to its history of composition. To discover the aesthetic value in a work of music, he suggests, one must have knowledge of something that cannot be heard: the composer's heuristic path: the factors that influenced and constrained his compositional action. Unless we know something of the extent of the composer's achievement—whether his work was original or derivative; whether he had to overcome substantial technical limitations; whether the work marked a new direction in his *œuvre*, and so on—we are unable to judge the work's aesthetic merit effectively. In short, in order to uncover a work's aesthetic qualities, we must have knowledge of the musico-historical context in which it was composed. As Currie himself puts it, '[i]f we knew absolutely nothing about the historical background to a work, then I think we would be in a position where we could not appreciate it at all' (1989: 76).

Currie takes this account of aesthetic appreciation to be supported both by examples and by a proper understanding of the nature of composition. And, for sure, examples that appear to make Currie's point are not too difficult to construct. Imagine, for instance, that a work sonically indistinguishable from *In This House, On This Morning* had been composed in 1935. Clearly its composer's achievement would have been greater than was Marsalis's in 1992; and, as a result, it is tempting to suppose that she would have composed a work that differed from Marsalis's with respect to certain of its aesthetic properties. The composer of the 1935 piece would have composed a work that possessed the properties of *being visionary* and *being ground-breaking*, neither of which is shared by Marsalis's, whatever its many other merits.

But what of the nature of composition? Why does Currie think that an understanding of what composition consists in pushes us towards his favoured aesthetic theory? Crucially, Currie draws an analogy between composition and scientific experimentation (1989: 41–2). A scientist

---

4 The term 'achievement property' is borrowed from David Davies (2004: 129).

conducts experiments in order to test scientific theories. Analogously, Currie claims, a composer composes pieces of music in order to test two things: certain artistic conventions and techniques, and his own abilities. Given that this is so, Currie's own account of the nature of aesthetic appreciation would seem to follow: to appreciate a work can only be to assess whether, or how well, this test has been passed. Hence, according to Currie, in judging a work of music, we are

weighing the evidence that it provides concerning what we should say about the artist's performance, taking 'performance' in that wide sense which includes not merely his actions ... but also his path to the conception and execution of the work, an understanding of which involves an analysis of the conventions and technical limitations that constrain his action. (Currie 1989: 42)

As a result, the intelligent critic helps us, not merely by enabling us to hear things in the music that we might otherwise miss, but also by 'help[ing] us to understand, by means of historical and bibliographical research, the way in which the artist arrived at the final product' (1989: 68).

For Currie, then, the aesthetic appreciation of a work of music requires us to evaluate the composer's achievement in composing it. And, naturally, once this aesthetic theory is accepted, empiricism is sunk: if Currie is right, acoustically indistinguishable works of the same category may yet differ aesthetically, if their respective composers' heuristic paths—and hence their respective levels of achievement—are different.

Having taken himself to have demonstrated that works' achievement properties play a role in determining their aesthetic value, the question Currie asks next is this: what must works of music be like, for such a theory to be true? A convincing account of the ontological nature of works of music must, he supposes, underpin the anti-empiricist aesthetic theory to which we have become committed. And now, in a bold step, Currie suggests that the most natural way of doing justice to the nature of aesthetic appreciation—as he sees it—is simply to *identify* works of music with action-types performed by composers (1989: 70–1).

It is this move that determines the exact details of Currie's proposal. Given that Currie believes works to have achievement properties that are relevant to their aesthetic value, we can see why he insists that *In This House, On This Morning* is a composing-type that has a certain (type of) heuristic path as a constituent. If we also note, once more, Currie's insistence that a work could have been composed at a different time and by a different composer (provided that the counterfactual composer's heuristic path was sufficiently similar), we can see why Currie claims that *In This House, On This Morning* is a composing-type with open places for a person and a time.

Currie's argument here is clear, lucid, and engaging, but I have to say that I disagree with its every step. First of all, the overall aesthetic theory from which Currie derives his ontological proposal is flawed. As I have noted already, Currie thinks that what is heard constitutes 'the evidence' (1989: 42) supporting an aesthetic judgement of a musical work, a judgement that concerns the composer's achievement. But when it comes to aesthetic appreciation, this way of viewing things misconstrues the relation obtaining between the composer's activity and that activity's end result. As Levinson has put it, '[w]hen all is said and done, in art we primarily appreciate the product...: we don't primarily appreciate the activity of production, as readable from the product' (1992a: 217).[5] In making aesthetic judgements about works of music, we do not *infer* from what is heard to something imperceptible that lies behind it: the composer's accomplishment. I hear *A Love Supreme* as spiritual, craggy, and, in places, sublime. These are some of my aesthetic responses to the piece, and they concern *how it sounds*. I am not making a judgement about the composer on the basis of what I hear; I judge what I hear.

True enough, having heard *A Love Supreme*, I come to think highly of the composer and marvel at how he could have composed the piece in 1964. But this is not to treat my aesthetic judgement as actually concerning the composer's achievement: it concerns the piece's sonic character. Nor is it to treat what is heard as mere evidence supporting an aesthetic judgement: a work's aesthetic properties are heard *in* it (by expert listeners). We are only interested in composers in so far as they are the people who have composed *those* pieces of music; and we are only interested in what they have done—their achievements, in other words—in so far as they have left us with *these* musical works.

The moral to be drawn from this should be obvious: since our appreciation of musical works sees us judging the thing heard, rather than the

---

[5] Levinson's use of the word 'product' here underlines his view that musical works—*qua* types—are created by their composers. Having taken on board the argument of Ch. 3 and the discussion of Levinson's views in §5.1, we may disagree with Levinson on this point, and yet second the sentiments expressed by his quoted remark.

composer's performance, any pressure to treat such works as types of composing is imagined rather than real. At this point, however, Currie might seek to reply by claiming that I have been attacking a straw man. I have been treating what is heard (which Currie regards as a sound structure) and the composer's achievement as distinct things, and have been portraying Currie as believing aesthetic judgement to involve inference from the heard sound structure to the composer's achievement in indicating it. But, in apparent contradiction of this portrayal, Currie goes on to claim that his is 'a position that denies that we can distinguish effectively between an appraisal of the work's appearance and an assessment of the kind of ability and technique that went into producing it. Aesthetically considered, the product and the act of production are a seamless whole' (Currie 1989: 43). This remark presents us with something of a puzzle. On the one hand, we have seen Currie claim that a work's appearance—its acoustic character—is the evidence from which we evaluate its composer's achievement. On the other hand, Currie is now suggesting that we cannot pick apart the one from the other. These positions are irreconcilable.

In fact, Currie is not entitled to claim that the product (i.e. the sound structure) and the act of production are a seamless whole. By 'act of production' here, Currie can only mean the composer's heuristic path. As Currie explains (1989: 67), it is the nature of a composer's heuristic path—whether, for example, he plagiarized his ideas, or whether he deployed a creative musical imagination—that informs us of the nature of his achievement. Nonetheless, it is plain that Currie himself regards a work's sound structure and its heuristic path as distinct entities. For Currie's view is precisely that a musical work has three distinct 'constitutive elements' (1989: 70): a sound structure (S), a heuristic path (H), and the three-place relation x *discovers y by heuristic path z* (D). *In This House, On This Morning*, remember, would be represented by Currie as $[x, S, H, D, \tau]$. If S and H are distinct constituents of *In This House, On This Morning*, they do not form a seamless whole.

If challenged in this way, a defender of Currie's position might nevertheless insist that this objection misses the point Currie makes in the previously quoted passage. There Currie claims that the product and the act of production are a seamless whole '[a]esthetically considered', so he could argue that this claim about the *phenomenology* of appreciation is quite consistent with the thesis that they are distinct constituents of the work. However, such a distinction, though nice in itself, does not help

Currie. For *S* (a sound structure) and *H* (a heuristic path) constitute significantly different kinds of evidence for the nature of the composer's achievement. The sound structure is something that is, supposedly, audible in performance: it is something that can be heard. The composer's act of production, by contrast, is a datable, locatable action that is not audible in performance, but of which we usually gain knowledge by testimony, documentary evidence, and the like. Given this difference, it is hard to deny that *S* and *H* are distinct aesthetically as well as ontologically: one can have knowledge of the one without having knowledge of the other. Hence, my original objection to Currie's account of aesthetic appreciation stands: in appreciating a work of music, we primarily appreciate what we hear, not the composer's achievement.

Currie's conception of the nature of composition fares no better. For the claim that composition is akin to scientific experimentation is, to my mind, particularly implausible. Composition is not such an academic activity. As I noted in §4.5, the composer is not an *enquirer*: the purpose of composing a piece of music is not to test hypotheses or otherwise *find things out* in a quasi-scientific spirit; it is to compose works with certain sonic, and hence aesthetic, features, with a view to their being presented to a musically literate public for their aesthetic appraisal. As we saw in §5.4, it is precisely because composers are not engaged in a project of enquiry that it makes no sense to say that Beethoven, for example, could have been mistaken in his composition of the Archduke Trio.

In addition, Currie's conception of the nature of composition seems to make it too much a self-reflective exercise. A composer can count himself as successful, so Currie would seem to suggest, just in case he tests his own abilities—together with the techniques and conventions that he has inherited—to the limit. But what this omits is the fact that music is a performance art. Works of music are composed with a view to affecting *an audience*. To be sure, in composing *A Love Supreme*, for example, John Coltrane was straining against the extant conventions in jazz, but this was not his primary aim. Much more important to Coltrane than this was that the work succeeded in communicating with its listeners, and that its audience could be moved by its solemnity and depth.

My point, then, is that Currie's aesthetic theory—the theory with which his ontological proposal is designed to cohere—is uncompulsory and unconvincing. So how could Currie have failed to recognize this? The answer, I think, lies in the way in which he draws a particular anti-empiricist moral from certain thought-experiments. In Currie's view, such thought-experiments provide clear counter-examples to musical empiricism and, at the same time, point us towards his own favoured view, in which aesthetic appreciation is constituted by appreciation of the artist's achievement. However, I am unconvinced that such cases really speak so unequivocally. One response to Currie's strategy would be to grant that the said thought-experiments refute empiricism, but to deny that this need commit us to viewing works as action-types.[6] But in my view, although such a response has a good deal of merit, it is unnecessary, since the thought-experiments in question fail to refute empiricism in the first place.

To see this, let us first of all return to our earlier example in which a work sonically indistinguishable from *In This House, On This Morning* is composed in 1935. It is easy to think that such a work would, indeed, differ aesthetically from Marsalis's work, and that this would be so because the respective composers' achievements would differ. The composition of such a piece in 1935 would be visionary, ground-breaking, and anticipatory of future developments in jazz; and it is tempting to suppose that this entails that the earlier piece, but not the later, would have these aesthetic properties too. But, as Currie himself acknowledges (1989: 36–7), there is a clear reason why this description of the case is controversial. For a convinced empiricist will simply deny that the kinds of properties in question—*being visionary, being anticipatory of later developments in jazz, being ground-breaking*, and the like—are genuinely *aesthetic*.[7] She will sharply distinguish genuine aesthetic value from both art-historical value and what we might term 'individual achievement value', and then insist that the aforementioned properties pertain to the latter two forms of evaluation rather than to the first. Judging that a work is ground-breaking, visionary, and anticipatory of later developments in jazz renders the work interesting from an art-historical point of view, and unquestionably makes us think highly of the composer's achievement; but an empiricist will insist that the properties in question no more pertain to the aesthetic value of a musical work than does its value in, say, improving a

---

[6] Such is the line taken by Levinson (1980*b*, 1990*c*), e.g. Levinson rejects empiricism, but takes this to indicate that works of music are indicated types: types individuated more finely than the second part of the simple view—sonicism—allows. For more on this, see Chs. 8 and 9 below.

[7] In fact, as we shall see in the next section and in Ch. 8, there is good reason to deny that such properties are genuinely properties of works at all. It is far better, I argue, to view them as properties of composers and their compositional acts.

child's academic performance. Examples such as these will not convince the empiricist that the composer's achievement is aesthetically relevant; which, in turn, means that we are not, as yet, under any pressure to identify musical works with types of composing. Consequently, Currie must come up with a more convincing thought-experiment if he is simultaneously to refute aesthetic empiricism and provide evidence for the action-type hypothesis.

With a view to doing just this, Currie constructs examples such as the following. To adapt Currie's own ingenious case (1989: 36–40), imagine that a race of Martians share our aesthetic sensibilities and interests, as well as our artistic categories. Now imagine, further, that these beings differ from us in having vastly greater compositional abilities, so that a 5-year-old Martian could easily compose a work indistinguishable from Marsalis's *In This House, On This Morning*.[8] Let us call Marsalis's work L_1 and the infant Martian's work L_2. Whilst we take L_1 to be a great work, imagine that the Martians—sharing both our musical sensibility and our musical categories—believe its acoustic doppelgänger, L_2, to have little value. Currie claims that if this is so, then the empiricist's view—namely, that L_1 and L_2 are aesthetically indistinguishable—cannot be maintained. Here is why.

If there is no aesthetic difference between L_1 and L_2, then either our judgement or that made by the Martians must be wrong. But, argues Currie, there is no objective standpoint from which it can be decided which judgement is the wrong one. As he explains, '[f]rom our perspective, our judgement that [L_1] is a great work seems as rationally defensible as their judgement that [L_2] is lousy seems to be from theirs' (1989: 37). Consequently, argues Currie, it would be 'completely arbitrary' (1989: 37) to say that one judgement was right and the other wrong. So, given that L_1 and L_2 can be aesthetically indistinguishable only if either our judgement or the Martian judgement is wrong, this demonstrates that there must be an aesthetic difference between L_1 and L_2.

Once it is granted that there must be an aesthetic difference between L_1 and L_2, the question arises of how the nature of this difference should be explained. Currie suggests that the moral to be drawn is that judgements of aesthetic value are relative to the class of artworks found in the community from within which such judgements are made. To be more precise,

---

[8] Here I change Currie's example. Currie has the infant Martian produce a canvas indistinguishable from Picasso's *Guernica* (1989: 37).

the only way to make sense of our judgments of aesthetic value in this and other cases is to interpret them as being relativised to the class of human works of art. The scale that *we* use is the scale defined by the kinds of artistic abilities found in *our* communities (and analogously for Martian judgments) ... When we say that [L_1] is a great work of art we mean that it is great for a human work of art, or, more precisely, that it is great for a work produced by a member of a community in which human levels of artistic skill prevail. (Currie 1989: 38)

So although L_1 and L_2 are sonically indistinguishable (and fall into the same artistic category), they have distinct aesthetic properties. And the reason why this is so is that the attributions of such properties to a work depend on facts about the level of skills and abilities in the communal setting in which the work was composed. *In This House, On This Morning* is a great work because its composition 'was a great achievement by human standards' (Currie 1989: 39); a conclusion which, of course, ushers us towards Currie's thesis that the aesthetic appreciation of an artwork is the appreciation of the artist's performance in composing it.

Currie's introduction and discussion of this case is, without doubt, resourceful and impressive. But be this as it may, once properly elucidated, it does not act as a counter-example to musical empiricism. The reason for this is that the scenario is described in question-begging terms from the very beginning. Currie's discussion of the thought-experiment is supposed to demonstrate that to appreciate a work is, in part, to appreciate the artist's achievement in composing it. This thesis is contentious, so it is at once striking and unsettling to find Currie assuming its truth in the way in which he sets up the example. For Currie assumes that the fact that L_2 is produced by an untalented Martian child (by Martian standards) entails that it would be judged by Martians as 'not at all valuable' (1989: 37). But why suppose that the Martians would make such a judgement, given that we regard the sonically indistinguishable L_1 as a masterpiece? It cannot be because the Martians have different, perhaps higher, aesthetic sensibilities than we do: Currie explicitly says that they have 'aesthetic interests and sensibilities much like our own' (1989: 36). So what other reason could there be for supposing that the Martians would regard L_2 as valueless. Just this, it would seem: the very thesis at issue: namely, that attributions of aesthetic qualities depend upon facts about the prevailing levels of skills and abilities in the community in which the work is composed.

An aesthetic empiricist will thus reply to Currie by denying his starting-point: that L_2 would be judged by the Martians as valueless. L_2, remember, is a sonic doppelgänger of *In This House, On This Morning*. So, since the Martians share our aesthetic sensibilities, they will, for example, hear the piece's thematic consistency, its joyfulness and depth, and will appreciate the way in which its movements form an integrated, unified whole. Such qualities are heard in the sounds, and so must be shared by L_1 (*In This House, On This Morning*) and L_2 (the Martian work). True, a Martian audience would judge L_2 to be *less valuable* than other pieces composed by adult Martians at the height of their powers, but it remains the case that L_2—like L_1—would merit the attribution of the (perceptible) aesthetic qualities just mentioned.

A way of putting my rejoinder is this. A musical empiricist denies that the aesthetic value of a work is to any extent determined by whether its composition occurred in a community in which the composition of such works *comes more or less easily*. Any value a work has is, he will maintain, *perceived in it*. Consequently, given that Currie's Martians share our aesthetic sensibilities and artistic categories, the empiricist will insist—*pace* Currie—that human beings and Martians would not, in fact, attribute conflicting aesthetic qualities to sonically indistinguishable works. Whilst Currie begs the question, the empiricist stands his ground. The argument is stalled as soon as it starts, and, with this, the motivation for the action-type hypothesis is undermined.

7.2.2 The Action-type Hypothesis Considered

Having questioned the motivation for Currie's account of the ontological nature of works of music, we can now go on to consider that account itself. To this end, one thing should be highlighted at once: in taking types to be things that have a sound structure, a heuristic path, and a three-place relation as 'constitutive elements' (1989: 70), Currie—like Levinson (1980b: 65)—commits the error of supposing types to have constituents. As we noted in Chapter 2, no sense can be made of this suggestion: the fact that a type's properly formed tokens must be structured in some way should not be interpreted as meaning that the abstract type itself is structured in that way. However, in what follows I shall put this criticism to one side. Even if Currie were right in thinking types to have constituents, he would nevertheless be wrong in supposing works of music to be types of composing. The two objections that follow—based on the initial worries introduced in §7.2—each point to a property possessed by musical works that cannot be shared by musical-works-according-to-Currie.

The first objection, in its original form, has been pithily made by Wolterstorff (1991: 80). Our intuitions tell us that works of music are things that musicians can perform. *In This House, On This Morning*, for example, has been performed by the Lincoln Centre Jazz Orchestra on countless occasions. But whilst the type/token theory can unproblematically explain what this phenomenon consists in—that is, the tokening of a type of sound-event—the action-type hypothesis cannot so much as allow for a work's performability. A group of musicians, however talented, could not play something which has a heuristic path and the relation *x discovers y by heuristic path z* as constituents. It is senseless to say that such entities as heuristic paths and relations can be played on musical instruments; so it is equally senseless to suggest that an entity that has such things as parts can be performed.

The ultimate explanation for why musical works-according-to-Currie cannot be performed would seem to be that their tokens are individual composings, not performances. Given that the type/token relation is taken by Currie to obtain between the work and token-composings, and not between the work and its performances, this relation cannot be used to explain how a work is performable. Indeed, given that works, *qua* action-types, have constituents that cannot be performed, it would seem to be the case that the work itself—the item that includes these unperformable items as parts—is unperformable. For Currie, the thing performed can only be *In This House, On This Morning*'s sound structure: an entity that Currie takes to be one of the work's constituents, not the work itself.

Having said this, one possible response to this objection would be to claim that it trades on a question-begging assumption about the nature of performability: namely, that a work's being performable *can only* be explained by its performances being its tokens.[9] It could be countered that Currie has a perfectly defensible account of what it is for a work W to be performed, namely, this: W is performed just when a token of the work's *sound structure* is produced. But this, it seems to me, will not quite do the job, since the original objection merely resurfaces, albeit in a new form. Even if this gloss on performability is granted, it remains false that *the entire*

---

[9] I owe this (typically) ingenious response to David Davies.

work is performable. For if the performance is a token, not of the work, but merely of one of its parts (viz. the work's sound structure), then it follows that only *one part* of the work, *and not all of it*, is capable of being performed. No sense can be made of the claim that a performer can perform a heuristic path by virtue of performing a sound structure, and so the work *in its entirety* cannot be performed. It goes without saying that this is a most paradoxical result: the idea that an orchestra could obey the totality of a work's score, yet fail to perform the complete work, runs contrary to our artistic and critical practice. Such a consequence should be avoided, if at all possible.

If it is true that Currie cannot allow for all of a musical work's being performable, it is equally true that—like the musical perdurantist—he cannot allow for such works being audible in their entirety; and this is my second objection. To be sure, Currie might argue that he, like the type/token theorist, can say that one can hear a work *by* hearing one of the work's performances. But he would be wrong about this: as we have just seen, according to the action-type hypothesis, it is not works that are performed, but constituents of works: sound structures. Consequently, performances are performances not *of* works, but of sound structures; and so the only gloss available to Currie of how a work can be heard is this: *W* is heard just in case a token of one of its constituents—its sound structure—is heard. But at this point, it is plain that an appeal to the type/token relation cannot explain how a whole work, rather than one of its constituents, can be heard. Too much has been conceded already. The type/token theorist can exploit the type/token relation to explain how a complete work can be heard in performance because it construes works as unstructured types of sound-event: a performance of a work—that is, a sound-sequence produced by the actions of performers—presents the work in its entirety because the work is nothing more than the unstructured type of which the particular sound-event is a token. Currie, by contrast, cannot say this. For, if Currie is right, the type presented by a performance of a work is not the work itself but one of its parts: its sound structure. Consequently, it is only a work's sound structure, and not the whole work, that one hears by hearing a performance. And, given that the action-type's other constituents—a heuristic path and *x discovers y by heuristic path z*—are not the sorts of thing that can heard by listening to a performance, it follows that the action-type hypothesis rules out the possibility of listening to a complete work (i.e. listening to all of its parts). The problem is a clear product of two theses definitive of Currie's position: that a work's tokens are composings, rather than sound-sequence-events; and that the type of which performances are tokens is a mere part of the work.

No doubt, as a final fling of the dice, Currie could challenge the type/token theorist to demonstrate that her theory is any less revisionary of our intuitions than is the action-type hypothesis. After all, the type/token theorist is committed to the idea that musical works exist eternally and, as a result, that composers creatively discover, rather than create, them. Furthermore, we have also seen that, if works are types of sound-event, they cannot bear many of the properties that we unreflectively ascribe to them: for example, a work of music, *qua* sound-event-type, cannot possess the property of containing a $C^{\#}$ in the seventh measure or the property of ending with an A minor chord. If musical works are types of sound-event, and if types are unstructured items that lack temporal parts, and hence cannot be said to *take place* or *occur* in time, then they cannot *contain* occurrences of chords and cannot *come to an end*. Only entities with parts can contain things, and only things that happen—events and processes—can be said to come to an end.

However, as I noted in §4.3, these consequences are less troublesome for the type/token theory than they might, at first, appear. We should first of all note that the action-type hypothesis is similarly revisionary of our intuition that works of music are created: as Currie himself puts it (1989: 75), action-types are not created by the people involved, but enacted by them. Second, and as we concluded at the end of Chapter 5, the fact that a theory compromises our intuition that composers bring their works into being is far less significant than many have supposed. The idea that composers create their compositions has been revealed as being both far less central to our concept of composition than many have claimed and defensible against the standard objections in the literature. Furthermore, the phenomenon of analogical predication enables the type/token theorist to explain elegantly how a work can lack a property that pre-theoretical intuition would have us ascribe to it, whilst preserving the intuitive truth-values of our everyday predications. No work can possess the property of containing a $C^{\#}$ in the seventh measure, but 'contains a $C^{\#}$ in the seventh measure' can be true of such a work, since this predicate, when ascribed to a work, expresses the property *being such that something cannot be a properly formed token of it unless it contains a $C^{\#}$ in its seventh measure*. A type/token theorist can thus say everything that common sense would have us say, without being committed to false doctrines concerning types. The action-type hypothesis, by contrast, simply saddles us with counter-intuitive commitments.

7.3 Davies's *Performance Theory*

One might suppose that Davies's elaboration of the view of musical works as process-like—namely, that they are compositional action-*tokens*, rather than types—stands even less chance of fending off objections than does Currie's action-type hypothesis; but, in fact, Davies does a highly impressive job of addressing such objections directly. However, as I shall argue in this section, his account is ultimately unpersuasive.

Modulo a flourish or two, the difference between Currie's action-type hypothesis and what Davies calls his 'performance theory' is that the latter identifies works with the actions that the former takes to be work-tokens.[10] For Davies, a musical work is an event: namely, the composer's unrepeatable compositional action. To use his own way of putting it, the performance theory has it that works of music (and artworks generally) 'belong to the class of performances whereby a content is articulated through a vehicle on the basis of shared understandings' (2004: 80). In composing the item usually assumed to be the work of music—what Davies calls the 'focus of appreciation' (2004: 26), 'work-focus' (2004: 179), or 'work-product' (2004: 97)—the composer makes an artistic statement that is articulated in an artistic medium realized by a vehicle (2004: 60).[11] But the work of

---

[10] Currie, as we have seen, characterizes his action-types thus: such an entity is the *discovering* of a structure-type by means of a particular heuristic path (1989: 70). Davies argues both that the notion of a structure has only limited application to the philosophy of art (2004: 135–6), and that the notion of a heuristic path cannot be satisfactorily cashed out (2004: 133–5). He also regards work-focuses—the things we listen to via performances—as things *created*, rather than discovered, by artists. As a result, he replaces talk of discovering a structure via a heuristic path with talk of an artist's specifying a focus of appreciation (2004: 149).

[11] These notions require some unpacking. To begin with, 'statement' is meant loosely, and should not be taken to imply that the statement made by an artist is propositional in nature. As Davies explains, 'the "artistic statement" articulated in a work standardly includes what would normally be described as representational, expressive, and formal properties of the object or structure generated by the artist' (2004: 53). Second, Davies's form of words—viz. that the artistic statement is 'articulated in an artistic medium realized in a vehicle' (2004: 60)—nicely encapsulates his distinction between artistic and vehicular media (2004: 56–62). An artist's vehicular medium comprises the physical means by which the focus of appreciation is produced (in music, the instruments, the sounds they can make, and the notation used to characterize these sounds (2004: 61–2)). An artist's artistic medium, meanwhile, consists in a vocabulary for describing the focus of appreciation produced, together with a set of shared

music is not the focus of appreciation itself—the item listened to via a performance—but the composer's unrepeatable 'generative performance' (2004: 152) by which this focus of appreciation was produced.

Davies elaborates and defends his unorthodox position with considerable vim and ingenuity. Having said this, I am unconvinced by his performance theory. First of all, the position faces powerful objections—some shared with Currie, but others unique to Davies's conception of works as action-tokens—that his detailed responses cannot succeed in fending off. But in addition, I shall also argue that Davies's attempt to explain the nature of the actions with which he identifies musical works is stymied by a flawed philosophy of action. Having made the case for this conclusion, I then take the chance to revisit his arguments for the performance theory.

7.3.1 Objections to the Performance Theory

In a nutshell, the most obvious problem facing Davies is that, *prima facie*, works of music have properties that are not shared by generative performances, and vice versa. The source of some of Davies's difficulties is his claim—shared with Currie—that musical works are (generative) process-*like*. If, for example, Duke Ellington's *Never No Lament* is the process by which the work-focus was composed (whether we identify the work with a process-type or a process-token), then the audibility and performability of the work are both immediately problematized. A present-day audience cannot hear Ellington's compositional action, and such an event cannot be played on musical instruments. A further source of problems is Davies's particular proposal that works of music be viewed as generative performance-*tokens*. If *Never No Lament* is the event that is Ellington's compositional action, then it follows that the work started and finished in 1940, lasted for two days (I'm guessing here), and was located in the United States. Such claims could not be more revisionary of our linguistic usage, seemingly violating the following 'pragmatic constraint' on the ontology of art that Davies, as we shall see presently, himself relies on to make his case:

(PC) [a]rtworks must be entities that can bear the sorts of properties rightly ascribed to what are termed 'works' in our reflective critical and appreciative practice; that are individuated in the way such 'works' are or would be individuated,

understandings as to the kinds of artistic statement that could be made with various manipulations of the vehicular medium (2004: 61–2).

and that have the modal properties that are reasonably ascribed to 'works', in that practice. (2004: 18)

However, as I shall now explain, Davies in fact denies that his proposal fails to meet (PC).

Davies attempts to turn the trick of reconciling the performance theory with (PC) by exploiting the constraint's normative character: (PC) demands that an ontology of art does justice to 'a theoretical representation of the norms that *should* govern the judgements that critics make', not to the judgments that are actually made (2004: 143). So Davies's suggestion turns out to be that the revisionism demanded by the performance theory is, in fact, justified once we reflect upon our critical practice. So how does Davies set about defending his revisionism? It would seem that his defence has three strands. First, he makes the kind of move that any holder of a process-like conception of musical works, including Currie, must make: that is, he claims that 'features of our discourse about artworks that, taken at face value, are incompatible with the idea that works are process-like rather than product-like entities are best reinterpreted, on reflection, as discourse ... about the elements that make up the work-focus, rather than as discourse about works themselves' (2004: 179). Second, and in order to trump the suspicion that his distinction between talk of works and talk of work-focuses is *ad hoc*, Davies promises something that Currie manifestly fails to offer: namely, 'a principled basis for the distinction' (2004: 180). Third, he argues that what he presents as the only serious alternative to viewing works as process-like—that such works are contextualized products[12]—is no less revisionary. I shall consider these three elements of Davies's response in turn.

According to Davies, then, *Never No Lament*, *qua* Ellington's generative performance-token, is inaccessible to listeners and performers. The thing listened to and performed is but the work-focus: the item specified by the generative performance, whose production brings this performance to an end. Now this is a highly counter-intuitive thesis. Nonetheless, Davies could reply, with some justification, that there exists no cogent theory that does justice to *all* of our intuitions in the ontology of art: we must make a critically informed decision about where to tolerate the inevitable lumps under the carpet. But to this response, a couple of rejoinders can be made.

---

[12] The most influential such contextualist approach is, of course, Levinson's conception of works of music as indicated types (1980b, 1990c).

To begin with, I think that the performance theory ends up with an account of musical works that is ontologically suspect, as we shall see presently. Furthermore, when it comes to evaluating the respective claims of competing theories to pull off the delicate task of reconciling our untutored intuitions with philosophical theory, I feel that Davies has severely underestimated the simple view that it is the business of this book to defend: that is, a sonicist type/token theory that identifies works with decontextualized, as opposed to indicated, types of sound-event. The simple view's appeal, when compared with the performance theory, is that it assuages a great many more of our intuitions. A work of music, for the simple view, is an abstract entity, thereby doing justice to our intuition that *Never No Lament* (unlike Ellington's compositional action) is not located in a particular region of space. Equally, given that the work is a type whose tokens are sound-sequence-events, there need be no denial that the (whole) work itself can be performed. Finally, as I noted in §4.2, the simple view's first component—the type/token theory—can exploit the notions of deferred ostension and analogical predication to explain, respectively, how an entire piece, and not just one of its constituents, can be listened to in performance, and how predications seemingly incompatible with the type/token theory can nonetheless come out as true.

Davies's reply to the simple view is that its commitment to musical empiricism, and consequent denial that works have properties that are provenance-dependent, is indefensible (2004: chs. 1–3). But, as I shall explain in greater detail in Chapters 8 and 9, such arguments admit of empiricist replies. As Davies himself notes (2004: 46–7), contextualists tend to try to make their case by means of the kinds of doppelgänger thought-experiments devised by Levinson (1980b: 68–73). That is to say, a contextualist will typically endeavour to describe a possible world in which two composers produce scores that represent the same pure sound-event-type but in which (as a result of differences in the musico-historical contexts in which the respective compositional acts take place) the composers concerned compose distinct works that differ in their respective artistic or aesthetic properties. But, as we shall see in Chapter 9, the empiricist's most obvious form of response to this kind of case is to present the would-be contextualist with a dilemma. If the property putatively possessed by one work and not by the other is either an *art-historical* property (e.g. *being influenced by Ellington*) or an *achievement* property (e.g. *being visionary*), then it is possessed by *composers* and *their actions*, rather than by their works, thereby presenting no problem for the empiricist. On the other hand, if the property is genuinely aesthetic (for instance, *being swinging* or *being eerie*), then the empiricist will insist that compositions that do not differ sonically cannot differ with respect to such properties. Either way, empiricism survives. Or so I shall argue.

Naturally, I do not want to be accused of underestimating the work that needs to be done by the empiricist to defend herself against Levinson-style thought-experiments. There are further epicycles of argument and objection to be considered before the empiricist's position can be made good. My aim, for the moment, however, is more modest: namely, that of assessing Davies's treatment of the simple view. And my worry here is that Davies's response to the kind of empiricist line just outlined sees him operating with a double standard when it comes to (PC). For his reply to the first horn of the dilemma pressed by the empiricist is to endorse Currie's claim that taking art-historical and achievement properties to be properties of the composer's compositional act violates the pragmatic constraint (2004: 46). But if (PC) has the normative, rather than purely descriptive, character Davies presents it as having, then what is to stop the type/token theorist from making the kind of revisionist move that Davies himself does? In other words, what is to stop her from claiming that such properties are not 'rightly' ascribed to works? A holder of the simple view will insist that her combination of the type/token theory and empiricism is much less revisionary of our intuitions than is the performance theory and, what is more, that the type/token theory can provide a principled rationale for denying that musical works genuinely bear art-historical and achievement properties. How, she will ask, can an abstract object really be, for example, *influenced by Ellington* or *visionary*? Strictly speaking, the only things that can have such properties are people and their actions. Once one appreciates that works of music are abstract objects, ascribing such properties to them becomes a strange business indeed.

Suffice it to say that I think that a thoroughgoing type/token theorist would remain unconvinced by the first element in Davies's reply to the charge of excessive revisionism. And the same would seem to go for the third such element: his claim that contextualism turns out to be no less revisionary. I suspect that this is true, but have noted already that the simple view I defend turns out to be a good deal less disruptive of our intuitions than Davies's performance theory. This just leaves the second part of Davies's defence of his revisionism: his claim that he has a principled motivation for distinguishing in the way he does between talk of works (*qua* generative performance-tokens) and talk of work-focuses. Such a rationale is provided by a fascinating argument whose starting-point is that 'talk of appreciating works is properly analogous to talk of studying or understanding natural phenomena, and to be contrasted with talk about physically interacting with such phenomena' (2004: 188). With this premise in place, Davies goes on to claim that to understand or study a natural phenomenon is characteristically to understand or study a physical process rather than the process's product. When it comes to corrosion, for example, Davies thinks that what scientists study is not the state of corrosion, but 'the process generative of that product' (2004: 187). Consequently, given that appreciating a musical work is akin to understanding or studying a natural phenomenon, and that the object of this latter understanding or study is a generative process, we are entitled to regard works of music themselves as generative processes, and hence to discriminate between talk of works and talk of work-focuses in the way in which Davies suggests.

However, although this argument is ingenious, I have doubts about both of its key premises. First, I dispute that scientists are always concerned purely with the process and never with its product. Consider diseases, for example. A scientific understanding of New Variant CJD explains *both* the degenerative process *and* the nature of the brain-state that is completed by it. Indeed, if scientists had not studied the brain-states of sufferers, they surely would not have noticed the striking similarities between the brains of New Variant CJD suffers and the brains of cattle that had fallen victim to BSE. The same considerations, it seems to me, apply to Davies's favoured examples. A scientific explanation of sunburn is not simply an explanation of how people come to be sunburnt; it involves an account of the state that sunburnt skin is in. Only if a scientist knows what sunburnt skin is like can she begin to formulate treatments for it. Once more, it seems that the scientific study of ψ, where 'ψ' exhibits a process/product ambiguity, involves a study of both process and product. And if this is the case, the examples Davies discusses cannot justify a process-ontology of musical works to the detriment of an account that takes such works to be the things composed by compositional actions.[13]

---

[13] Having said this, it could be argued that my discussion of such scientific examples misrepresents the performance theory. For a performance theorist could claim, I suppose, that a generative performance

So much for Davies's claims about the nature of scientific study. Even if we were to let these claims go, we would still be justified in questioning the intended analogy between appreciating an artwork and studying a natural phenomenon. Davies admits that this claimed analogy is 'controversial in abstract' (2004: 188), and I am sceptical whether such doubts can be put to bed—as Davies thinks they can (2004: 188)—by endorsing the idea that elements of provenance feature essentially in the individuation of artworks. In §7.2.1 I noted that Currie's picture of the composer as a quasi-scientist misconstrues the compositional enterprise, and similar considerations apply to the analogous claim concerning the listener's activity. A listener's appreciation of *Never No Lament*, it seems to me, is very *unlike* a scientist's study of corrosion. For one thing, the scientist tries to uncover facts, but the listener is engaged in no analogous project of enquiry. Whilst we are happy to talk of a discerning listener's *understanding* the work, the understanding in question is decidedly non-propositional in nature. Aesthetic understanding is a matter of responding in ways merited by the music, where the kinds of response involved may include exercises of the emotions. It is appropriate, I would claim, to feel a strange mixture of melancholy and upliftedness when listening to *Never No Lament*. Such understanding is of a different kind altogether from that gained by a scientist explaining the process of corrosion.

All in all, I remain unconvinced of Davies's treatment of the standard objections to process-ontologies of art. He fails to motivate a principled distinction between talk of works and talk of work-focuses, and we are left with the feeling that his performance theory is too disruptive of our intuitions to be acceptable. But, as I said earlier, my worries do not end here. For, as I shall now explain, his specific proposal as to the actions

---

is not separable from the product that completes it, but is, rather, *the process completed by the product*. On such a view, the product is the final part of the process (i.e. the process's completion); and, if this were right, then the kinds of scientific examples we have been considering would not conflict with Davies's intended analogy, since *both* appreciating a musical work and studying a natural phenomenon would involve an appreciation of both process and product.

However, I doubt whether such a reading of Davies's performance theory is sustainable. Davies explicitly claims that scientists study processes *rather than* their products. As he himself says, when scientists study a phenomenon, 'it is characteristically the process generative of the product, *not the product so generated*, that is the subject of study, understanding, or investigation' (2004: 187; my emphasis). And in any case, Davies nowhere suggests that a work's focus of appreciation—the work's product, in other words—is a *part* of the process. Indeed, such an idea makes dubious sense. A product produced by a process of manufacture is not a part of that process; it is not itself the process's final stage. The product 'completes' the process only in the sense that the process's final stage is the completion of the product.

with which works of music are identified is threatened by ontological obscurantism.

7.3.2 Which Actions are Musical Works?

Actions are events (Davies 2004: 169): datable, locatable occurrences. More precisely, an action is an event that can be described in a way that makes it intentional.[14] With this in mind, the question for Davies is this: what kind of event is an artwork supposed to be? An example will help to sharpen our sense of what is at stake. Ellington composed *Never No Lament* by executing certain manipulations of a pencil and score paper (thereby producing the finished score). According to Davies's performance theory, the work itself is not the type of sound-sequence-event characterized by the score; it is, presumably, Ellington's action (or series of actions) that were completed by the creation of the finished score. Given that this is so, the natural move for a performance theorist to make would be to identify the work with just those manipulations of pencil and score paper by which Ellington produced the score. However, Davies is quite right to regard such a thesis as having a severely counter-intuitive consequence (2004: 168–9).

The consequence in question is this: if *Never No Lament* were the event comprising Ellington's manipulations of the pencil and score paper, it would follow that the work could not have been composed at any other time. That such a consequence is counter-intuitive is obvious: the piece could surely have been composed by Ellington some five years earlier or later, for instance. Why, then, would the performance theory have this counter-intuitive consequence if it were to identify the work with the said event? The answer, as Davies himself recognizes, concerns the ontological nature of events.[15] For events have their temporal location necessarily: no event could have happened at any time other than the one at which it occurs actually. And the reason why this is so is that events are perduring entities *par excellence*: that is, fusions of temporal parts. Fusions, like sets, have their parts essentially (Caplan and Bright 2005). So it follows that there is no possible world in which an event, *qua* fusion of temporal parts, differs

[14] This way of putting it is, of course, due to Davidson (e.g. 1971: 46). An example may help the point to stick: I did not disturb my neighbours intentionally, but, given that we can redescribe this unfortunate event as 'Julian's first attempt to play *Never No Lament* on his alto saxophone', we can see that the event in question was, indeed, an action of mine.

[15] Although I doubt whether he quite puts his finger on the precise reason (Davies 2004: 168–9).

in its temporal parts from those it has actually. But now consider the nature of such temporal parts. A perdurant's temporal parts are 'modally inductile' (Van Inwagen 1990: 253): they have their temporal extents (i.e. the times at which they begin and end, and the times for which they last) essentially. (It makes no sense, for example, to say that the temporal part of the 1975 Cup Final that occupied the period of time from 3 p.m. to 3.05 p.m. on 3 May, 1975 could have lasted longer, or could have begun or finished at different times. The temporal part in question is nothing more nor less than whatever was taking place in Wembley Stadium *between those times*.) But if events are perdurants,[16] if perdurants have their temporal parts essentially, and if a perdurant's temporal parts are modally inductile, then events cannot but have the temporal location and extent that they have actually.[17]

One thing is clear, as Davies himself realizes: he cannot treat artworks as events in this sense (2004: 172). So, seemingly drawing upon the 'basic actions' literature (2004: 172),[18] Davies argues that a piece of music is not a basic action (i.e. an action by an agent that is brought about otherwise than by another of the agent's actions), but what he calls a 'doing' (2004: 173). Two presumed features of doings—themselves, supposedly, a subset of non-basic events or 'happenings' (2004: 173)—are worth stressing. First, doings are non-basic; they are actions accomplished 'by executing' basic actions (2004: 172). Second, and supposedly as a result of their being non-basic actions, doings are events that are not essentially tied to the times at which they actually occur. According to Davies, a doing could have 'occurred at different times and through different basic actions, as long as the conditions for performing *this* non-basic action were met' (2004: 173). So the idea is this, it seems: rather than Ellington's composition of *Never No Lament* being *identical with* the manipulations of pencil and score paper

---

[16] Of course, it may be denied that events are perduring entities. Kim (1976), for one, takes an event to be, or be modelled by, an ordered triple of an object, a property, and a time. But, granted that set-theoretical entities such as triples have their members essentially, this view leads us to the same thesis—i.e. that an event's time is essential to it—albeit by a different route. If an event, e, is $< \alpha$, $F, t >$, or is modelled by this triple, then there is no possible world in which it occurs at any other time. Kim is less sure of this than me (1976: 321), but, tellingly, agrees that the appearance of modal flexibility with respect to an event's time can be explained away in the way I go on to recommend.

[17] Peter Van Inwagen accepts that one may escape this argument if one takes a counterpart-theoretic approach to modal statements about individuals (1990: 253–4). But I agree with him that such a rejoinder is a dead end. As we saw in §1.2, counterpart theory is implausible in itself.

[18] I say 'seemingly' because Davies does not explicitly refer to the work of Danto in this area. Danto's defence of the doctrine of basic actions can be found in his 1963 and 1965.

that took place—a series of events that could not have taken place at any other time—his compositional action is, in fact, a distinct action that was brought about by these bodily movements, and which could have been realized by other basic actions at other times.[19]

In my view, however, such a distinction between basic actions and doings cannot be maintained. To begin with, the motivation for it is flawed. Davies supposes that some such distinction is required, if we are to do justice to much of our modal talk about events and, thereby, works: talk that appears to presuppose that certain event-tokens (i.e. happenings) could have occurred at different times and could have been 'realized' by different basic events (2004: 169–73). For example, we come out with truths such as the following:

(53) More people would have been saved if the sinking of the *Titanic* had occurred a few hours later;

(54) Ellington might have composed *Never No Lament* on a glockenspiel;

and it might be supposed that both commit us to Davies's distinction. (53), it might be alleged, sees us truly describing an event-token—the sinking of the *Titanic*—as modally flexible with respect to its time of occurrence in a way that standard events are not (Davies 2004: 169–70), thereby pressing upon us the distinction between basic and non-basic events that Davies applies to actions. And when it comes to (54), it could be claimed that its truth presupposes that a certain action-token—Ellington's composition of the piece—is capable of being 'realized by' other basic actions.

But such reasoning is by no means obligatory. The truth of (53) does not demonstrate that an event-token might have occurred at an alternative time; for in coming out with (53) we are saying merely that there could have been an event that was a sinking of the *Titanic* and which took place a couple of hours after the event-type in question actually came to be instantiated. The counterfactual claim, in other words, does not concern the very event that occurred, but another event of the same type. In the

---

[19] At this point, a lack of precision in Davies's use of 'basic action' should be recognized. Strictly speaking, a basic action is, supposedly, an action by an agent that is not brought about by another action by the agent; so the kinds of actions Davies describes as basic—manipulations of piano keyboards and the like (2004: 172)—are not genuinely basic. If there are such things as basic actions, they can only be pure bodily movements characterized without reference being made to objects beyond the agent's skin. For our present purposes, however, nothing much hinges on this nicety, so I have followed Davies's lead in describing the supposedly simpler actions by which works of music are composed as basic.

same vein, to say that Ellington might have composed *Never No Lament* on the glockenspiel is not to say that the very same action-token might have been realized by a different set of basic actions; it is to say that there could have been an action that was a composing of *Never No Lament* and which involved Ellington's playing the glockenspiel. Once more, the putative motivation for Davies's distinction is undercut once we understand what is said by (53), (54), and such like.

So much for the motivation for Davies's distinction between basic actions and 'doings'. Might there not be benefits to this theory, nonetheless? I don't think so, for the distinction between basic actions and 'doings' faces two serious objections. First of all, the relation supposedly obtaining between a basic action and a doing is far from clear. The most obvious account has it that the relation in question is causal: if one's ψ-ing is a non-basic action that one performs by ϕ-ing, then it is hard to avoid the conclusion that one's ϕ-ing is an event that *brings about* the distinct event that is one's ψ-ing. Such a position, however, has a highly counter-intuitive consequence: namely, that Ellington *caused himself* to compose the work. But if Ellington performed this action freely, then surely *nobody* caused him to do it (Davidson 1971: 56). Whilst it may be true to say that he *brought it about* that he composed the piece, this use of the locution is not genuinely causal: it is equivalent to the claim that he brought himself to compose the piece (Davidson 1971: 57).

So if the relation is not causal, what is it? Davies himself draws an analogy between the way in which a 'doing' is supposedly 'realized' by a basic action or actions and the way in which a statue can be *constituted by* a lump of bronze (2004: 174–5). Assuming that there is a cogent argument for the thesis that the latter relation of constitution is not that of identity, and claiming that 'to the extent that the argument for a constitutive rather than an identity relation in an object ontology of art is good, a similar argument can be constructed in the event ontology of art defended here' (2004: 175), Davies takes 'doings' to be composed by the basic actions that realize them in a similar way. But at this point, I doubt whether appealing to authority on the question of the nature of the constitution relation can really help.[20] For one thing, the case against viewing constitution as identity is not itself watertight. Tellingly, Lynne Rudder Baker, a chief defender of distinguishing constitution from identity, herself doubts that the premisses

---

[20] Davies refers the reader to two papers: Rudder Baker 1997 and Thompson 1998.

of her argument can be defended non-question-beggingly.[21] Second, it is unclear, to me at least, whether the proposed analogy between a statue's being constituted by a lump of bronze and a non-basic action's being 'realized' by a basic action or actions holds good. A clear sense can be attached to the claim that a statue is constituted by a piece of bronze: the statue is a particular substance, and bronze is the stuff of which it is made. Events, by contrast, are not constituted by anything in this sense. True enough, events can be composed of other events: a football match has other events—shots, goals, kicks, and headers—as temporal parts. But an event's temporal parts are not the substance of which the event is made: events have a substance only in a very attenuated sense. And in any case, the supposed constitution relation obtaining between a basic action and a 'doing' is not intended by Davies to be mereological. Ellington's manipulation of his pencil and score paper is not supposed to be a temporal part of his composition of Never No Lament; the former is the action which 'realizes' the latter. The problem, however, lies in disentangling the nature of such 'realization'. We are beggared for an account that is both clear and objection-free.

The second reason for rejecting Davies's appeal to the theory of basic actions is what one might call 'the missing action problem'. Basic actions theory tells us that Ellington's movement of his fingers (by which he manipulates the pencil and score paper) brings about another action of his: his writing of the score. But, as Davidson vividly explains, once Ellington

---

[21] The argument in question goes as follows, where Discobulus is a statue and BP the piece of bronze that constitutes it:

(55) Discobulus is essentially a statue
(56) BP is not essentially a statue.
∴ (57) BP ≠ Discobulus. (Rudder Baker 1997: 601)

One problem here is that it is not clear why we should accept (55). Why is it true that Discobulus is essentially a statue? Rudder Baker defends (55) by claiming that its falsehood would also commit us to the claim that 'all the other artworks that do exist could exist without being artworks' (1997: 620). This latter consequence she takes to be objectionable because she regards it as counter-intuitive to suppose that there is a possible world without art that is nonetheless ontologically indistinguishable from the actual world. She regards it as obvious that we should think of a world without art as 'ontologically impoverished compared to our world' (1997: 620).

Both steps of this defence of (55) are questionable. First, it does not follow from the falsehood of (55) that all existent artworks could exist without being artworks. Some artworks—i.e. those that are types rather than particulars—are not constituted by any kind of stuff, so no puzzle analogous to that of the statue and the bronze arises for them. Second, even if it did follow that a denial of (55) committed us to the existence of a world without art that was ontologically indistinguishable from the actual world, Rudder Baker has not given a decisive reason for regarding such a commitment as a reductio. As she herself admits, she is only wielding an intuition pump, and it is a familiar point that our pre-theoretic intuitions may be outweighed by mature philosophical theory.

has performed the said movements of his fingers, there is nothing left for *him* to do—no action for him to perform—before the score is written. Ellington's movement of his fingers was by itself enough to bring about the creation of the score. Whether or not the pencil leaves marks on the score paper, is 'up to nature' (Davidson 1971: 59). Ellington has done his work; it remains for the pencil to do its (Davidson 1971: 57–8). The crucial point to grasp is this: although the score paper's becoming marked is an event subsequent to, and brought about by, Ellington's action, the action itself is something that can be variously described as 'Ellington's movement of his fingers', 'Ellington's manipulation of the pencil and score paper', 'Ellington's creation of the score' and, of course, 'Ellington's composition of *Never No Lament*' (Davidson 1971: 59).

The end result is that Davies faces a nasty dilemma. Either he admits that identifying works of music with generative performances entails that these works could not have been composed at any other time. Or else, if he seeks to avoid this result by appealing to the theory of basic actions, he ends up embracing ontological obscurantism. The need to make such a choice is well worth avoiding.

7.3.3 Davies's Arguments Considered

It is one thing to object to a theory; a fully satisfying critique will also seek to undermine the arguments presented in its favour. Given that I believe the performance theory to be false, I must, therefore, try to explain where Davies's detailed and ingenious arguments for it go awry. This is the task of the present section.

There would seem to be two main arguments offered for the performance theory.[22] The first is an argument from artistic intentions (2004: ch. 4);

---

[22] There are two others, but they have much less weight than the two I consider in the main body of the text. First, Davies believes that a view of artworks as generative performances best enables us to view late modern works as continuous with artistic tradition (2004: 189–200); second, he thinks that the performance theory nicely explains our treatment of forgeries (2004: 200–5). The latter argument is, I believe, irrelevant to the case of music since, I take it, musical works—unlike scores—cannot be forged. As Christopher Janaway (1999) has, to my mind, demonstrated, no putative case of a forgery of a musical work *W* meets both of the following necessary conditions for a forgery having occurred: that a work distinct from *W* is composed; and that the composer of this other work intends to claim falsely that it is *W*.

The suggestion that the performance theory best explains the fact that late modern works are continuous with more traditional works is, of course, predicated on the assumption that such continuity is actual. And one might wonder whether this is so, as Davies admits (2004: 1–6). Inasmuch as the second is that the performance theory best allows us to accommodate the putative work-relativity of modality (2004: ch. 5): the (supposed) phenomenon according to which whether a feature of provenance is essential to a work depends upon the particular work in question (2004: 107). Let us begin our discussion by focusing on the former. Following an insightful and impressively nuanced critique of both actual intentionalism and hypothetical intentionalism (2004: 84–9), Davies concludes that we should favour an 'uptake' theory, in which the meaning-properties of an artwork (i.e. the 'artistic statement' it makes) are determined by 'the meaning that a properly informed receiver, correctly applying the appropriate norms, would ascribe to a vehicle taken to be intentionally used to make a given kind of utterance' (2004: 89). However, he nonetheless holds that an artist's intentions, 'where all of the relevant features of provenance are held constant, can effect the appreciation of a work' (2004: 90). Specifically, Davies considers the following kind of pair of cases (2004: 92–3). They concern literary works, but the conclusions transfer harmlessly to the case of works of music.

Case 1 has it that Smith authors a text T_1 with the intention of its containing a story N_1, in which it is true that Stanley is motivated by fear of emotional commitment: something which is a recurrent theme in Smith's characterization throughout her work. But imagine that, in this case, Smith's intention is unfulfilled: although she intends that readers view Stanley as being motivated by fear of emotional commitment, our 'uptake theory' determines that it is true in N_1 that Stanley is motivated by self-centred ambition. Case 2, by contrast, is identical with Case 1 except that Smith authors a text T_2, word-for-word identical with T_1, but this time with the intention of its being true in N_2 that Stanley is motivated by self-centred ambition.

Now let us consider how we would appreciate the works in the two cases. One thing is for sure: T_1 is identical with T_2: as well as being word-for-word identical, they have the same meaning-properties: in both, Stanley is motivated by fear of emotional commitment. But, still more crucially, Davies believes that we would regard the *works* as distinct, since we would appreciatively evaluate them differently (2004: 93–4). In Case 1

it is defensible to argue that late modern works are discontinuous with earlier works—because understanding them requires one to be *au fait* with contemporary art theory—one might deny the thesis upon which Davies's argument is premissed. (It is not implausible, e.g. to regard Cage's *4'33"* as a work contributing to a debate about the nature of music, rather than as a work of music itself.)

we would regard the work as Smith's failed attempt to illustrate her usual thematic preoccupation. In Case 2, by contrast, we would regard the work as a deliberate attempt to express a view of human motivation different from that expressed in the rest of her *œuvre*. The work produced in Case 2 would thus have a ground-breaking and innovative quality that the work produced in Case 1 lacked. The point, then, is that 'the actual semantic or narrative intentions of the author, even if they do not determine the meaning-properties of the authored text, do enter crucially into the appreciative evaluation of the *work*' (2004: 94).

In Davies's view, this conclusion has an ontological corollary, which he argues for by means of a *reductio* (2004: 97–8). The following argument, he claims, is valid, but has a false conclusion:

> (58) The proper object of critical evaluation of a work is what the author achieves, not what she tries to achieve.
>
> (59) What the author achieves is the product of her creative activities, the 'work-product'.
>
> So (60) The proper object of critical evaluation of a work is the work-product.
>
> (61) If (60), then the author's actual semantic intentions can affect the critical evaluation of her work only by determining the meaning-properties of the work-product.
>
> (62) For any type of meaning-property P for which an 'uptake' analysis is correct, actual authorial semantic intentions with respect to P do *not* determine the P-type meaning-properties of the work-product.
>
> So (63) For any type of meaning-property P for which an 'uptake' analysis is correct, actual authorial semantic intentions with respect to P are irrelevant to the critical evaluation of works.[23]

That (63) is false is the moral Davies draws from his discussion of Cases 1 and 2. Consequently, given that the argument is valid, it seems that we must deny one of the argument's assumptions: (58), (59), (61), or (62). As Davies points out (2004: 98), (62) is true by definition, whilst (58) is too intuitive to be rejected except *in extremis*; so we seem to be left with a choice of rejecting either (59) or (61). To deny (61), according

---

[23] I have changed Davies's numbering here to fit my sequence in this book.

to Davies, would be a mistake. One might suppose, for example, that a work-product could have the relational property of *being created with the intention that it mean P*, and that in evaluating this work-product we must take into account the fact that it was created with this intention. But the worry here is that, since the work-product's having this property in no way determines the work-product's meaning-properties, it is hard to see how it could bear upon the appreciation of the work-product, at least if an 'uptake theory' is correct. The work-product's having this property merely bears upon what the artist *attempted*, rather than what she *achieved*, and so, by (58), is irrelevant to the evaluation of the work. In order to argue that the work-product's being created with the intention that it mean *P* bears upon the evaluation of the work itself, we must deny (58), which we have agreed already to be highly intuitive. If the work is, indeed, the work-product, facts about what the artist attempted have a bearing only on how we evaluate the artist, not the work (2004: 99).

Davies's conclusion is thus that we should avoid a commitment to (63) by denying (59): that is, by holding that the thing the author achieves—the work, in other words—is the artist's generative performance (2004: 99). The author's actual intentions are relevant to our appreciation of the work, without determining the work-product's meaning-properties, because these intentions are 'aspects of the work so conceived' (2004: 99).

But it seems to me that Davies has underestimated the strength of the aesthetic empiricist's case, his assumption being that the question is merely *how* we should acknowledge the role of provenance in the individuation of works. As I suggested in §7.2.1, I am unconvinced by arguments designed to show that the *aesthetic* appreciation of a work of music need involve the evaluation of the artist's achievement. And when it comes to the argument at present under consideration, the empiricist will surely just insist that (63) is true, and hence that the argument is perfectly sound. The empiricist, remember, works with a strict distinction between, on the one hand, art-historical and achievement properties and, on the other, properties that are genuinely aesthetic. Consequently, for the committed empiricist, the difference between Case 1 and Case 2—a difference in Smith's aesthetic intentions—pertains only to our evaluation of the artist's activity, and not to our aesthetic evaluation of the work itself. Davies's response to this move—namely, that, in relegating much of our 'art-criticism' to the level of biography, it violates the pragmatic constraint (2004: 96)—strikes me as a little quick. An empiricist will, no doubt, respond by claiming such a revision of our critical practice to be in accordance with (PC), since such art-historical and achievement properties are not *rightly* ascribable to works. Such revision, the empiricist will argue, is the price that must be paid for accepting a theory that is actually a lot less revisionary than the performance theory. And, as we have noted already, she questions the coherence of the ascription of art-historical and achievement properties to works themselves.

Davies's other major argument for the performance theory starts with the fascinating claim that '*aspects of provenance bear upon our modal judgments with a variable force that reflects our overall sense of what is to be appreciated in a given work*' (2004: 112). To illustrate what Davies is getting at here, he regards it as plausible to suppose that Warhol's *Brillo Boxes* could only have been produced in the artistic-cultural context of the American art scene of the 1950s and 1960s, but that a hypothetical work, *Prairie Snowscape*, produced by a naïve artist at the same time as *Brillo Boxes*, could have been painted a good deal earlier or later (2004: 108). Why is this so? According to Davies, because the 'artistic statements' made by the respective works are crucially different (2004: 108). The statement made by *Brillo Boxes* is context-dependent: it is a contribution to a culturally bound artistic exploration concerning the nature of art. *Prairie Snowscape*, by contrast, was produced naïvely, without its artist conceiving of herself as working within a cultural-artistic context.

Standard contextualist ontologies cannot allow for the putative work-relativity of modal properties. If, for example, we take a work of music to be a Levinsonian object—that is, an indicated type—then *all* works will have their time of origin essentially. So the question is: how can we best allow for work-relativity? By endorsing the performance theory, according to Davies (2004: 114–20). The modal difference between *Brillo Boxes* and *Prairie Snowscape* is grounded in the difference in the extent to which features of the context of creation must enter into an adequate characterization of their respective artists' generative performances (2004: 114). Since *Prairie Snowscape* is a naïve work, its artist's generative performance can be adequately characterized without ascribing action-guiding mental states to her, states whose content makes reference to the cultural-artistic context in which she is situated. By contrast, since Warhol's creation of *Brillo Boxes* certainly *was* a self-conscious attempt to contribute to a certain *milieu*, the same cannot be said for his generative performance, which goes to explain why we see his work as analytically tied to that context. But having explained the work-relativity of modal properties in this way, an ontological pay-off hoves into view. Given that construing works as contextualized products cannot account for this work-relativity, the best option, Davies claims, is simply to accept that works *just are* the relevant generative performances (2004: 117).

What are we to make of this? In my opinion, this argument faces two serious problems. First, an empiricist will, of course, question Davies's starting-point: namely, that features of provenance determine the identity of artworks to any extent. Armed with the distinction between aesthetic value, individual achievement value, and art-historical value, she will argue, once again, that there are no genuine context-dependent properties possessed by works: those properties that appear to be context-dependent are really art-historical, or else pertain to the composer's (or performer's) achievement, and hence are not genuinely possessed by works at all. However, whatever the rights and wrongs of this position, the second problem facing Davies's argument from the work-relativity of modality is, it seems, inescapable. For, as he himself admits, he can only make good his claim that the performance theory allows for work-relativity once he has provided us with an account of the ontological nature of the events with which such works are to be identified (2004: 116). But, if my argument of §7.3.2 is correct, it is precisely this that he has failed to do. The time at which an event occurs is essential to it, and Davies's attempt to circumvent this objection by identifying generative performances with a species of supposedly non-basic actions fails to yield a clear, defensible conception of the events with which he wishes to identify works of music.

7.4 Conclusion

Both versions of the conception of musical works as process-like are seriously flawed. Whether we are tempted to view a work of music as a composing-type or as a composing-token, we are faced with highly counter-intuitive consequences: on either elaboration of the process-idea, works (in their entirety, at least) can be neither performed nor listened to. Given that the type/token theory can allow for both the performability and the perceptibility of whole musical works, and that the paradoxical features facing it can be ameliorated by appeal to the doctrine of analogy, it is clear where our loyalties should lie.

The rejection of the accounts offered by Currie and Davies completes our defence of the type/token theory. As well as being the theory that is *prima facie* correct, it turns out to do the best job of balancing mature philosophical explanation with our pre-theoretical intuitions. But whilst claiming musical works to be (norm-) types of sound-event provides us with a convincing answer to the categorial question, it leaves the question of such works' individuation open. What is it for a work of music W and a work of music W^* to be identical? As I said in the Introduction, I endorse a species of *sonicism*: the view that W and W^* are one and the same work of music just in case they have the same sonic properties normative within them: just in case they sound exactly alike, in other words. This book's last two chapters are devoted to an elaboration and defence of this claim.

8

Sonicism I: Against Instrumentalism

8.1 Sonicism Introduced

The categorial question in the ontology of music has now been settled. Musical works are norm-types whose tokens are sound-sequence-events. This conception, better than all its rivals, captures such works' repeatability, performability, and audibility, whilst avoiding metaphysical obscurantism. But it is one thing to provide an answer to the categorial question; it is quite another to give an account of how musical works are individuated: that is, to provide an informative account of when we have one and the same work of music and when we have numerically distinct such works. However, such an account is provided by the simple view's second conjunct—*sonicism*—and my final two chapters are devoted to its motivation and defence.

With a view to laying out the sonicist's individuative claim, let us first of all return to the crucial way in which types differ from sets. A type, by contrast to a set, is individuated according to the condition that a token has to meet in order to instantiate it (Rumfitt 1993: 448). Factoring in the thesis that musical works are norm-types, a musical work is individuated according to the condition a sound-event must meet to be one of its *properly formed* tokens. This being so, the sonicist's distinctive claim can be put thus: whether a sound-event counts as a properly formed token of W is determined purely by its acoustic qualitative appearance. Nothing else matters. The properties comprising the set Σ of properties normative within any work W are all wholly acoustic in character: properties such as *being in 4/4 time, ending with a C minor chord*, and so on.

Having clarified the sonicist's position, we can now formulate it in the usual way in which such individuative claims are made: as an account of the identity conditions for the kind of entities with which the theory is concerned. Given what has been said already, the sonicist's stand on the identity conditions of works of music is clear. A work of music W and a work of music W^* are numerically identical if and only if W and W^* are acoustically indistinguishable: just in case, that is, they have exactly the same acoustic properties normative within them.

Having set out sonicism in this way, it is plain that two highly controversial consequences ensue. First of all, suppose that a composer, Twin Beethoven, whilst ignorant of Beethoven's work, composes a piece that is an acoustic facsimile of the *Hammerklavier* Sonata, but with a score that specifies that the work be performed on a Perfect Timbral Synthesizer that makes sounds that exactly duplicate those made by a piano. According to the sonicist, Beethoven and Twin Beethoven compose the same work. Given that sonic equivalence alone makes for work-identity, what we have here are not numerically distinct sonic duplicates but one and the same work composed for different instruments. True enough, the respective scores differ in their instrumental specifications, but it is one and the same work that is scored twice.

Now, to vary the example somewhat, imagine that Twin Beethoven independently produces a score that varies not one jot from Beethoven's score for the *Hammerklavier*, but that Twin Beethoven composes his piece in 2007. According to the sonicist, once more, Beethoven and his twin have composed the same work even though their compositional acts occurred almost 200 years apart. Since works are identical just in case they are acoustically indistinguishable, our example sees a single work composed in two distinct musico-historical contexts.

Conventional wisdom has it that each of these consequences demonstrates that sonicism individuates musical works insufficiently finely.[1] With regard to the first consequence, the position that we may term *instrumentalism* claims that works of music written for different instruments cannot be identical because they lay down distinct conditions for the production of properly formed tokens: to return to our example, a properly formed token of the *Hammerklavier* must be produced by a piano, whilst a properly formed token of Twin Beethoven's work can only be the product of a Perfect

---

[1] This moral has been drawn, in one form or other, by Currie (1989: Ch. 3), David Davies (2004: Chs. 1 and 2), Stephen Davies (2001: 60–86), and Levinson (1980b, 1990a, 1990c).

Timbral Synthesizer.[2] So, whereas the sonicist claims that the set Σ of the properties normative within a work W comprises merely acoustic properties, the instrumentalist takes Σ to include properties concerning how the token sounds are *produced*: *performance means-properties*, such as *being produced by playing a piano in the conventional fashion*. Clearly, if the instrumentalist is right about this, then it cannot simply be sonic equivalence that makes for work-identity. For once it is granted that performance means-properties are normative within works, we have no choice but to admit that W and W^*, to be identical, must also have the same performance means-properties normative within them.

When it comes to the second consequence, the position we may term *contextualism* denies that it is possible for one and the same work to be composed by two composers occupying diverse musico-historical contexts. For the contextualist, any differences between the settings in which compositional acts take place will automatically bring about differences in the works composed, even if those works sound exactly alike. So, however the contextualist expresses her claim—as the thesis that 'distinct composers determining the same sound structure ... inevitably produce different musical works' (Levinson 1980*b*: 68); as the thesis that W and the acoustically indistinguishable W^* are distinct if composed in distinct musico-historical settings; or as the conjunction of the previous two claims—she insists that acoustic equivalence is insufficient for work-identity. And what follows from this is a distinctively contextualist account of what it is for a sound-sequence-event to be a token of a work. As Levinson explains, for such a sound-event to count as a token of W at *all* (whether well-formed or otherwise), it must not merely have a certain acoustic character, but must bear a certain (presumably causal-intentional) relation to the *actual process* of W's composition that took place.[3]

Swimming against a strong intellectual current, the remainder of this book will see me arguing that a suitably nuanced sonicism can repel the challenge presented by both instrumentalism and contextualism. And my route to this conclusion will be via two claims. First, I shall present sonicism (or, more precisely, a version thereof) as the face-value theory when it

---

[2] Those who argue vigorously and ingeniously against sonicism from the perspective of instrumentalism include Stephen Davies (2001: 60–71), Godlovitch (1998), Levinson (1980*b*, 1990*a*, 1990*c*), and Walton (1988).

[3] For more on this, see Levinson (1990*c*: 249, 1980*a*: 98).

comes to the individuation of musical works. It is, I shall claim, the theory that we should accept unless it is defeated. Second, and crucially, I shall argue that the arguments offered by both instrumentalists and contextualists are insufficient to defeat it. To be sure, sonicism is unfashionable. But then again, aestheticians, of all people, should not be fashion victims.

8.2 Sonicism Motivated: Moderate Empiricism

Let us treat Σ as the set of properties normative within the *Hammerklavier*: the set of properties which a sequence of sounds must have to be a properly formed token of the piece. The sonicist, we have seen, takes these properties to be purely acoustic in nature: features concerning the pitch and duration of notes; melodic, harmonic, and articulational features; and such like. Such a view, I have claimed is *prima facie* correct. Why is this so? First of all, sonicism is acknowledged as the default position on the question of the individuation of works of music. This is the position from which we should be budged only by cogent argument. Indeed, it is worth noting that even sonicism's most eloquent opponents accept that there is something deeply intuitive about taking musical works to be pure types of sound-event: entities individuated along sonicist lines. As Levinson, a famous enemy of sonicism, puts it, 'the most natural and common proposal [in the ontology of music] is that a musical work is a *sound* structure—a structure, sequence, or pattern of sounds, pure and simple' (Levinson 1980b: 64). Now, such items, Levinson insists, are types, and, as we saw in §2.4, it can lead only to incoherence to follow Levinson in assuming that types have parts, which is why I have set up sonicism without any talk of 'sound structures' or the like. But whatever view we take on the ontological nature of types, Levinson's suggestion that sonicism is intuitive and natural is surely correct.

To see this, we should first of all note that someone unencumbered by developments in analytical aesthetics will surely insist—*pace* the contextualist—that two composers who produce identical scores compose the same work, *whatever the differences in the respective contexts in which they were working.* Having produced identical scores, the two composers provide performers with the same instructions for producing properly formed performances; and if performers must do *the same things* to produce a correct performance of the works, then those works are one and the same.

In the same vein, this time against the instrumentalist, our pre-theoretical intuitions have it that a performance of the *Hammerklavier* Sonata on a Perfect Timbral Synthesizer, indistinguishable to the ears from a performance on a piano, would be no less satisfactory a performance of the piece. True enough, if such a synthesizer were easier to play than a piano, we might think less of the *performer's achievement*, but the respective patterns of sounds the performers produced—*qua* representations of the piece—would surely be regarded as being on a par. After all, we would not be able to tell them apart. This being so, it would seem that our intuitions suggest that Σ does not include performance means-properties, and hence that the sonicist's account of what it is for W and W^* to be identical may stand.

But although this explanation of sonicism's status as the face-value theory is fine as far as it goes, it does not go far enough. As yet, all we have is a bald statement of our intuitions concerning the individuation of works of music; we have not yet been told what *grounds* these intuitions: what explains why we have them. This lacuna, however, can be filled relatively quickly. In my view, the intuitive appeal of sonicism consists in the fact that it follows from a highly natural account of musical appreciation, as I shall now explain.

The starting-point of this account is the *musical empiricism* that we met in §7.2.1: roughly speaking, the view that to appreciate a piece of music, we need only use our ears. The limits of musical appreciation, the empiricist claims, are what can be heard in the work, or derived from listening to it (Beardsley 1958: 31–2). Facts concerning the context in which the piece was composed are of art-historical interest, and perhaps shed light on the extent of the composer's achievement; and facts concerning how the sounds are actually produced enable us to determine the nature of the performer's achievement; but such facts as these play no role in determining a musical work's aesthetic value.

Such a theory, it seems to me, is enshrined in some of the responses typically made by ordinary listeners in a variety of situations. For example, a modern jazz *aficionado*, unimpressed by what seem to her to be the gauche and corny mannerisms of the New Orleans jazz of the 1920s, will not in the least be swayed on being told how contemporary jazz evolved from such music and how original and ground-breaking this earlier music was at the time. Such considerations, though they might make our modern jazz lover better disposed towards the *achievements* of the New Orleans jazz men, will be regarded by her as irrelevant to the question of its worth as *music*. What matters, she will argue, is how the music *sounds*; and to her it sounds crude and lacking in sophistication.

Our modern jazz lover, then, will not be swayed by appeals to matters art-historical. Nor should she be. In our ordinary discourse about music, we regard with suspicion those who change their opinion of a piece's aesthetic value after finding out who composed it and when. For example, as Kivy has mentioned (1987: 246), there is a prelude and chromatic fugue in E flat that was thought to be an early work of J. S. Bach, but was later discovered to have been a mature work of his cousin, J. C. Bach.[4] Now, someone who changed her mind about the work's aesthetic value upon finding out the true history of its composition would, I think, be regarded—by ordinary listeners, at least—as something of a cheat. To claim subsequently to discovering its true origin, and in contrast to one's earlier opinion, that the piece is powerful and complex would be to reveal oneself to have failed to examine the work on its own merits. Whether the piece was composed by the middle-aged J. C. Bach, or is a piece of J. S. Bach's 'juvenilia', is a question that should not be allowed to cloud our judgement of the work's aesthetic value.

Musical empiricism thus determines that our appreciation of a perform-ance of a musical work *as music* requires neither that we be cognizant of the way in which the sounds are produced, nor that we be able to place the work in its musico-historical context. But if this is right, and if we grant the highly plausible thesis that the nature of such works reflects our aesthetic practice, then sonicism results. If a work's sonic character alone determines its aesthetic properties, then works can only be pure types of sound-event: things individuated purely acoustically. A plausible thesis about our appreciation of music—musical empiricism—and a doctrine concerning the nature of works of music—sonicism—go hand in hand.

That said, clarification and reformulation must take place before musical empiricism can be allowed to stand. And to begin with, it has to be accepted that musical empiricism requires that we reinterpret the discourse of music criticism as it is done at the beginning of the twenty-first century. As David Davies has remarked, and as I noted in §7.3.3, if facts concerning a work's place in an *œuvre*, the composer's intentions, influences upon

---

[4] That is, Johann Christoph Bach (1642–1703), who is not to be confused with J. S. Bach's son, Johann Christian Bach (1735–82).

the composer, and the musical styles prevalent at the time the work was composed are irrelevant to a musical work's aesthetic merit, we thereby treat much of what is regarded as art criticism as biography (Davies 2004: 96). The empiricist insists upon a distinction between the aesthetic and the art-historical, so her point is that such contextual factors are of interest, if we are to tell the story of how a composer came to compose works with the character that they have, or to evaluate her achievement in doing so. But the empiricist nonetheless insists that to tell this story is to change the subject from giving an account of the aesthetic value of a composer's works.

True enough, to distinguish genuinely aesthetic value from both art-historical value and individual achievement value is to set one's face against the assumptions typically made by music critics. But two points need to be made at this juncture. First, the concept of music—which includes within it the concept of a musical work—is not owned by professional musical critics; it belongs to all of us. And what this means is that the theoretical beliefs of music critics—a small minority of the concept's constitu-ency—can be trumped by the practices of ordinary consumers of music. Second, to argue that much of what counts as music criticism is really art-historical is not to downplay its interest: the empiricist's point is merely that music critics misfile its interest as aesthetic. Of course, it is of great moment that a fugue assumed to be written by a youthful J. S. Bach was really composed by his cousin in his mature years; it is just that it is an important discovery concerning the history of music that should in no way change our view of the work's aesthetic merit.

Neither need the empiricist deny that knowledge of features deemed to be art-historical may help us to come to appreciate a work (Currie 1989: 21). The empiricist claims that a work's aesthetic properties can all be appreciated merely by listening to it (and to other works); she leaves it open that a subject's ability to recognize such features may be aided upon learning facts about the work's composition, its influence upon other composers, and the like. The melodic complexity of Charlie Parker's 'Relaxin' at the Camarillo' is there to be heard; but those who fail to appreciate it when they first hear it may come to fully discern it once they have been told, for instance, of the influence it had on later jazz musicians and of the difficulty that two high-class musicians, Wardell Gray and Howard McGhee, had in playing it in the celebrated Los Angeles session of February 1947. The empiricist denies that such facts themselves *justify* aesthetic judgements; she does not doubt that they can sometimes prompt the listener to make them.

As for art-historical features, so for knowledge of music theory. To hold, as does the empiricist, that the limits of the aesthetic are the limits of what can be heard is quite compatible with the fact that theoretical knowledge enables us to find things in what we hear that would be difficult to find otherwise. As Kivy explains, '[t]he ability to describe music in music-theoretic terms provides us with tools for distinguishing, in the musical object, events that are closed to the listener without such tools, (Kivy 2002: 83). One example should suffice. The ability to redescribe our experience of harmony music-theoretically enables a particular harmony's expressive effects to become evident. As Scruton observes, noticing 'the little gesture to the bass' that augments a D flat major chord in Art Tatum's 'Aunt Hagar's Blues' enables the musically literate listener to fully appreciate the way in which it 'reinforces an existing sense of lazy consonance and delicious relaxation' (Scruton 1997: 67). The totality of what is aesthetically valuable in a piece of music can be heard in it, but a knowledge of music theory enables us to hear more in a work than we would do otherwise.

My claim is thus that sonicism is enshrined in an independently plausible account of the nature of our appreciation of music: musical empiricism. But it is important to realize that musical empiricism's formulation requires amendment if it is truly to be defensible. First of all, it would be naïve to think that a work's aesthetic properties can be heard in it *simpliciter*. As David Davies has remarked (2004: 29), a property that is manifest to one person may be hidden from another: an auditor familiar with modern jazz, for example, may hear balance, intricate rhythm, and expressiveness in a piece that a jazz innocent hears as mere noise. Consequently, we need some way of specifying *to whom* a work's aesthetic properties are manifest. Second, as Frank Sibley has pointed out (1959: 314–22), a work's aesthetic properties are in some sense dependent upon, though not reducible to, its acoustic features. Whilst we justify an aesthetic judgement by making appeal to a work's non-aesthetic audible characteristics, 'there are no non-aesthetic features which serve in *any* circumstances as logically *sufficient conditions* for applying aesthetic terms' (Sibley 1959: 314). We cannot, for example, define what it is for a melody to be elegant using purely non-aesthetic vocabulary. However, since this is so, it behoves the empiricist to explain the precise nature of the relation obtaining between a work's aesthetic properties and the acoustic properties upon which the former depend.

Fortunately, both of these problems have a relatively simple solution. To begin with, we can follow Sibley (1959: 312), once more, in claiming that a work of music's aesthetic properties can be heard in it by those with the requisite *discriminative abilities* or, as he himself puts it, *taste*. The empiricist's position, properly formulated, is not that *just anyone* can hear the balance, intricacy, and expressiveness in a piece of modern jazz; it is that these qualities are there in the music to be heard by an auditor whose familiarity with the style of music has given her the requisite ability to hear it as it should be heard.

What, then, of the relation between a work's aesthetic properties and its acoustic properties? Here the empiricist will make a supervenience claim. That is to say, she will argue that two works with the same acoustic properties must have the same aesthetic properties: that two works cannot differ aesthetically unless they differ acoustically. More precisely, as Currie formulates it (1989: 23), if 'x' and 'y' range over works of music, and 'w' and 'u' range over possible worlds, then

(ST) $(\forall x)(\forall y)(\forall u)(\forall w)(x$ has the same acoustic properties in u as y has in $w \rightarrow x$ has the same aesthetic properties in u as y has in w).

This way, it is guaranteed that, as long as one listens to a work, and one has adequate discriminatory abilities, one can retrieve its aesthetic properties. The empiricist intuition remains standing.

There is, however, one final epicycle of objection and response that must be considered before musical empiricism becomes fit to be defensible. The objection in question, offered by Kendall Walton (1970), starts by introducing the notion of a *category* of art. An artistic category is determined by which features are *standard*, *variable*, and *contra-standard* within it. A feature F is *standard* with respect to a category C just in case a work's lacking F would (tend to) disqualify the work from counting as a C; F is *variable* with respect to C just in case whether a work is a C has nothing to do with whether or not it has F; and F is *contra-standard* with respect to C just in case an object's having F (tends to) disqualify a work from being a C (Walton 1970: 334–6). So, for example, the category *painting* is such that being two-dimensional is standard, having moving parts contra-standard, whilst a work's distribution of colour is variable within the category.

Now, it is Walton's contention that it is too simplistic to say that an artwork's aesthetic properties supervene upon its manifest properties (as (ST) suggests), since, when we assess the aesthetic merits of a work of art, we not only consider its manifest properties, but make a judgement relative to the *category* of artwork it falls under. In particular, Walton points out that our aesthetic assessment of a work is coloured by whether its manifest properties are standard or variable. Given that this is so, it is possible for two artworks to be indistinguishable with respect to their manifest properties, yet differ aesthetically. Such a difference occurs when two works, whilst sharing their manifest properties, differ with respect to whether one or more of these properties is standard or variable: in other words, when the two works differ with respect to the artistic categories they fall under.

Walton's own example of this phenomenon concerns a culture that does not go in for producing artworks of the kind we call 'paintings', but instead produces works of art termed 'guernicas'. Such items all look exactly like Picasso's painting of the same name when viewed from above, but may vary considerably with regard to their topology. Their surfaces, explains Walton (1970: 347), protrude from the wall 'like relief maps of different kinds of terrain'. Now let us compare Picasso's *Guernica* and an indistinguishable artwork produced as a totally flat guernica. Whilst Picasso's *Guernica* has its flatness as standard, the guernica's flatness is variable for it. And this has profound aesthetic implications (Walton 1970: 340). Picasso's *Guernica*—considered as a painting—is 'violent, dynamic, vital, disturbing to us' (1970: 347). The guernica, meanwhile, though it looks exactly like Picasso's painting, would be viewed by consumers of guernicas—even if they shared our tastes and sensibilities—as 'cold, stark, lifeless, or serene and restful, or perhaps bland, dull, boring—but in any case *not* violent, dynamic and vital' (1970: 340). The idea that the aesthetic supervenes merely on what is given in perception breaks down.

As for works of visual art, so for works of music. To come up with a counter-example to (ST), all we have to do is imagine a culture in which it is not musical works as we understand them that are composed, but, for instance, items that we might call 'chaconnes': works that would be taken by us to be instances of Bach's Chaconne movement from his Partita No. 2 for solo violin, and which do not vary amongst themselves in how they sound, but which differ according to the visual patterns invented by artists to accompany the playing of CD recordings on a computer screen. Now imagine that an ordinary CD recording of a performance of Bach's Chaconne is played on a computer and, without an accompanying pattern having been invented, the screen is a uniform black. Compare this with a sonically indistinguishable chaconne with an accompanying uniform black screen. As in Walton's example, artworks that share their manifest properties nonetheless diverge in their aesthetic properties. The chaconne is boring and dull, whilst Bach's Chaconne is anything but; and the reason why this is so is that the indistinguishable works have different properties as standard and variable and hence fall under different categories of art.

What does such a counter-example demonstrate? Not that musical empiricism is misconceived, but that it needs further modification. As Walton himself concludes, we should preserve the idea that 'sonatas are to be judged solely on what can be ... heard in them—when they are perceived correctly (i.e. in the correct category)' (1970: 354), but that our empiricism should be *moderate*, acknowledging that a work's aesthetic properties supervene on its acoustic properties *and* its category. In other words, we should replace (ST) with

(SM) $(\forall x)(\forall y)(\forall u)(\forall w)($($x$ has the same acoustic properties in u as y has in $w \wedge x$ and y fall under the same artistic category) $\rightarrow$ x has the same aesthetic properties in u as y has in w).

It is (SM) that is the defensible elaboration of the empiricist intuition with which we started. And such a position—moderate empiricism—still points us towards sonicism. For if a musical work's aesthetic properties depend purely upon how it sounds and the artistic category to which it belongs, and if matters of individuation track our appreciative practice, then neither the instrumentation specified in a work's score, nor the musico-historical context in which a work is composed, play a part in its individuation.[5]

---

[5] In fact, things are little more complicated than this, but, as it turns out, harmlessly so. Following the kind of move suggested by Walton himself (1970: 341–2), one might seek to make the case for a version of instrumentalism by making play with the very machinery of standard, variable, and contra-standard properties that is used to formulate moderate empiricism. Whilst accepting (SM), Walton nonetheless suggests that performance means-properties are standard with respect to certain categories of musical work, and hence that works of those categories can be properly performed only if the performers make use of certain kinds of instrumentation. He insists (1970: 341), e.g., that *being properly performable only by means of a piano* is standard relative to the category of 'piano sonata', and hence that any correctly formed token of the *Hammerklavier* should comprise sounds made by a piano. (I thank an anonymous reader for directing me to this passage.)

However, this argument for instrumentalism only goes through on the assumption that performance means-properties are indeed standard within works, and this, I think, is nothing but an alternative way

Of course, it would be wrong to suppose such musical empiricism, even in this moderate form, to command convergence among aestheticians. In fact, it is usually presented as a simple-minded theory: the first port of call for someone thinking about the nature of aesthetic appreciation before conclusive counter-examples compel her towards a more subtle position.[6] However, two things need to be remembered at this point. First, it is acknowledged, even by those who end up denying it, that moderate empiricism is the natural and pre-theoretically intuitive position to take on the question of the appreciation of music. Second, if the efforts of Currie are anything to go by,[7] the supposedly compelling arguments and puzzle-cases taken to demonstrate moderate empiricism's inadequacy should be taken with a pinch of salt. Indeed, we shall see both in this chapter and the next that the arguments designed both to disprove both sonicism and moderate empiricism, and to push us towards instrumentalism and contextualism, are unsound.

8.3   Instrumentation: *Timbral Sonicism* Introduced

For now, though, let us return to the question of a work's instrumentation. The sonicist claims that only acoustic properties are normative within works, and hence takes works to be identical just in case they have exactly the same *purely acoustic* properties normative within them. The instrumentalist, by contrast, argues that whether a sound-sequence is a properly formed token of W depends not only on how it sounds, but upon whether these sounds are produced by the instruments specified by the piece's composer. Consequently, the instrumentalist, unlike the sonicist, believes that performance means-properties are normative within works, and hence

---

of expressing the very crux of the dispute between the instrumentalist and the sonicist. Presumably, someone keen to make the case for performance means-properties being standard with respect to categories of musical work will appeal to precisely those considerations—i.e. the specification of instrumentation on scores, and the thesis that a work's aesthetic qualities depend upon specific instrumentation—that I go on to discuss (and reject) in the remainder of this chapter. One way of putting this chapter's main point is this: what is standard with respect to the category of 'piano sonata' is not the property *being properly performable only by means of a piano*, but that tokens of such sonatas should comprise piano-*like* sounds. It thus turns out that Waltonian arguments for instrumentalism are notational variants of the arguments propounded by Davies and Levinson that I discuss in §§8.4–8.5 below. Consequently, there is no need for us to revisit these arguments in their Waltonian guise.

[6] Philosophers who take this attitude include Currie (1989: Ch. 2) and David Davies (2004: Ch. 2).
[7] See the discussion in §7.2.1 above.

thinks that exact acoustic facsimiles will be numerically distinct if they were composed for different instruments. Which view is to be preferred?

Now, as we saw in §8.2, sonicism is itself a natural and intuitive theory, as well as being supported by a plausible and attractive view of aesthetic appreciation: moderate empiricism. But when it comes to the dispute the sonicist has with the instrumentalist, further weight may be lent to the sonicist's cause by considering how well it coheres with a plausible account of the nature of musical experience. Roger Scruton describes our musical experience as *acousmatic* (1997: 2−3); and what he means by this is that, in hearing sounds as music, we attend purely to the sounds themselves, and not to their causal origin. Scruton believes that our experience of sounds as music sees us detach these sounds from the circumstances of their production, and hear them as organized according to pitch, rhythm, melody, and harmony (1997: 20). We hear the sequence of sounds as an organized whole, something that develops and progresses, so that, rather than focusing on the fact that a middle C is produced by an oboe, for example, we hear it as the response to the B that preceded it, and as calling for the E that follows it (Scruton 1997: 19). For Scruton, although we *happen* to conceive of the constituent sounds of a musical performance in terms of their characteristic causes, in principle a purely qualitative description would do just as well.

Obviously, if this view of our musical experience is correct, instrumentalism takes on a hugely uncompulsory air. For if hearing the music as it ought to be heard requires us to attend merely to its qualitative nature, and not to the ways in which the sounds are produced, then nothing about the nature of our musical experience threatens to dislodge us from the default position that is sonicism. Having said this, Scruton's account of our experience of music is flawed. For, as we have seen, he believes the only essential features of our musical experience to be *organizational* features: pitch, rhythm, harmony, and melody. As a result, he comes to regard timbre as an inessential feature of our musical experience, even though he accepts that it can contribute to musical meaning (1997: 77). In my view this is a mistake: timbral properties, as we shall see in a moment, are normative within works, for the reason that their presence determines many of a work's aesthetic properties; so, even though timbre is not itself an organizational feature of sound-sequences, an appreciation of timbre is essential to our experience of sounds as music.

What follows, if we depart from Scruton's position this way? As Scruton himself notes (1997: 77), timbral features are specified by reference to their customary origin: if we are to avoid recourse to metaphor, we have no choice but to conceive of a certain timbre as 'the sound of a middle C played on an oboe', for example. Consequently, it follows that Scruton is wrong in thinking that our musical experience can always be described *without making any reference* to sounds' usual origin. But, as it happens, this turns out to be a relatively small amendment, for what we might term a *modified acousmatic* account of our musical experience is still compatible with a denial of instrumentalism. Whilst it is true that we must make reference to certain sounds' usual causal origin in order to put our finger on their timbral aspects, and thereby properly appreciate the work performed, what does *not* follow from this is that we need be *cognizant* of the sounds' *actual* origin; and this leaves it open for these sounds to have been produced by non-standard means. We do 'not have to identify [the sounds'] cause in order to hear them as they should be heard' (Scruton 1997: 3); we need only *characterize* them in terms of their customary means of production.[8]

---

[8] But why, it might be objected, need an audience think of a sound as, say, *an oboe-like middle C*, if sonicism is true? Once sonicism is assumed, and it is held that a work could be properly performed using perfect timbral synthesizers rather than oboes, it might seem mysterious why an audience should have to think of the sound in terms of its customary origin in order to properly appreciate the said work. In principle, at least, someone could surely appreciate the performance properly, yet think of the sound using some other, purely qualitative, vocabulary.

Well, the response to this concern is point out, as we shall see in §8.5, that our appreciation of many of a work's aesthetic and expressive qualities depends precisely upon our conceptualizing sounds in terms of their customary origin. To pick up on a piece's insouciant quality, e.g., we may well have to imagine a run of tones as a genuine *glissando*: i.e., as a series of sounds produced by a *flicking gesture* on a piano. To appreciate the music's insouciance, we must hear the gesture in the music, and this requires us to imagine the sounds to have been produced with that particular gesture.

One response to this kind of move will be discussed in §8.6, but is worth highlighting now. It might be alleged that what I have said serves only to undermine the thought that a work's aesthetic properties are genuinely (i.e. objectively) possessed by it. For if hearing a work's aesthetic qualities requires us to think of a performance's constituent sounds in a particular way, and yet there is an alternative, and equally acceptable, way of thinking about these sounds (i.e purely qualitatively) that does not enable auditors to hear these perceptual qualities in the work, then the said properties are not genuinely possessed by the work at all.

For the time being, I shall just say this: that properties only detectable by certain kinds of perceiver, and detectable because such perceivers occupy a particular *point of view* on the world, may yet be objective in the sense that matters to us. A work's aesthetic qualities are response-dependent, and it is the responses of sensitive listeners (i.e. listeners classed as such *by our own standards*) that enter into such qualities' analysis. To put their finger on tone colours, such listeners conceptualize sounds in terms of their customary origin: a way of thinking about sounds that constitutes a cosmically parochial point of view on them. This, however, in no way impugns the idea that the aesthetic qualities uncovered as a result of thinking of sounds in this way are genuinely possessed by the object. Such properties are, indeed, defined as the kinds of properties that sensitive listeners—i.e., listeners counted as such by *us*—are liable to detect in works. But, first of all, '[i]t is pointless to chafe at the fact that what we believe is what *we* believe' (McDowell 1983: 14); and, second, it remains the case such qualities are

And if this is right, and if we grant the highly plausible thesis that how a musical work should be heard is revelatory of its ontological character, then our modified acousmatic account of the nature of musical experience strongly suggests that we need go no further than sonicism. In order for an audience to hear a performance as it ought to be heard, the performers need not use certain specific instruments; they need only produce sounds that *seem* as if they have been produced by such instruments.

Be this as it may, the sonicist is obliged to explain what she takes the 'auditory character' definitive of a work's identity to consist in. *Which* acoustic properties comprise set Σ: the set of properties normative within *W*? According to the view that Stephen Davies calls 'pure sonicism' (2001: 60), the members of Σ are the sorts of properties one would expect—melodic, rhythmic, harmonic, articulational, tempic properties, and the like—but with one notable exception: timbral properties. On such a view, a performance of the *Hammerklavier* would be in no way defective if produced on a Hammond organ, as long as the resultant sound sequence had the tonal structure and other (non-timbral) acoustic properties indicated by its score. In my view, though, such a position is too extreme to be acceptable. Indeed, as I shall now explain, it is implausible in itself, inadequately motivated, and subject to a serious objection. However, an appreciation of pure sonicism's demerits opens up the possibility of there being a version of the doctrine that avoids these pitfalls.

That the pure form of sonicism is counter-intuitive (almost) goes without saying. A performance of the *Hammerklavier* on a Hammond organ or, perhaps, by a flute quartet,[9] might capture the piece's tonal make-up, but such a performance would ignore the specification of a piano in the score. As I shall argue presently, the fact that a score instructs performers to use specific instrumentation does not entail that a properly formed performance *must* use the instruments specified. Such an instruction is essentially context-bound and provisional, its purpose being that of instructing performers how to produce a properly formed sound-sequence *given the instruments available at the time*. The goal of such an instruction—the production of sound-sequences of a certain qualitative character—would be met even if such a sound sequence were produced without such instrumental instructions

---

genuinely *discoverable* in works by us. This, it seems to me, is sufficient for such qualities to be regarded as objective.

[9] This example is Levinson's (1990c: 240).

having been followed. Having said this, Beethoven's specification of a piano on the score of the *Hammerklavier does* at least demonstrate that a correctly formed performance of the piece should be constituted by *piano-like* sounds. His scoring of the piece for piano was not completely arbitrary; in specifying a piano, he was making it clear that performances of it would be inadequate if constituted by the kinds of sounds made by organs, violins, or flutes. The fact that Beethoven specified that a piano be used, whilst not entailing that *being produced by a piano* is normative within the work, *does* serve to characterize the qualitative nature of the sounds that must constitute a proper instance. Such sounds should have the timbral quality typical of sounds produced by such an instrument.

Saying this, of course, serves merely to invite the sonicist to retreat from the pure version of the doctrine to its timbral counterpart. As Levinson has noted, it is a decisive objection against pure sonicism that it renders some of a composer's choices—for instance, trumpet or oboe, or bassoon or cello—motiveless and arbitrary (Levinson 1990c: 244). But the timbral sonicist precisely avoids this charge by ensuring that timbral properties *are* normative within musical works. Elsewhere, Levinson recognizes that timbral properties, though generally specified via performance means-properties, are in principle 'physically and logically separable from them' (1990c: n. 9); and an appreciation of this possibility enables us to formulate the weaker, timbral version of sonicism that can account for the importance of the choices that composers, in practice, make.

It is true, of course, that a performance of the *Hammerklavier* on a Hammond organ would still be recognizable as a performance of the piece; and this, perhaps, is the source of the pull that pure sonicism exerts over some philosophers.[10] But, having set out the type/token theory in the way in which I have, such a motivation for this version of sonicism is swiftly revealed to be misconceived. A performance using the Hammond organ could, indeed, count as a performance of the piece; but acknowledging that this is so is quite compatible with recognizing that a *properly formed* performance must be made up of piano-like sounds. A work of music is a norm-type, remember: its identity is determined by the properties that are normative within it. Consequently, the mere fact that there could be a performance of the *Hammerklavier* on a Hammond organ (if such a performance had a

---

[10] Over Kivy, for example (1988: 55).

sufficient number of the other properties normative within the work) does not demonstrate that timbral qualities are not members of Σ. It is a familiar fact that a work may have instances that are improperly formed. After all, that there can be performances (albeit imperfect ones) of the piece that miss out certain passages, play wrong notes, or misconstrue the rhythm does not show that a properly formed token of the work should not have these features.

Pure sonicism is thus an undermotivated doctrine. But it also faces a decisive objection whose origin lies in the work of Levinson (1980b: 73–8). For Levinson draws our attention to the fact that many of a work's aesthetic and expressive properties depend upon their timbral, in addition to their more broadly sonic, features.[11] The *Hammerklavier*, Levinson notes, is a 'sublime, craggy and heaven-storming piece of music' (1980b: 76), but a sound-sequence would fail to represent it as such if it were produced by a Hammond organ or (worse still) by a recorder ensemble.[12] Likewise, John Cage's *In a Landscape* would lose much of its gentle, exploratory, contemplative character, if played on a trombone. What examples such as these reveal is that a properly formed performance of a piece—one that, among other things, does justice to the work's aesthetic content—must have a specific timbral character. It is insufficient merely for such a performance to be properly formed with respect to its other audible features.

This being so, it is my contention that a philosopher appreciative of sonicism's status as the face-value theory, yet sensitive to the problems besetting sonicism in its purest form, must adopt timbral sonicism. But, be this as it may, the instrumentalist insists that a proper understanding of the role played by scores, and of the features determinative of a work's aesthetic content, reveals that performance means-properties, as against merely timbral properties, are normative within the types that are works of music. In the next two sections I explain why such a conclusion is unwarranted.

8.4 Scores

As we have seen, the crux of the dispute between the timbral sonicist and the instrumentalist concerns whether performance means-properties are normative within works. If they are, then, *pace* timbral sonicism, a work

---

[11] The distinction between aesthetic and expressive properties is outlined in §9.3 below.

[12] The latter example is Stephen Davies's (2001: 64).

W and a Work *W** may be exact acoustic sound-alikes, yet numerically distinct (if they differ with respect to the performance means-properties normative within them). Consequently, given timbral sonicism's status as the face-value theory of musical works' individuation, we need to consider whether the instrumentalist's arguments for performance means-properties being normative within works are sufficiently strong to warrant our giving up what amounts to the default position.

The first such argument concerns the nature of a work's score. And indeed, it might be supposed that the line taken in the previous section inadvertently leads us towards such an argument. In §8.3 I charged the pure sonicist with disregarding the fact that composers specify the use of certain instruments to produce sounds. Could it not be argued that this manœuvre equally demonstrates the falsehood of even timbral sonicism? Does not such an appeal to the specification of instruments in scores throw one directly into the arms of instrumentalism? Levinson, for one, thinks that it does. In his view, scores are definitive of musical works, and so, if Beethoven's Quintet Op. 15 calls for a clarinet to be played, this means that 'the Quintet Op. 15 without a clarinet is not the same piece—even if all sound-structural characteristics (including timbre) are preserved' (1980*b*: 75). Levinson's point, in other words, is that Beethoven's specification of a clarinet means that the work essentially involves the clarinet, and hence that a sound-event cannot be a properly formed instance of the piece unless a clarinet has been used in the production of the sounds. If Levinson is right, *being produced by a clarinet* is normative within the work.[13]

However, as I explained briefly in §8.3, this way of understanding the instrumental instructions in scores is not obligatory. Indeed, the best way to make sense of the fact, for example, that the *Hammerklavier*'s score calls for a piano is to see this *apparently* exceptionless instruction as having an altogether more provisional nature. A work's score specifies how a sound-sequence-event must sound if it is to be a properly formed instance of the work; and the instruction to use certain instrumentation should be seen in this context: as exclusively serving the aim of facilitating the production of sound-sequence-events with certain specific timbral features. True enough, the *Hammerklavier*'s score contains an instruction to produce such sounds *in*

---

[13] This position is endorsed by Currie, who claims that '[a] performance that violates the composer's directions as to how the sounds are to be produced is not a correct performance of it' (1989: 49).

certain specific ways, that is, by means of a piano. But this in no way entails that a properly formed performance *must* involve the specified instrumentation, as opposed to some other aurally indistinguishable means of sound production. For this instruction was aimed at a particular *constituency*—namely, potential performers of the piece at the time the piece was composed—and is wholly in the service of the production of sound-sequence-events of a certain qualitative nature. In short, the score was instructing performers in 1818 to use a piano simply because no other means of producing sounds with the requisite timbral features existed at that time. However, since the purpose of such an instruction was merely to specify the tone colour that must be had by a well-formed instance of the work, it is an instruction that can, in principle, be overruled as long as sounds with the right timbral qualities are produced.

A predictable objection to this is to point out that composers often *believe* their own instrumental instructions to have the status of exceptionless instructions for performers. It may well be the case, for instance, that Beethoven, had he been given the choice, would have preferred, for whatever reason, a performance of the *Hammerklavier* on the piano to one that made use of a Perfect Timbral Synthesizer. But the important point is that such a consideration cuts little ice against the timbral sonicist's arguments. Convinced by her doctrine's status as the default position, and impressed by the way in which it coheres with the modified acousmatic account of our musical experience, the timbral sonicist concludes that performance means-properties cannot be normative within works, and hence that instrumental specifications in scores should be interpreted in the alternative way suggested.

Indeed, it seems to me that our objector may well have been misled by a misunderstanding of the sonicist's claim about the instrumental specifications in scores. That such specifications serve solely to characterize the qualitative nature of the sounds constituting a properly formed occurrence of works is not a *psychological* claim concerning the nature of composers' intentions; it is a claim concerning how such specifications should be *interpreted* in the light of well-grounded philosophical theory concerning both the individuation of works of music and the nature of our musical experience. The timbral sonicist denies that the proper way to perform a work can simply be read off from the composer's actual (or hypothetical) preferences, and hence allows that composers can misconstrue their own works.

Naturally, saying this will not of itself placate the instrumentalist. Stephen Davies, for example, would be tempted to reply by drawing our attention to the kinds of scores that seem especially concerned with the production of sounds on specific kinds of instrument. One such example is provided by sixteenth-century lute tablature, in which the notation tells the performer where to place his or her hands on the neck of the lute. Such a score, Davies suggests, can only be '[i]nstrument specific. Rather than thinking of his piece as an abstract sound structure and being indifferent to the manner of realizing it, [the composer] is addressing himself expressly to a musician who is holding a lute in his hands' (Davies 2001: 62). But such an example provides no new challenge to the timbral sonicist. Right enough, the producer of such a score addresses himself to someone holding a lute, but it does not follow from this that a properly formed token of the piece must be produced by a lute rather than by an artefact that produces lute-like sounds. The same kind of response as before suffices to make the point: although the composer addresses himself to lute players, his instructions are (punningly) to be interpreted instrumentally;[14] they function merely as a means for specifying the qualitative nature of the sounds that performers must produce. So, given that sounds with such a qualitative nature could also be produced by non-lutes, a performer may ignore *the letter* of the score's instrument-specific instructions, just as long as she is able to produce sounds indistinguishable from those produced by a lute player. Whether he recognizes it or not, how the sounds are produced is only of practical, *de facto* interest to the composer: an interest in performance means subserves the aim of specifying the acoustic appearance of the sounds themselves.

Levinson makes a similar objection to Davies's, but, ultimately, to no greater effect. Levinson too objects to the sonicist's conception of a score as a recipe for providing an instance of a type of sound-event *for its own sake*. As he sees it, '[w]hen Beethoven writes a middle C for the oboe, he has done more than require an oboelike sound at a certain pitch—he has called for such a sound as emanating from that quaint reed we call an "oboe"' (1980b: 74). And one reason why Levinson takes this line is that he believes it to be the only position that makes sense of the way in which composers actually think of the sounds that they wish to see produced. As he himself puts it:

Composers are familiar with tone colors only insofar as they are familiar with instruments that possess them. We do not find composers creating pure combinations of tone color, and then later searching about for instruments that can realize

---

[14] This joke is Kivy's (1988: 85).

or approximate these aural canvasses; it would obviously be pointless or at least frustrating to do so. (Levinson 1980b: 74)

To my mind, though, this objection sees Levinson mistaking an epistemological fact for a metaphysical one. For that a work's composer *describes* the kinds of sounds he wants produced by referring to their customary origins does not entail that only sounds with such origins can figure in a correct performance. A timbral sonicist, I noted in §8.3, *accepts* that sounds must be thought of in terms of their customary origin, if their timbral aspects are to be characterized. What she *denies* is that this connection *in thought* between sound and customary origin need *actually obtain* for a performance to be properly formed. As we have just seen, there is a defensible interpretation of scores available to the timbral sonicist, according to which instrumental specifications serve merely as a means for characterizing how correct performances should *sound*. In the light of this, pointing out what we all know—namely, that we think of tone colours by means of thinking of their customary origin—is beside the point.

Once this response has been made, Levinson's attempts to bolster what we might call *the argument from scores* against timbral sonicism are doomed. No doubt, he is right to point out that composers often conceive of a use of instrumentation prior to conceiving of pure types of sound: double-stopping is an example of this, as is pizzicato. We may agree with Levinson that 'ideas for pizzicato passages do not first occur to composers and then, only later, what will serve, for the nonce, to realize them' (1990c: 244). But, to reiterate, this evident fact does not have the implications for the conditions of correct performance that Levinson takes it to have. That a work's composer conceives of sounds in terms of their customary origin does not entail that a correct performance of the work incorporating such sounds should see them actually have that origin.

What, then, is left of the instrumentalist's appeal to the authority of scores? Not much. One might try to bolster it by adopting what Stan Godlovitch describes as a 'socio-historical perspective' on the question (1998: 56). According to Godlovitch, once one understands that musical communities are akin to guilds—defining their own conditions for membership and rank—one comes to appreciate that such communities will automatically be hostile to the idea of performing the *Hammerklavier* upon a Perfect Timbral Synthesizer, even if such a performance were an exact acoustic replica of a performance on a piano. Guilds, reports Godlovitch, 'systematically resist instrumental innovations in order to preserve their own structure which requires the establishment and maintenance of a skill hierarchy based on handicaps legitimised by the Guild' (1998: 53). According to the music-making establishment, then, the value of a performance is not determined simply by how it sounds, but by how it is achieved. In particular, the performer must demonstrate skill in overcoming the handicaps presented by playing the piece on the kind of instrument sanctioned by the musical community (Godlovitch 1998: 57).

Now, I see no need to disagree with any of this. Godlovitch, it seems to me, makes a convincing case for his sociological account of the values held dear by musical communities. But we need to be clear that such a descriptive account of how music-making communities come to the opinions that they do on matters of instrumentation can in no way support a philosophical thesis concerning the individuation of works of music. That the practice of musicians embodies a commitment to instrumentalism does not entail that this doctrine is correct. To make good this latter thesis, we need to come up with sound philosophical arguments, not a sociology of belief. Merely reporting the beliefs embedded in musical practice does not help us decide whether these beliefs are true.

Having abandoned such a sociological approach, it might be tempting to try to buttress the argument from scores by arguing that the norm of authenticity demands that performers use the instruments specified by the composer. As Stephen Davies sees it, '[i]f the composer determinatively instructs that certain instruments should be used, they must be played if the performance is to be fully authentic' (2001: 69). And Davies thinks this because he believes that there exist conventions in music that necessarily connect the scored sounds with the specified instrumentation:

[I]mprovisation, the creation of works, the public specification of works, the performance of works, the reception of works—all these assume, involve, and rely on practices and conventions, some of which are predominantly musical and others which have more to do with social structures and purposes. As a result, connections that otherwise might be merely contingent take on a different status because they become normative within the relevant practice. ... Within the relevant practices, playing the appropriate instruments is not merely a useful means to the production of the desired result, which is supposedly the creation of an abstract sound structure. Instead, the use of those instruments is part of the end, which is to articulate the specified sound structure on the required instruments. To do otherwise is to 'cheat' and thereby to undermine the playing's status as a performance. (S. Davies 2001: 64–5)

I remain unconvinced, however. For one thing, and as I have explained already, the composer's instruction to use certain instruments can be viewed as provisional. To be true to the piece, a performer need only produce sounds with the same timbral features as sounds produced using the specified instruments. Authenticity in performance is, indeed, a *desideratum*, but what I am suggesting is that the features required for a performance to be authentic cannot simply be read off from the score in the way in which Davies suggests. The simple specification that a piano be used, for example, must be *interpreted* in the light of two things: the fact that (timbral) sonicism is the face-value theory when it comes to the question of the relation between works of music and the instrumentation specified in their scores; and the fact that this theory coheres with our overarching account of the nature of our musical experience.

Davies would, I expect, remain unsatisfied by this. Indeed, at this point he would surely seek to press his claim that the conventions and practices underlying the making and appreciation of music give composers, performers, and listeners an interest in how sounds are produced, not just in their qualitative appearance. But the case that Davies presents as an example of such a convention is nothing of the kind, as we shall now see. Davies claims that we regard a performer who uses alternative instrumentation to that specified in the score as having *cheated*, and that such a decision on the part of the performer undermines the playing's status as a performance (2001: 65). This claim, though, needs careful handling. To begin with, the timbral sonicist, by contrast with his pure sibling, will agree that a performance of a piece on instruments that produce sounds of a different tone colour to those produced by the specified instruments is inauthentic and deficient. So let us focus on a case in which the instrumentalist's and the timbral sonicist's positions diverge: our imagined example in which the *Hammerklavier* is performed on a Perfect Timbral Synthesizer. Davies argues that such a performance would be a less adequate performance of the piece than a sonically indistinguishable performance making use of a piano; and he takes this to be demonstrated by the fact that we would regard the performer of the synthesized performance as having cheated in some way.

As a matter of fact, it seems to me that we can distinguish *two* kinds of case here, neither of which has the implications that Davies believes it to have. In the first kind of case, the synthesized performance is produced with the aim of *deceiving* the audience into thinking that a piano has been used. Clearly, in this case, if we discovered the deception, we would, indeed, regard the performer as having cheated; but, equally, the source of our resentment would not be that the performer had misrepresented the piece by playing it on a synthesizer, but that the performer had, in effect, lied to us about what she was doing. In the second kind of case, by contrast, the audience is well aware that the performer is using a synthesizer, but is also aware that such an instrument is easier to play than the piano, thus making the performer's task less demanding than is usual. Here too we might regard the performer as having *cheated*, but, once more, our sense of having been short-changed does not have its origin in such a performance's being inauthentic; this time, the audience would feel cheated because the performer had not been tested to the degree that other performers of the piece, using conventional instrumentation, have been. In this instance, the performer's decision to use a synthesizer does, indeed, 'undermine the playing's status as a performance' (Davies 2001: 65); but, once more, this is not because such a performance lacks authenticity, but because the performer's feat is less impressive than it would have been had traditional instrumentation been employed.

So my point is this: although we could feel cheated by synthesized performances, the fact that this is so is explicable in ways that do not entail the truth of instrumentalism. At this juncture, Davies may seek to reply by insisting that there is a possible case of our feeling cheated by a synthesized performance that I have not considered, and that *does* entail the falsehood of timbral sonicism. He might, in other words, claim that we would still feel cheated by a synthesized sonic doppelgänger of an acknowledged authentic performance of the Hammerklavier even if we were aware of the sounds' causal origin and even if such an instrument were as difficult to play as a piano. But I simply deny that we would feel in any sense cheated by such a performance. The performance would be a sound-sequence indistinguishable from a performance on a piano; and it would make demands of the performer that are on a par with the demands faced by pianists. What would there be for an audience to feel resentful about? Short of simply begging the question, I cannot see a reply for Davies here. There is no case in which our sense of having been cheated by a synthesized performance tells against timbral sonicism.

8.5 Instrumentation, Artistic Properties, and Aesthetic Content

So much for variants of the argument from scores. They by no means force us to admit that performance means-properties are normative within works, and hence do nothing to undermine the timbral sonicist's identity criterion. The timbral sonicist is not yet home and dry, however. For an instrumentalist may also argue for her position by claiming that *a performance's transmission of a work's aesthetic content and artistic import* requires not only that it *sound* a certain way, but that the sounds be *produced* in a certain way. Arguing along these lines, and in such a manner as to simultaneously attack sonicism and moderate aesthetic empiricism, Levinson claims that a work's aesthetic content and artistic properties are 'determined not only by its sound structure ... but also in part by the actual means of production chosen for making that structure audible' (Levinson 1980*b*: 76). According to Levinson, the kind of thinking about the determination of aesthetic content that prompted my move from pure to timbral sonicism ultimately commits us to instrumentalism; so, if he is right, the line cannot be held where the timbral sonicist wishes to hold it. A consideration of what is required of a performance, if it is to transmit a work's aesthetic and artistic content, reveals that performance means-properties—and not just acoustic properties—are normative within works. And this can only mean that—contrary to the sonicist's identity criterion—there can be numerically distinct works that are acoustic facsimiles of each other.

Some examples should help Levinson's style of argumentation to stick. First, consider Paganini's Caprice, Op. 1, No. 17. This piece, Levinson claims, has the artistic property of being virtuosic and, hence, a correct performance of it should have a virtuosic quality too. But, argues Levinson, such a performance could only have this quality, if it made use of a violin:

if we did not conceive of the Caprice No. 17 as essentially for the violin, as inherently a *violin piece* (and not just a *violin sounding piece*) then it would not merit that attribution. For, as executed by a computer or by some novel string instrument using nonviolinistic technique, its sound structure might not be particularly difficult to get through. (Levinson 1980*b*: 77)

For Levinson, then, the Caprice, Op. 1, No. 17, is virtuosic, but a performance could only transmit this artistic quality, if the sounds were actually produced by a violin rather than by some kind of violin-substitute.

As for artistic properties, so for aesthetic and expressive properties. For according to Levinson,

> The aesthetic qualities of the *Hammerklavier* Sonata depend in part upon the strain that its sound structure imposes on the sonic capabilities of the piano; if we are not hearing its sound structure *as* produced by a piano, then we are not sensing this strain, and thus our assessment of aesthetic content is altered. (Levinson 1980b: 76–7)

And the same goes, if Levinson is right, for works' expressive content too. Mozart's Serenade in E flat, K. 375, begins with a passage which has an 'assertive, attention-getting quality' (Levinson 1990a: 396); and, Levinson contends, the reason why the piece's opening has this expressive content is that the sounds produced by the winds have a *honking* aspect: that is to say, air is forced through narrow openings in tubes in the same way as that in which a goose—a literal honker—forces air though its windpipe (Levinson 1990a: 396). Now, according to Levinson, in order to appreciate the passage's assertive content, the audience must hear the sounds *as* honkings; but they can only do this, if they hear these sounds *as produced* in the way in which honkings are produced; which is to admit that the passage's expressive content is dependent upon its being played by wind instruments and not, for example, by Perfect Timbral Synthesizers:

> Would those sounds—i.e. those produced on the Perfect Timbral Synthesizer—*be* a honking in the quasi-literal sense in which the accented outputs of oboes and clarinets are such? I suggest not. If it is aesthetically appropriate to take sounds in performance for what they are, and not for what they aren't, and if the opening's particular assertiveness is partly a matter of its properly coming across as a honking, in the sense described, then part of the aesthetic character of that opening is distorted or undercut if the performing means that Mozart directly specifies are bypassed and only the resulting sound (or timbral complex) that he indirectly specifies is adhered to. (Levinson 1990a: 396–7)

So, if Levinson is to be believed, it turns out that *being performed using wind instruments* is normative within the piece because a performance on Perfect

Timbral Synthesizers would fail to produce genuine honking sounds at the piece's beginning, and hence would fail to deliver the assertive content that Mozart intended.

Needless to say, further examples of this kind are easily constructed. The appreciation of a piece's expressive content, so it is claimed, requires us to hear passages as making musical gestures akin to human expressions of emotion: we must hear phrases as *sighing*, *crashing*, *booming*, or such like (Levinson 1990a: 399–401). But in Levinson's view, in order to hear gestures in music, one must hear the sounds produced *as* made with the relevant gestures; and this, in turn, requires that the sounds really *are* produced by means of an instrument with which such gestures can be made.[15] Hence, if a work is to be performed properly, such a performance must not merely perfectly ape the sounds made by the specified instrumentation; it must use those very instruments to produce those sounds.

So how should a timbral sonicist reply? Two points need to be made at this stage. First, and contrary to the spin that Levinson himself occasionally places on these examples, they cannot of themselves demonstrate a work's instrumentation to be *essential* to it. Even if it is shown, for example, that a performance of Paganini's Caprice No. 17 can only transmit the work's aesthetic content if its constituent sounds are produced on a violin, it would only follow that the work essentially involves the violin if a work's aesthetic content were essential to it, and this is a thesis that Levinson does not defend (1990c: 221–2). At best, then, the examples can demonstrate only that performance means-properties are normative within works, not that they are so normative in each possible world in which the works in question exist.

Having made this point, such examples are still a threat to the sonicist's account of the identity conditions of musical works, of course. The sonicist's distinctive claim is that acoustic properties alone are normative within works, so she repudiates the suggestion that a properly formed performance of the Caprice, for example, must make use of a violin. However, and this is my second point, Levinson's examples do not even show this much, as we shall now see.

[15] One example of this putative phenomenon should suffice. Drums can contribute a *pounding* or *battering* content to passages of music; and one might be tempted to follow Levinson (1990a: 400) in supposing that this expressive content can only be fully transmitted if the sounds are actually made with a pounding or battering gesture.

To begin with, let us focus on Levinson's argumentative strategy. For Levinson takes his discussion of his various examples to demonstrate the truth of the following claim: that it is a necessary condition of a work W's having certain aesthetic, expressive, or artistic properties that certain performance means-properties are normative within W. In other words, he points to certain features that works are taken to have indisputably, and then claims that works can have these features only if performance means-properties are normative within such works. However, in what follows I argue that Levinson's examples are insufficient to justify this claim. To this end, my strategy will be disjunctive. First of all, I shall argue that the kinds of artistic properties to which Levinson appeals are not genuinely possessed by works at all. When it comes to artistic (i.e. art-historical or achievement) properties, I thus precisely deny the thesis whose presumed truth supposedly requires instrumentalism to be true. Aesthetic and expressive properties, on the other hand, certainly *are* genuinely possessed by works of music; but in this case, my complaint against Levinson is that his examples do not demonstrate that a work's having such a property is genuinely contingent upon performance means-properties (as opposed to merely timbral properties) being normative within it.

Let us start by considering artistic properties and, in particular, by returning to Levinson's own example. Paganini's Caprice, Op. 1, No. 17, he says, deserves the attribution 'virtuosic', and hence a performance, if it is to do justice to the piece's virtuosic quality, must make use of the violin rather than, say, a sonically indistinguishable instrument that, perhaps, demanded less of a performer. But I think that the starting-point of Levinson's discussion of this example—namely, his presumption that the work literally possesses the property *being virtuosic*—should simply be denied by a sonicist. True enough, a *performance* may be virtuosic (if the performer plays a violin rather than a space-age sound-alike that is easier to play); but a sonicist will not accept that *being virtuosic* is normative within the *work*: that is, that *any* well-formed performance should be virtuosic. For, since the sonicist takes the Caprice to be a pure type of sound-event—a type whose normative properties are all acoustic in nature—she thereby repudiates the suggestion that a property concerning how sounds are *produced*, as opposed to their qualitative nature, can be normative within it. Of course, *if* it were true that the piece itself were virtuosic, it would follow that it should only be played on an instrument that required technical excellence of the performer. But it is the antecedent of this conditional that no self-respecting sonicist will accept. It is *performances* of works that can be virtuosic, not the works themselves.

A similar response can be made to other putative examples of the same kind. Levinson asks us to imagine a piece written for violin to be played in such a way as to make certain passages sound as if they were played by a flute. Would not this piece, by contrast with a sonically indistinguishable piece written for violin and flute, be *original* and *unusual*? And would not this demonstrate that a correct performance of the former piece—one that preserved its artistic import—would have to be played on the violin alone (Levinson 1980b: 77–8)? But to this we can make what is essentially the same reply as before, albeit with a slightly different twist. Once again, Levinson's mistake is to suppose that a sonicist will agree that *works themselves* possess artistic properties such as unusualness and originality. Since the sonicist takes works to be pure types of sound-event, she denies that they can be analytically tied to instruments at all, and hence repudiates the idea that such works can themselves be unusual by virtue of involving surprising instrumentation. By contrast, a sonicist will insist that it is *composers and their compositional acts* that, strictly speaking, have the artistic properties concerned. What is unusual and original in Levinson's example is not the work itself, but a particular composer's scoring of such a work for solo violin rather than for violin and flute. The work itself is a pure sound-event-type, and hence cannot have properties such as these.[16]

One thing is clear, however: the same sonicist strategy will not work for examples taken to illustrate the fact that performance means-properties are

---

[16] David Davies (in correspondence) has alleged that this account of the predication of 'unusual' is implausible. In his view, if timbral sonicism is correct, and if the proper function of the instrumental specification in scores is merely that of identifying the timbral qualities that a sound-event must have in order to be a properly formed token of the work, then the actions of Levinson's hypothetical composer—in scoring a work for violin imitating flute—are not so much unusual as *bizarre*. There could, Davies contends, be no *point* to scoring the work in this way, if timbral sonicism were true.

In my view, such an objection is misconceived. The hypothetical composer may, e.g., score the work for violin imitating flute because he wishes to set the performer a challenge: that of sounding as flute-like as possible. Such an ambition is rational, not bizarre. The key point, however, is that this challenge *need not be taken up* by performers who see their business as being that of producing a properly formed performance that thereby transmits the full extent of the work's aesthetic content. A performance involving violin and flute would do just as well in this regard. The composer himself may, of course, *believe* his instrumental specification to lay down a genuine condition of correctness in performance, but he would be wrong about this for the sorts of reason that I have laid out in the present chapter. So, as long as it makes sense for individual composers to misconstrue the import of their specifications of performance means, it is possible for the timbral sonicist to acknowledge that Levinson's hypothetical composer makes a perfectly rational decision in scoring the piece for the instrumentation that he does.

normative within works by virtue of determining such works' *aesthetic* or *expressive* qualities. Works certainly *can* be sublime, craggy, and assertive, so a timbral sonicist cannot reply by denying this. Nevertheless, replies *are* available, and we shall now see that Levinson is mistaken in thinking that a work's having such an aesthetic or expressive quality may be dependent upon performance means-properties being normative within it.

Consider, once more, the *Hammerklavier*'s sublimity and cragginess. It is Levinson's contention that unless we hear the piece *as* played on the piano, we will have no sense of the strain that the piece places on the instrument, and hence will fail to pick up its true awesomeness. In this sense, according to Levinson, '[t]he aesthetic qualities of the *Hammerklavier* sonata depend in part on the strain that its structure imposes on the sonic capabilities of the piano' (1980b: 76–7).

But this latter conclusion is resistible. Whilst it is true that we must hear a performance of the piece *as* played on the piano if we are to grasp the full gamut of its aesthetic qualities, it does not follow that a properly formed performance must *actually* make use of the piano. A truth about aspect perception is surely this: to see or hear *o* as (an) *F* does not entail that *o* really is (an) *F*. I can see a smile as friendly, yet the smile be contemptuous; I can hear what is really a cry of surprise as a cry of pain. So, taking her cue from facts such as these, a timbral sonicist will insist that all that is required for a performance of the *Hammerklavier* to transmit the piece's cragginess and awesomeness is that its constituent sounds sound *as if* they originate from a piano. As long as the sounds produced sound just like those that a piano would produce, it is of no consequence whether they are actually produced by a piano or not. All that is required is that they sound *as if* they have, rather than *actually* have, that origin.

Exactly the same response is available in the case of works' expressive qualities. Let us return to the assertive character of the opening of Mozart's Serenade in E flat, K. 375. Levinson's claim, remember, is that this passage would not have this content, were it not for the fact that it has a honking quality; and that the sounds would not have this honking quality—that is, would not be a honking in the required 'quasi-literal sense'—unless they were actually made by oboes and clarinets (1990a: 396–7). However, this second claim is false, since a sound can have a honking *quality,* and yet not be a literal—or even quasi-literal—honking. Just as long as a sound *sounds* just like a genuine honking, it has a honking quality; it is not necessary for the sound to be the result of air being forced through a tube. And such a reply to this case yields a generalizable moral. We may grant Levinson the fact that understanding a piece's expressive content requires us to hear gesture in music (1990a: 398); but we should deny that 'expressive content in music is not detachable from the means of performance that are written into musical compositions' (1990b: 399). As long as we hear the music *as* embodying a certain gesture, it does not matter whether the sounds have actually been produced *with* that gesture. So, for example, if we hear a run of tones *as* a genuine *glissando* on a piano, it will succeed in conveying the insouciance associated with such a flicking gesture, even if the sounds are produced by pressing buttons on a Perfect Timbral Synthesizer. The music's insouciant quality requires only that we imagine the sounds to have been produced by a flicking or sweeping gesture (i.e. hear them as having been so produced); and, given our familiarity with the customary origin of such sounds, it would be extremely difficult for us *not* to do this. To suggest that the sounds must actually be produced by a piano—that the *glissando*-like sequence actually *be* a *glissando*—is to insist on more than suffices.

Levinson's reply to such a sonicist move ultimately cuts no ice. Envisaging a case in which a sound-sequence exactly duplicates a *glissando* but is produced by other means of performance, he says this:

If this imaginative construal [of the sounds as having been produced by a *glissando*] is in fact unsupported by performance in the appropriate manner, that is, on a keyboard, and we are aware of this, the resultant effect is not that proper to the music, but rather some degree of cognitive dissonance. (1990a: 399)

But the crucial clause here is 'and we are aware of this'. Once this clause is inserted, the sonicist can acknowledge that such cognitive dissonance may occur. Granted, if the sounds are *glissando*-like, yet we *know* them not to have been produced by such a gesture, the music *might*—though need not[17]—fail to have the abandon for us that it would have had otherwise. But such a difference in perceived expressiveness admits of an explanation that avoids any commitment to instrumentalism. Rather than being explained by the fact that the sounds are not produced by a *glissando*, an audience's failure to hear the passage as expressive of abandonment is caused by a

---

[17] This qualification is crucial. Levinson seems to regard it as being extremely difficult for an audience to imagine sounds to have a certain source whilst knowing these sounds to have another origin (1990a: 403). As we shall see in §8.6, Levinson overestimates the difficulty in what is an everyday phenomenon.

failure of imagination on their part: a failure to hear the sounds *as if* made by a *glissando*. Putting things this way, sonicism is unscathed. For the fact remains that a sound-sequence produced on a Perfect Timbral Synthesizer *could* be heard as a *glissando*, and hence *could* have the same expressive content as a sonically identical sequence produced in the characteristic way. All Levinson has shown is that we might fail to hear a sound-sequence *as* making a certain gesture, if we know it not to have been produced by means of such a gesture; and this need not be denied by a sonicist.

Ultimately, then, Levinson faces a dilemma. If, in the *glissando* example and others like it, he argues that the music may fail to have the appropriate expressive content for us if we *know* it to be produced by non-standard performance means, the sonicist can, as we have just seen, grant such a possibility without it damaging her position. If, on the other hand, Levinson claims that the music would fail to have the appropriate content even if we heard the sounds *as* having been produced by a genuine *glissando*, this claim would seem to be false. For, as we have seen already, sounds can be heard as embodying a certain gesture, and hence have a certain expressive content, even if they are not made with that gesture. All that is required is that the sounds are *qualitatively indistinguishable* from sounds produced with that gesture.

Having said this, an objector may, nonetheless, allege that the position occupied in the above response to Levinson fails to account for works themselves genuinely having aesthetic qualities.[18] As we have seen, a key element in the sonicist's response is to point out that a proper appreciation of a performance of, say, the *Hammerklavier* requires us to hear it *as* played on a piano even if the sounds are really produced by a Perfect Timbral Synthesizer. Only if we engage in such an act of imagination will be able to hear the full gamut of the work's aesthetic properties. It is, of course, also quite possible for listeners to hear such a performance *as synthesized* and, as a result, to fail to pick up on what a sensitive, knowledgeable listener would regard as the full extent of the work's cragginess and awesomeness. And it is at this point that the critic of sonicism sees his chance. For, given the assumption that the work itself is as the timbral sonicist describes it—in other words, that the conditions for correct performance are purely acoustic—the objector insists that neither way of hearing the performance (as involving a piano, or as involving a Perfect Timbral Synthesizer) can be

---

[18] An objection pressed, in correspondence, and with characteristic acuity, by David Davies.

privileged. And what this means, the objector continues, is that there is no basis for saying that the work is genuinely awesome and craggy (or, at least, *as* awesome and craggy as the auditor hearing the performance's constituent sounds as produced by a piano takes the work to be). It is fully awesome and craggy for those listeners who hear it as played on a piano, but less so for those who—with equal justification—hear it as played on a Perfect Timbral Synthesizer. So it turns out that the aesthetic properties in question are not objective properties of works at all: works do not have them *anyway*.

What this objection fails to register, however, is something that I alluded to earlier (in n. 8): namely, the way in which for aesthetic properties, as for secondary qualities (McGinn 1983: ch. 2; McDowell 1985), the responses of a certain class of perceiver enter into their analysis. It would be wholly implausible to think that an object's having an aesthetic quality could be explained other than by making reference to the way the said object strikes a certain sort of perceiver: aesthetic qualities are not like primary qualities. But once we appreciate this point, and, in particular, the role played by the notion of a *properly sensitive listener* in cashing out the nature of aesthetic qualities, the sonicist *can* allow that the *Hammerklavier*, for example, has genuinely objective properties which can be detected only if we hear a performance as performed on a piano. Let us see how such an explanation goes.

The starting-point is this: given the history of music and our familiarity with the traditional means of sound production, we come to think of sounds' tone colours in terms of their characteristic causes: we hear certain sounds as *the kinds of sounds produced by a piano*, for instance. It is a brute fact about the kind of beings we are that we think of sounds in this way in order to put our finger on their timbral, qualitative nature. Furthermore, it is by means of conceptualizing sounds in this way that the sensitive listener comes to exercise her capacity for detecting the aesthetic properties of works whose performances comprise such sounds. Inevitably conceiving of certain sounds as the kinds of sounds made by a piano, the sensitive listener hears a performance of the *Hammerklavier* (even if such a performance uses a Perfect Timbral Synthesizer), thinks of its sounds as *piano*-like and, as a result, finds the work's awesomeness and cragginess in it.

Of course, the objection that we are presently considering disputes our right to think of such experience as a kind of *finding*. And the basis for this rebuttal is the evident fact that there could be listeners who conceptualized sounds differently from ourselves (i.e. purely qualitatively), who, as a result, failed to hear the work in the same way as do the people we class as sensitive listeners, and who thereby failed to hear the same aesthetic qualities in it. But to this we may reply by pointing out that an account of what it is for something to have an aesthetic property will make essential reference to the responses of people we class as sensitive listeners—the responses of those who occupy, one might say, a certain *point of view*—just as much as will an account of what it is for an object to have a colour or a taste. Specifically, a work is awesome and craggy just in case, in suitable conditions, it would be found to be such by a competent, sensitive listener: a listener who not only has a properly functioning auditory system, but who has a developed musical sensibility and who shares *our* way of conceptualizing what is heard. Because it is the responses of sensitive listeners that enter into the analyses of aesthetic qualities, because such sensitivity is sensitivity by *our lights*, and because such listeners will think of certain sounds as *sounds typically made by a piano*, it follows that hearing a performance of the *Hammerklavier* as produced by a piano is the conduit to the full range of its aesthetic qualities. To appreciate a work properly, one must hear it as the sensitive auditor hears it; and such a sensitive listener, to get her mind round the timbral quality of the sounds, will think of them as *piano sounds*.

Now, what follows from this account is that if one is to be sensitive to a work of music's aesthetic properties, one must take up a certain perspective: the perspective of the sensitive and musically literate listener. But it no more follows from this that a work does not genuinely have such properties than it follows from the fact that pigs lack colour vision that objects are not really coloured. The fact that colours fails to show up from the porcine point of view does not undermine our confidence that grass is green *anyway*; neither does the fact that one must take up a certain perspective in order to uncover a work's aesthetic properties. Aesthetic qualities are defined in terms of the responses of listeners *we* class as sensitive, and it does not impugn the objectivity of such qualities that one must use our conceptual system, and exercise taste (again, according to our lights) to pick them out. As McDowell has insisted (1983: 16; 1985: 112), someone who takes seriously the analogy between evaluative properties and secondary qualities should insist that an object's being thus and so *anyway* (i.e. objectively) requires, not that this fact be accessible from no point of view, but that it be *discoverable* (i.e. that it obtain independently of any particular representation of the object as such). And this much is guaranteed by the way in which I have been thinking of musical works' aesthetic qualities. The perspective from which a work's aesthetic qualities are detected is the perspective from which certain sounds are heard as produced by their customary performance means.[19]

8.6 Levinson's Rejoinder

Having assuaged any worries that the sonicist may fail to allow for works genuinely possessing aesthetic properties, let us return to Levinson's opposition to sonicism. As we saw in §8.5, and as Levinson himself recognizes (1990a: 402–3), the sonicist responds to his argument by claiming that a performance of a piece can transmit its aesthetic and expressive content, just as long as the sounds produced are *imagined* to be produced in certain specific ways (i.e. heard as being so produced). To insist that the sounds *should* be so produced is to insist on more than suffices. Levinson, though, is dissatisfied with this reply, for three reasons. First, he claims that its cogency depends upon the audience's not learning the real origin of the sounds they are hearing, or else being willing to be fooled concerning their source, 'neither of which is a viable stance vis-à-vis a performance' (1990a: 403). Second, he states that a sonic doppelgänger of, say, a *glissando* will present

---

[19] It follows from this that a piano-less possible world *w* in which the *Hammerklavier* is composed for Perfect Timbral Synthesizer is a world in which the work's cragginess and sublimity are inaccessible to listeners. To detect these qualities, we must hear the work as played on a piano, and in a world in which the piano has not been invented, this would be impossible.

Given that aesthetic qualities are response-dependent, does it follow from this that the *Hammerklavier* lacks cragginess and sublimity in *w*? No. For whilst aesthetic qualities are defined in terms of the responses of competent, sensitive listeners in suitable circumstances, this idea may be cashed out in either of two ways. If we were to say that a work has an aesthetic property *F* at *w* just in case it is such as to be taken to be *F* by listeners classed as competent and sensitive, and in circumstances classes as suitable, according to the standards operating *at w*, then the *Hammerklavier* would indeed lack sublimity and depth at *w*. But this is not the only way of explicating aesthetic qualities' response-dependence. For equally, we might say that a work has *F* at *w* just in case it is such as to be taken to be *F* by observers that are counted as competent and sensitive, and in circumstances counted as suitable, according to the standards in place *now*, in *the actual world*. On this second construal of the response-dependence of aesthetic qualities, the *Hammerklavier* comes out as sublime and craggy at *w* because it is true, at *w*, that a musically sensitive listener in the actual world would, in conditions deemed appropriate in the actual world, find it sublime and craggy.

It is this latter explication of response-dependence that I prefer. A piano-less world is a world in which people are not competent to detect the *Hammerklavier*'s aesthetic properties: a world in which the conditions for doing so are not suitable. Hence, the fact that optimally sensitive listeners in *w* cannot detect the work's cragginess and sublimity does not entail that the work lacks those properties in *w*. Aesthetic qualities are defined by *us* from *here* (the actual world). The standards of competence, sensitivity, and suitability that apply are those in operation now. (The thrust of this note has been influenced by William Child (1991: 169).)

merely a *simulacrum* of the expressive gestures that belong to the passage, rather than the gestures that really belong to it (1990a: 404). Finally, he contends that such a sonic doppelgänger cannot count as authentic because it would effectively stymie our ability to compare and evaluate performances (1990a: 404–5). I shall consider these objections in reverse order.

Let us start then, by examining Levinson's third objection. A performance of the *Hammerklavier* on a Perfect Timbral Synthesizer, even if indistinguishable from a properly formed performance on a piano, would be inauthentic, Levinson claims, because it would present us with a severe critical quandary. In short, we would not know how to evaluate it. As Levinson puts it, if a piano were not involved,

we would be pretty much completely at sea in regard to assessing the particular expressiveness of the performance ... its particular manner of bodying forth [the work's] inherent expression. For an important dimension of assessment would have been removed: how have the instrumentalists, given their control over and way of internalising the gestural capacities of their instruments, related themselves, at each turn, to the demands of this music, which is conceived for and referred to those capacities? (Levinson 1990a: 405)

But inasmuch as there is a genuine worry here, it would seem to be irrelevant to the point at issue, which is, remember, whether a performance of the work on a Perfect Timbral Synthesizer could transmit the full extent of the piece's aesthetic content. It may well be difficult to evaluate such a performer's achievement in transmitting such content, given that we tend to make such evaluations according to how well the performer has overcome the limitations of the instruments for which the work was written. It would, indeed, be easier said than done to compare the achievements of an Ashkenazy with a performer who produced a sonically indistinguishable sound-sequence on a synthesizer: we are accustomed to the problems posed by playing the piece on a piano—our familiarity with both the instrument itself and the attempts made by pianists down the years give us a reasonably clear sense of this—but until we had a clear idea of the problems and constraints faced by a player of a Perfect Timbral Synthesizer, any such comparison with performances by pianists would be obstructed. Having said this, it is far from clear why the existence of such a puzzle would demonstrate the synthesized performance to be inauthentic: that is, to fail to present the full extent of the performed work's aesthetic content. For the puzzle to which Levinson draws our attention in fact concerns how we would evaluate a performer's achievement *in* transmitting a work's aesthetic content; it is irrelevant to the question of whether a synthesized performance *could* deliver this content. And, of course, to this latter question, the timbral sonicist has a clear answer: such content is determined wholly by how a performance *sounds*, and to no extent by how these sounds are produced.

What of Levinson's second objection to the sonicist's reply to his argument? *Must* a synthesized performance inevitably fail to present a work's aesthetic substance as it *is*? I don't think so. Naturally, a timbral sonicist agrees with Levinson that 'an authentic performance should seek to present a piece's aesthetic substance as it *is*' (1990*a*: 404). But her claim is precisely that this aesthetic substance is not dependent upon specific means of performance in the way in which Levinson supposes: as long as a sound-sequence sounds exactly like a *glissando* on a piano, so that the audience can *imagine* the sounds to have been produced with a sweeping gesture along a piano keyboard, the resultant sounds will have exactly the same aesthetic substance as a genuine *glissando*. The *glissando*-like sounds express the sweeping gesture, and hence give the music an insouciant quality, even though they were not produced with such a gesture. Aesthetic substance is determined by how the music sounds, not how it is produced. To put it another way, the vehicle of a work's musical meaning is not, as Levinson assumes (1990*a*: 404), sounds-as-produced-by-specific-instruments, but those sounds themselves, whatever their actual origin. His claim that a sonic doppelgänger of a *glissando* 'gives the appearance, but not the reality of the complex of soundings that are the true vehicle of a piece's musical meaning' (1990*a*: 404) sees him, once more, beg the question against the timbral sonicist.

Nonetheless, Levinson will insist that a synthesized sonic doppelgänger— even if it manages to convey the right expressivity to an audience—inevitably 'falsifies or disguises the *basis* for that expressivity' (1990*a*: 404), and, as a consequence, cannot be authentic. And this, in essence, is his one remaining objection to the kind of sonicist response to his original argument that I outlined towards the end of §8.5. This objection emerges once the following kind of case is considered. Imagine that an audience attends a performance of Mozart's Serenade in E flat, K. 375, well aware that it is performed using a Perfect Timbral Synthesizer rather than wind instruments. As a result, in order to hear the assertive quality of the piece's opening passage, an audience must hear the sounds produced *as* a sequence of honkings whilst at the same time knowing the sounds not to be honkings—that is, not to have been produced by forcing air through narrow holes in tubes. But this, Levinson suggests, is none too easy a thing to do: we must imagine the sounds to be honkings while knowing them not to be (1990a: 403); that is, we must allow ourselves to be *fooled* concerning the sounds' origin. And, in any case, even if an audience *could* succeed in doing this, a performance that required such a thing of its auditors could not be counted as authentic, and hence could not be properly formed:

A performance that enforces mental acrobatics on listeners in order that an intended expressiveness should emerge, which expressiveness should emerge effortlessly and unconsciously, can hardly be thought to further authenticity. On the contrary, to ensure that a listener's experience of a performance be informed by the thought of certain performing actions *in the right way*, the performance should actually involve those very actions and the very instruments that make them possible. (Levinson 1990a: 403–4)

But I have two replies to this reasoning. First of all, an audience's hearing sounds it knows to be synthesized sounds *as* honkings is not thereby allowing itself to be *fooled* as to the sounds' origin. On the contrary, the audience is imagining these sounds to have an alternative source to that which it knows them to have actually. The audience knows the sounds to be synthesized, but imagines them to be produced by clarinets and oboes. And before we are tempted to look askance at such a phenomenon, we should remember that imaginative engagement of this kind is not unfamiliar to audiences of the performing arts: the way in which an audience imaginatively engages with a play—imagining that the people on-stage are in real situations, but knowing the participants to be actors—is another example of the same genus.

Second, such a reflective exercise of the imagination is not an instance of 'mental acrobatics'. Quite the opposite. Given our familiarity with the typical way in which such sounds are produced, the musically aware listener gets her mind round the timbral aspect of a certain sound, say, by thinking of it as the sound produced by playing a middle C on an oboe. True enough, for the expressiveness of the music to emerge in a synthesized performance, the audience must employ greater imagination than if the sounds are produced by the wind instruments that the composer had in mind. It must put the actual means of performance out of its mind and concentrate on the sounds' qualitative aspect, thereby calling to mind their customary origin. But the exercise of such a capacity is both effortless and perhaps even unconscious: one just sits back in one's seat, shuts one's eyes, and lets the sounds, what one knows about such sounds' customary origin and one's imagination do the rest. I fail to see why a synthesized performance of a piece that required this of its audience would not be authentic. After all, this requirement, so easy to meet, ensures that such a performance would succeed in transmitting the piece's aesthetic content.

8.7 Conclusion

Given timbral sonicism's status as the face-value account of how musical works are individuated, we should only give it up once it has been shown to be untenable. But there is nothing in the instrumentalist's arsenal of arguments that forces us to take such drastic action. Specifically, the fact that a work's score specifies certain instruments does not entail that a properly formed token of the piece has to be produced by such instruments. As long as a performance uses means of performance to produce sounds aurally indistinguishable from sounds produced by the instruments specified in the score, the demands of authenticity can be met. Equally, the attempt to argue that a work's possession of certain aesthetic and artistic properties is dependent upon instrumental properties being normative within it falls crucially short of its target. All that is required for a work to have the content that it has is that it has a certain set of acoustic properties normative within it. Nothing the instrumentalist has said should force the sonicist into acknowledging that performance means-properties are normative within musical works, so the sonicist's way of individuating such works may stand.

However, as I said in §8.1, adopting instrumentalism is only one way of denying the truth of sonicism. The other way of doing so is by embracing a form of contextualism and, in so doing, arguing that composers working in different musico-historical contexts inevitably produce distinct works, even if these works are acoustically indistinguishable. Naturally, what counts as sameness of musico-historical context may be disputed; but however this notion is explained, the contextualist's threat to sonicism is clear. If the contextualist is right, then the sonicist individuates musical works in too rough-hewn a manner. It is this, the most potent challenge to sonicism, that I shall confront in my final chapter.

9

Sonicism II: Against Contextualism

9.1 Introduction: Formulating Contextualism

Timbral sonicism, to recap, consists of the following claim concerning the individuation of works of music: work W and work W^* are numerically identical if and only if they have exactly the same acoustic properties normative within them (where these acoustic properties include timbral properties). In other words, the condition that a sound sequence must meet to be a properly formed token of W is purely acoustic. One source of dissatisfaction with this thesis was disposed of in the previous chapter. The arguments for thinking that the set of properties normative within a work includes performance means-properties in addition to acoustic properties, are unsound: the sonicist need not give up her pre-theoretically intuitive position in favour of instrumentalism. But what of the contextualist's response to sonicism? Like instrumentalists, contextualists claim that acoustic indistinguishability is only necessary for work-identity, not sufficient, though for a different reason. According to the contextualist, for composer A and composer B, to compose the same work of music independently, it must not merely be true that their compositions sound exactly alike; it must also be the case that A and B occupy the same musico-historical context.

Needless to say, such a response provokes two questions. First, what considerations could push one towards contextualism? Second, what exactly counts as 'the same musico-historical context'? On the first question, much of the following chapter will be given over to considering numerous instances of the contextualist's style of argument; but, for now, suffice it to say that the main weapon in the contextualist's arsenal is the kind of sonic doppelgänger thought-experiment that was introduced in §8.1.[1] Typically, the contextualist asks us to imagine a possible world in which composers, working independently and at different points in the history of music, produce identical scores and, hence, compose works that are acoustically indistinguishable. The sonicist, of course, has no choice but to claim that such an example sees one and the same work composed twice. As we shall see, however, the contextualist argues that the sonicist's identity criterion fails to individuate works sufficiently finely in such cases. According to the contextualist, the respective composers compose not one and the same work, but numerically distinct sonic duplicates. Although the two works have exactly the same acoustic properties normative within them, the contextualist points to alleged differences in their respective aesthetic or artistic attributes, and invokes Leibniz's Law to establish their distinctness.

Coupled with counter-examples of this kind is a diagnosis of why they occur. For the contextualist contends that her style of argument reveals something important about the way in which a work of music's aesthetic and artistic properties are determined. Rather than simply supervening upon a work's acoustic character (and its artistic category), 'the aesthetic and artistic attributes of a piece of music are partly a function of, and must be gauged with reference to, the total musico-historical context in which the composer is situated while composing his piece' (Levinson 1980b: 68–9). A work's aesthetic and artistic properties are in part determined by the position that its composer occupies in musico-historical space; and this is why composers occupying different such positions will inevitably produce distinct works, even if these works sound exactly alike.

We shall return to cases of this kind in §9.3 below. However, before we examine the contextualist's arguments for his position, we had better be clear about that position's details. That is to say, we would do well to consider the second question raised in the paragraph before last. It is all very well claiming that composers must occupy the same musico-historical context if they are to compose identical works; but we are no further forward, if it has not been explained what makes for sameness of such

---

[1] A notable exception to this trend is David Davies (2004: Ch. 2), who explicitly distances himself from such arguments. However, I take myself to have dealt with his particular version of contextualism in Ch. 7.

context. On this matter, one natural suggestion is that 'a musico-historical context is a function of time and person', and hence that 'given a time and person, musico-historical context is fixed' (Levinson 1980b: 80). On this view, difference in either person or time makes for difference in context and, hence, 'musical works are necessarily distinct if composed either by different people or at different times' (Levinson 1980b: 80), even if the composers produce identical scores. And, indeed, it is precisely Levinson's one-time commitment to this particular spin on contextualism that determined the details of his original ontological proposal. Seeking to enshrine this version of contextualism in an account of musical works' ontological nature, Levinson suggested that we view a musical work as a compound of a sound structure and a performing means structure,[2] ψ, that is analytically tied to its composer and the time at which it was composed. The work, according to Levinson, is not ψ itself, but ψ-as-indicated-by-A-at-t (1980b: 79).

The problem with individuating musico-historical contexts like this, however, is that it fails to speak to the way in which we naturally think of them, and hence carves them too finely. Levinson himself thinks of the musico-historical context in which a composer is situated at a time t as including cultural, social, and political history up to t; musical development up to t; musical styles prevalent at t; dominant musical influences at t; the musical activities of the composer's contemporaries at t; the composer's œuvre, repertoire and apparent style at t; and the musical influences operating on the composer at t (Levinson 1980b: 69). But once the notion of a musico-historical context has been informally characterized in this way, it becomes apparent that sameness of context does not require *either* sameness of time *or* sameness of person. Let us focus first on time. If the musico-historical context in which a composer is working in is informally characterized in the rich way in which Levinson suggests, one thing is clear: such contexts last for weeks, months, perhaps even years. If, as Levinson believes, sameness of context really does require sameness of time, then a composer would wake up in a new such context each morning. The reason why such a consequence is absurd is precisely that a composer's repertoire, style, and œuvre, together with the other, more general aspects of a musico-historical context, rarely *change* so swiftly.

---

[2] It is Levinson's commitment to instrumentalism that leads him to regard his indicated types as involving performing means structures in addition to sound structures (1980b: 78).

Similar considerations apply to the thesis that sameness of context requires sameness of person. Ruling out the possibility that two people can ever occupy the same musico-historical context, as this proposal does, ignores the fact that it is possible for two distinct individuals to share the same features that Levinson himself uses to spell out informally the notion of such a context. All we need do is further develop the Beethoven/Twin Beethoven case we considered in §8.1. Building in a few more details to the example, now imagine a possible world in which Twin Beethoven lives at the same time as Beethoven, shares his musical influences, and produces, secretly and independently, a body of work indistinguishable from Beethoven's own. Such a state of affairs is, admittedly far-fetched, but it is not impossible. In the wake of this thought-experiment, only dogmatism could motivate the claim that Beethoven and Twin Beethoven inhabited distinct musico-historical contexts.

This being so, the contextualist is, perhaps, best served by sticking with the less formal construal suggested in the paragraph before last. Rather than seeking to reduce the notion of such a context to a person and a time, the contextualist should regard the musico-historical contexts in which two composers A and B are working as identical just in case A and B share the same influences, œuvre, and repertoire and style; and are in the same situation in musical, cultural, social, and political history.

9.2 Contextualist Ontological Proposals

Contextualist approaches to the individuation of works of music typically bring with them an ontological proposal as to their nature, Levinson's construal of musical works as indicated types being the most notable example.[3] The thesis of the present section is twofold. First, the way in which Levinson thinks of indicated types is inherently problematic. But, second, the failure of (variants of) his ontological proposal does nothing to undermine the idea that musical works may nonetheless be *individuated* contextually. A contextualist about individuation need not be committed to any particular such ontological proposal (Rohrbaugh 2005: 211).

---

[3] Levinson's approach (if not its precise details) is endorsed by Thomasson (1999: 131–2). Similar views are held by Danto (1981), Walton (1988), and Margolis (1980).

But what *of* Levinson's conception of works of music? As I noted in §5.1, the leading idea is that the types that are musical works consist of a performed sound-structure, ψ, together with contextual elements that feature ineliminably. The indication of ψ in a specific context allegedly brings into being a contextualized entity distinct from ψ itself. Given that the contextualist is, I think, best served by treating neither a person nor a time as an essential component of a musico-historical context, it might seem that the obvious move to make is to construe a musical work as the following kind of type:

(MW*) ψ-as-indicated-in-musico-historical-context-C. (Levinson 1980*b*: 82)

Significantly, though, Levinson resists this treatment, eventually settling upon the following formula:

(MW) ψ-as-indicated-by-composer-A-at-t-in-C. (1992*a*: 220)

To my mind, however, it is (MW*) that is to be preferred by the would-be contextualist. (MW), but not (MW*), commits one to thinking that a work of music could not have had a different composer, and could not have been composed at a different time. As Levinson explains,

Could someone else have composed Beethoven's Quintet Op. 16, according to MW? For example, could Hummel have done so? No, because if ψ is the [performed sound structure] of the Quintet Op. 16, then all Hummel might have composed is ψ-as-indicated-by-Hummel-in-1797, and not ψ-as-indicated-by-Beethoven-in-1797. (1980*b*: 83)

Similar considerations apply to the case of the piece's time of composition. If, as (MW) demands, the time at which Beethoven indicated ψ is constitutive of his Quintet Op. 16, it follows that it could not have been composed at any other time.

Both of these consequences are highly counter-intuitive. As Levinson himself admits (1980*b*: 83), it goes against the grain to suppose that a work's composer is essential to it. And it is quite easy to construct thought experiments that place such a commitment under considerable strain. One such is the Twin Beethoven case discussed earlier. Another has been suggested by Currie (1989: 62): if there were a Twin Earth (a complete spatio-temporal duplicate of Earth) containing a Twin Beethoven who enjoys a life exactly duplicating that of Beethoven himself, it would be excessively doctrinaire to deny that Beethoven and Twin Beethoven *both* composed the Quintet Op. 16. Likewise, it conflicts with our pre-theoretical way of thinking about composition to suppose that Beethoven could not have composed the piece in 1798. To the ordinary man or woman in the street, it seems *obvious* that Beethoven might have composed the work a little earlier or later than he, in fact, did.

In the wake of such stark counter-intuitiveness, Levinson's insistent defence of (MW) fails to convince. On the question of the apparent inessentiality of its time of composition to the Quintet Op. 16, Levinson suggests that we should treat the notion of sameness of time with 'a degree of freedom or looseness, perhaps varying from case to case' (1992a: 219). But the worry about making this move is its accompanying whiff of *ad hocism*. On the face of it, there is nothing to stop Levinson from treating 'same time' as a movable feast: something that is not so much explanatory of our intuitions about work-identity as led by the nose by them. For a contextualist, it is far neater simply to accept that a work's time of composition does not of itself feature as a constituent of the relevant indicated type.

Levinson's response to the paradoxical consequences of taking composers to feature ineliminably in works fares no better. We should, he argues, *positively welcome* the consequence that works are essentially composed by their actual composers, since this 'gives composers *logical insurance* that their works are their very own. ... Why not adopt a construal of "musical work" ... which, while maintaining musical works as abstract types, guarantees this individuation by artist for them as well?' (Levinson 1980b: 83–4). But the answer to this question is simple. Unless it can be demonstrated that there is a clear philosophical need to individuate musical works this finely, we should avoid doing so, since such a move would contradict our firmly held intuitions that such works need not have had the composers they have actually. And, clearly, such a philosophical need is not provided by Levinson's claim that it is desirable to provide composers with an insurance of a *logical* kind that their works are their own. Composers do not need such insurance. It in no way undermines the brilliance of Beethoven's achievement to point out that someone else could have composed the Quintet Op. 16: such a counterfactual composer of the piece would have to have been as masterful as Beethoven. The thesis that we must preserve what Levinson calls 'the uniqueness of compositional activity' (1980b: 83) is unsupported by argument.

All in all, if the contextualist is to offer an ontological proposal as to the nature of works of music, she should adopt (MW*) or something like it. But at this point, the sonicist might take herself to sense a way of short-circuiting the contextualist's challenge to her favoured account of the individuation of works of music. For it has been suggested that Levinson's indicated structures—however their precise details are mapped out—lack a metaphysical pedigree, since they are either ontologically extravagant or ontologically obscure, or both. If such charges can be made to stick, and if contextualism is inevitably committed to such an ontological proposal, then contextualism is doomed from the start. But in fact, as we shall now see, the contextualist can nuance her ontological proposal in order to cope with such objections. That is, she may preserve her distinct account of the *individuation* of works of music, yet avoid commitment to the troublesome aspects of Levinson's particular ontological proposal.

With a view to demonstrating this, let us start by considering the charges that are commonly laid at the contextualist's door. The first—that of ontological extravagance—is made by both Currie and Predelli. Predelli, with characteristic elegance, puts the case against (MW) and, by extension, (MW*) like this:

[I]t does not appear to be true *in general* that, whenever an agent *a* enters into a relationship *R* with an object *o* at a time *t*, a novel entity comes into existence, one which may be denoted by an expression of the form '*o*-as-*R*'d-by-*a*-at-*t*'. For instance, in the absence of evidence to the contrary, it does not appear to be the case that, if you show me the tallest building on campus you thereby bring into existence a new object, that is, the building-as-shown-by-you. (Predelli 2001: 289)

As for '*o*-as-*R*'d-by-*a*-at-*t*', so with '*o*-as-*R*'d-in-musico-historical-context-*C*': the worry is that indicated types have been gerrymandered into existence. And Currie, in an extension of this objection, suspects Levinson to be operating with a double standard, admitting indicated types into his ontology only when it suits him:

Fleming discovered penicillin, in the process of doing so did he bring into being penicillin-as-discovered-by-Fleming? What sort of entity would that be, if it is not simply identical with penicillin? If Levinson's arguments establish the existence of indicated structures in the arts, they seem to establish their existence in a number of other areas where they are not wanted. (Currie 1989: 58)

According to Currie, the fact that Levinson's proposal generalizes so easily, and with such implausible results, merely serves to suggest that such items are cooked up rather than being genuine elements of the universe.

The second complaint—namely, that Levinson's indicated types are ontologically mysterious—has as its target Levinson's suggestion that his contextualized types have times, individuals, or contexts as constituents. For Levinson, remember, indicated structures are 'things *in which* a particular person and time figure ineliminably' (1980b: 82; my italics). This has led some commentators to doubt whether such structures are *bona fide* types at all: if an entity has a time as a *constituent*—as one of its parts—it must surely be an *event* rather than a type, at least, if Kim (1976) is right about events (Dodd 2000: 439–40; D. Davies 2004: 64). To such critics, Levinson's indicated types look like strange, cross-categorial entities: ontologically suspect things that look suspiciously made to measure for the purpose of solving a philosophical problem.

In my view, though, such a move is too quick. If we are correct in thinking that the contextualist's ontological proposal should take the form (MW*) rather than (MW), then there need be no commitment to *times* being constituents of contextualized types: the things that such a type comprises are simply a (performed) sound-event-type and a musico-historical context. Having said this, however, a reformulated version of the objection stands. For, as I noted in §2.4, types are, by their very nature, unstructured entities: they do not have constituents. Consequently, Levinson's attempt to provide a contextualist ontological proposal by writing contextual elements into the structure of such entities can only be misconceived.

So, in the wake of these concerns, is the contextualist beggared for an ontological proposal as to works of music? No. For she may agree that types are ontologically simple, yet defend the thesis that such types are *individuated* contextually. On such a view, two composers, A and B, can only compose the same work (= sound-event-type), if they inhabit the same co-ordinates in musico-historical space, but these co-ordinates do not enter the work as *constituents* of it. Rather, such contextual features enter into an explanation of the *individuation* of such entities; they do not literally figure as parts of them.[4] The point, then, is that the contextualist's proposal

---

[4] An analogy should make this point clearer. It is one thing to agree with Quine (1985) that events are identical just in case they occur in the same place at the same time; it is another thing entirely to suppose that events have spatial points and times as constituents.

concerning the individuation of works of music need not be accompanied by Levinson's own ontological proposal as to their nature: the contextualist could—indeed, *should*—treat indicated types as ontologically simple.

A similarly bullish response can be given to the charge that indicated types are the products of ontological gerrymandering. True enough, if Levinson admits indicated types in the arts, he must recognize their existence elsewhere.[5] This consequence, though, need not be viewed as so damaging. For if the contextualist has been brought to accept the ontologically thin account of types that I recommend—if, in other words, she has come to view them as merely the structureless associates of the properties by which they are individuated—then she is entitled to ask what harm there could be in acknowledging their widespread existence. Predelli is, no doubt, right to observe that we do not *ordinarily* admit the existence of contextualized types, if this is taken to mean that most people do not admit such things into their ontology. However, given that contextualized types—once properly understood—are so slight, existing at a time merely if their property-associates do, the contextualist should reply by pointing out that there is no harm in admitting such things into our ontology across the board. There are, the contextualist should say, as many contextualized types as there are contextualized conditions that a token must meet to be a token of a type. For a thoroughgoing contextualist, then, the controversial issue is whether we should identify types of a certain class (artistic, cultural, or scientific) with pure or contextualized types; that contextualized types exist in these areas is, she should insist, a near truism.

That said, it is clear that the sonicist would be wrong, if she thought that she could simply pack up now and go home with the prize. The game is very much back on. Individuating works of music contextually does not automatically commit us to an obscure or profligate ontology; so we must

---

[5] Levinson himself seems to wish to hold back from this, arguing that there is a *theoretical need* for such items in the arts but not in the area of the discoveries of science. His own preferred response has it that 'indicated structures may simply not be *needed* in such areas; that is to say, perhaps we haven't cause, at present, to recognize such things as penicillin-as-discovered-by-Fleming' (1992a: 219). But this move is a strange one, since it appears to be predicated on the assumption that whether a given class of entities exists or not is determined by whether our philosophical theories have need of them. This, of course, is something that Levinson officially denies: we must, he thinks, acknowledge the existence of indicated types in the artistic field, not because we have need of such entities to solve a philosophical conundrum, but because the merest discovery and indication of a pure type of sound-event is sufficient to bring an indicated type into being. It is precisely because Levinson takes *so little* to be required for an indicated type to come into existence, that he has no choice but to acknowledge the existence of myriad indicated types in other areas.

assess the contextualist's challenges to the sonicist's individuative claim on their own merits. With a view to doing just this, Levinson, as we have noted already, takes a particular style of thought-experiment to demonstrate that musical works are individuated more finely than the sonicist allows. In his view, such examples show, *pace* sonicism, that such works are in part individuated by matters contextual. It is time to examine this style of argument now.

9.3 Levinson's Doppelgänger Thought-Experiments

The sonicist insists that work of music W = work of music W^* just in case W and W^* are acoustically indistinguishable. The contextualist, as we have seen, takes such acoustic equivalence to be merely necessary, not sufficient, for work-identity: in his view W and W^*, even if acoustic doubles, will be distinct works if their respective composers composed them in different musico-historical contexts. Levinson's style of argument for the contextualist position is simple and, it seems, compelling, as we shall now see.

Answers to individuation questions concern the identity and distinctness of entities *within* a single possible world (Rohrbaugh 2005: 211).[6] So a counter-example to the sonicist's claim will be a genuinely possible world in which there are acoustically indistinguishable works that are, nonetheless, numerically distinct. Recognizing this very fact, Levinson's strategy is to come up with convincing counter-examples of just this stripe. In each such case he first of all imagines a possible world in which composers working in distinct musico-historical contexts compose acoustically indistinguishable works, W and W^*; then claims that W and W^* differ with respect to their artistic or aesthetic attributes (as a result of having been composed in distinct musico-historical contexts); and then applies Leibniz's Law to derive the conclusion that W and W^* are distinct entities. As he himself puts it,

For all we know there *are*, and at any rate easily *could be*, works containing (incorporating) *identical sound sequences* and yet presenting nontrivial aesthetic

---

[6] Questions concerning the individuation of entities are distinct from questions concerning their essences (i.e. questions concerning the identity of entities *across* possible worlds). To see this, it is necessary only to note that an acceptance of Davidson's dictum that events are identical just in case they have the same causes and effects (1969: 179) does not commit us to any doctrine concerning how they *might have been*, least of all that events have their causes and effects essentially.

differences. ... A sonic doppelgänger, residing in another aesthetic-complexion generating musical matrix can be posited for any given, concretely situated musical work, thus demonstrating that the work is not the sound sequence: There are two works but only one such sequence (1990c: 222)

So, if Levinson is right, sonically indistinguishable works composed in different musico-historical contexts are inevitably distinct. In essence, the reason why this is so is that 'the aesthetic and artistic attributes of a piece of music are partly a function of, and must be gauged with reference to, the total musico-historical context in which the composer is situated while composing his piece' (1980b: 68–9). A work's aesthetic properties, Levinson believes, do not supervene on how it sounds (plus its artistic category); such properties supervene on the conjunction of these factors together with the context in which it was composed. What this means is that works cannot be individuated purely acoustically. As Levinson explains, 'musical works must be construed more narrowly, and counted more discriminatingly, than sound structures *per se* if we are to make sense of a significant range of critical descriptions of pieces of music, of attributions to them of artistic and aesthetic properties' (1990c: 221). The sonicist's spin on such cases—namely, that the sorts of cases imagined by Levinson see a single work composed twice—simply cannot be maintained. What we have here are numerically distinct sonic sound-alikes, not a single, multiply composed work.

So much for the argument in the abstract; it is time to focus sharply on the range of examples available to the contextualist. With this in mind, it will be useful to distinguish between four kinds of property that works of music may be taken to possess.[7] *Aesthetic* properties are properties bearing upon a work's value as an artwork and which are perceivable in the work: properties such as unity, delicacy, elegance, coherence, and beauty. *Expressive* properties, too, are perceivable properties bearing upon a work's aesthetic value, but they are qualities of a work that consist in its being expressive of emotions, such as sadness, despair, or hope. *Artistic* properties, by contrast with both aesthetic and expressive qualities, are not perceivable in the work itself, but are, supposedly, possessed by virtue of the relations in which the work stands to other works and to the musico-historical context in which the work is situated. So properties that pertain to the nature of the artist's achievement (such as originality and derivativeness)

---

[7] This paragraph leans heavily on Levinson's explication of such properties (1987: 182–4).

and art-historical properties (such as influence and revolutionariness) count as artistic. Finally, a work's putative *representational* properties see it refer to, depict, or portray objects, events, processes, and phenomena. If it is true that Honegger's *Pacific 231* represents a steam locomotive in motion, then its depiction of such a thing is a representational property of the work.

Having laid out this typology of properties, we may note that we can construct Levinson-style examples that make play with any of the four kinds of property. First, consider examples designed to reveal the inadequacy of sonicism by virtue of demonstrating that there are possible worlds in which sonically indistinguishable works differ with respect to their *aesthetic* properties (1980b: 70–1). A possible world in which Schoenberg's *Pierrot Lunaire* (1912) is joined by an exact sound-alike composed by Richard Strauss in 1897 is a world in which Strauss's work, according to Levinson, is the more bizarre, upsetting, and eerie. In such a world, Strauss's composition (let us follow Levinson (1980b: 70) in calling it '*Pierrot Lunaire**') is both contemporaneous with Debussy's Nocturnes and the next step after his *Also Sprach Zarathustra*. As a result, Levinson claims, *Pierrot Lunaire** is the more extreme musically when 'perceived against' (1980b: 70) the relevant musical tradition in which it is situated, its place in Strauss's œuvre, and the time at which Strauss composed it. If this is right, then, contrary to sonicism, *Pierrot Lunaire* and *Pierrot Lunaire** are distinct works.

In the same vein, Levinson claims that a possible world in which there exists both a certain Johann Stamitz symphony and a sonic duplicate of it—complete with 'Mannheim rockets'—composed by a modern-day composer is a world in which the modern piece is *funny* at the precise moments at which the piece by Stamitz is *exciting* (1980b: 71). Perceived in the knowledge that the piece is contemporary, a knowledgeable audience would find the later work *kitsch*. Stamitz's work is exciting, *given its place in the history of musical development*; the contemporary sonic doppelgänger would be heard as some kind of joke by an audience familiar with its provenance. Once more, according to Levinson, we have a demonstration that acoustic equivalence does not make for work-identity.

Further examples of this kind are easily constructed in which sonically indistinguishable works supposedly differ with respect to their respective expressive properties. To return to a case that arose briefly in §5.4, imagine a possible world in which Marsalis's *In This House, On This Morning* exists alongside a sonic doppelgänger composed in the sixteenth century by a

German artist. (True enough, such a world is very distant from the actual world, but, as we agreed in §5.4, it exists: it is metaphysically possible for such a piece to have been composed then.) In the imagined world, are the piece composed by Marsalis in 1992 and the composition composed by the sixteenth-century composer one and the same work of music? Here is a reason why a contextualist could say not: Marsalis's work is expressive of pride in the Black Americans of the Deep South; the sixteenth-century piece does not—*could not*—express that emotion because the object of the emotion did not exist at the time the piece was composed. Once more, there would seem to be a difference in the works' respective properties, a difference that entails that we have numerically distinct sonic doppelgängers, not a single work composed in two musico-historical contexts.

As for aesthetic and expressive properties, so for artistic properties. Once it is agreed that musical works possess properties such as *originality, being Liszt-influenced*, and *satirizing Shostakovich's Seventh Symphony*, we have no choice but to accept that works have such properties, not simply by virtue of sounding a certain way, but because they were composed at a particular point in musico-historical space (Levinson 1980b: 70–1). As a result, a possible world in which Mendelssohn's composition of his *Midsummer Night's Dream Overture* (1826) is joined by the independent composition, in 1900, of a sonically equivalent piece would seem to be a world containing two distinct works, not a single work composed at two different times. For, as Levinson describe the case (1980b: 70), the later work lacks the originality that characterizes Mendelssohn's piece: what makes the piece by Mendelssohn original is that a work sounding like *that* was composed *then*. Once more, the context in which the work was written partly determines the artistic properties it possesses: its artistic properties do not simply supervene on how it sounds and its artistic category; and this result is incompatible with sonicism.

A contextualist may attempt to draw the same moral from a different angle, once it is granted that musical works may have *representational* qualities. These too—if works genuinely possess them—would seem to be a function of the musico-historical context in which a work's composer is situated. As I have mentioned already, Honegger's *Pacific 231* is commonly taken to represent a steam locomotive starting up, moving at top speed, and then slowing down to a stop. Indeed, the piece has been called 'an orchestral picture of a steam locomotive' (Latham 2002: 591). But if this is right, then it looks like we can exploit this fact to produce a swift refutation of sonicism. Imagine a possible world in which, as in the actual world, Honegger composes *Pacific 231* in 1923, but in which a sonic equivalent is composed in the fifteenth century. The latter piece, it is plausible to think, could not have possessed the property of representing a steam locomotive (since steam trains had not yet been invented), and hence, by Leibniz's Law, we have two distinct works. If this example is to be taken at face value, the obvious moral to be drawn is that composers must be located in the same musico-historical context if they are to compose independently one and the same piece of music.

The sonicist thus faces quite a challenge. She must argue either that the contextualist's thought-experiments are based on some kind of mistake, or else come up with a convincing strategy for countering them. Ultimately, I think that a mixed strategy works best: the thought-experiments involving artistic, representational, and object-directed expressive properties trade on misconceptions, whilst those cases involving aesthetic properties need, but admit of, substantive replies. However, for the remainder of the present section, I shall consider the responses of Kivy and Wolterstorff. Neither succeeds; but understanding why they both fail will enable us both to comprehend how the thought-experiments work and to appreciate the size of the sonicist's task.

Kivy detects what he takes to be a whiff of sophistry in Levinson's examples. First of all, he takes Levinson to presuppose that works have their aesthetic properties *essentially* (1987: 245). According to Kivy, without this assumption in place, the case of *Pierrot Lunaire* and *Pierrot Lunaire** admits of a simple reply: to wit, that it shows merely that, if the work had been written by Strauss in 1897, it would have been more bizarre, upsetting, anguished, and eerie than it actually is. According to Kivy, the fact that Strauss's counterfactual composition has different aesthetic properties from Schoenberg's would only show the pieces to be distinct if such properties formed part of the work's essence; but they do not.

To put the point another way, Kivy objects to the way in which Levinson invokes Leibniz's Law in his examples. To Kivy's mind, Levinson's application of this principle across the board offends against our intuition that works might have been different:

Leibniz's Law, notoriously, makes no distinction between essential and accidental properties, whereas common usage and ordinary intuition do. ... On Leibniz's principle, *Don Giovanni* is a different work in a possible world in which Mozart was poisoned by Salieri from what it would be in one in which he was not, since there would be something true of it in the former case, not in the latter, namely, 'Don Giovanni was written by the composer Salieri poisoned'. No one, short of Leibniz himself, would be willing to accept such a conclusion. (Kivy 1987: 245–6)

In other words, Kivy supposes that Leibniz's Law applies only to essential properties, and hence that Levinson's examples demonstrate works to be distinct only if the properties wherein they differ are possessed essentially.

However, this response commits errors concerning both Levinson's examples and the nature of Leibniz's Law. To begin with, it is a mistake to think that Leibniz's Law applies only to essential properties: it applies to properties across the board. Having said this, it does not follow that Leibniz's Law, so understood, commits us to the thesis that works could not have differed in their aesthetic properties.[8] For the point, as Levinson makes clear, is that Leibniz's Law does not concern the identity of objects *across* possible worlds; it concerns their identity in *a single* possible world (Levinson 1990c: 222–3). Its claim is that if A and B differ in any genuine respects, they are not identical; it remains silent on what *would* be different from what in counterfactual circumstances.

Having made this point, we can see that Kivy misconstrues the nature of Levinson's thought-experiments. For, as I have noted already, these too concern identity within a possible world, not cross-world identity. Levinson is not asking us to consider *two* distinct worlds: the actual world in which Schoenberg composed *Pierrot Lunaire* in 1912 and a possible world in which Strauss composed a sonic doppelgänger in 1897. He asks us to consider a *single* world in which these two acts of composition take place (1980b: 70 n. 17). Given that this is so, he is entitled to invoke Leibniz's Law in the way he does, and is not guilty of presupposing that works have their aesthetic properties essentially. For all Kivy has shown, Levinson's attack on sonicism stands.

What, then, of Wolterstorff's response to Levinson? Unlike Kivy, he does not take himself to have uncovered hidden misconceptions in the way in which Levinson sets up his thought-experiments. On the contrary, he

---

[8] I take it that a work's aesthetic properties, since response-dependent, are extrinsic in the sense introduced in §2.5. Evidently, it follows from this that the fact that a work does not have its aesthetic properties essentially is consistent with the type/token theory's commitment to such works being modally inflexible (i.e. incapable of differing with respect to their *intrinsic* qualities).

takes them to issue a challenge that must be met. But, having admitted this, he replies by arguing that the putative difference in properties possessed by the acoustically indistinguishable works in Levinson's examples is *apparent* only. As Wolterstorff sees it, once we understand that the properties possessed by works are relativized to compositional acts, the patina of difference vanishes. For example, when it comes to the property of being Liszt-influenced, a property that Levinson takes a work to have partly as a result of the composer's occupancy of a certain musico-historical context, Wolterstorff says this:

> In saying that Brahms's sonata was Liszt-influenced, one might mean that Brahms's composing of this sonata was influenced by Liszt (and therefore derivative). But if so, why shouldn't it be the case that someone else's composing of it was not influenced (and highly original)? Why shouldn't this structure have the property of being such that someone's composing of it was influenced and derivative, and *also* have the property of being such that someone's composing of it was not Liszt-influenced and was highly original? (Wolterstorff 1991: 80)

Wolterstorff's idea, then, is this: the properties that the acoustically indistinguishable works composed in different contexts seem not to share are really shared properties relativized to acts of composition.

However, one inevitably suspects that this solution is altogether too *ad hoc* to command acceptance. As we shall see in §9.4, the idea that our apparent attribution of artistic properties is not what it seems can be defended relatively straightforwardly; but the same cannot be said for a revisionary account of our attribution of *aesthetic* properties to works. It is highly counter-intuitive to suggest that the aesthetic properties we ascribe to a piece of music are anything but monadic. We do not describe *Pierrot Lunaire* as 'eerie-as-composed-by-Schoenberg', or a Stamitz symphony as 'exciting-as-composed-by-Stamitz'; we apply monadic predicates to such works. All of which suggests, of course, that the properties they express are monadic. Now it is true that a sentence's grammatical form may mislead as to its logical form. And it is equally true that a sentence's logical form does not dictate the philosophical analysis we should provide of its constituent expressions.[9] But that said, it is nonetheless clear that we should depart from the idea that a one-place predicate expresses a monadic property only

---

[9] We may agree, e.g., that ' "*p*" is true' has the logical form of a name and a one-place predicate, yet take the concept expressed by the truth-predicate to be analysed in terms of a dyadic truth-relation.

if there is a good philosophical reason for doing so. Yet in this case, there exists no such reason: our critical practice has it that we treat works of music as possessing monadic aesthetic properties, and denying this for the sake of rebutting Levinson's contextualist arguments is just too convenient to be plausible. Wolterstorff's position is not independently motivatable.

The moral to be drawn from Wolterstorff's response to Levinson's thought-experiments is this: we should not give up the idea that musical works genuinely have monadic aesthetic properties. The sonicist must acknowledge that properties such as *being exciting, being funny, being eerie*, and the like are genuinely ascribed to works, and yet deny that works possess these properties partly in virtue of their occupancy of a given musico-historical context. To put it another way, the sonicist must insist that the (moderate) supervenience of the aesthetic on the sonic outlined in §8.2 holds, despite the apparent evidence to the contrary provided by Levinson. She must be bullish, in other words, denying that Levinson's examples are examples in which there are genuine aesthetic differences between sonic doppelgängers.

This is the line that I shall defend in §9.5. In the next section, however, I shall focus on the attempt to refute sonicism by imagining worlds in which there exist sonic doppelgängers that differ artistically, with respect to their representational properties, or with respect to their (object-directed) expressive properties. These cases, I suggest, really are flawed, but not in the way Kivy supposes. My response to Levinsonian thought-experiments is thus essentially the same kind of disjunctive approach recommended in §8.5. Those involving the ascription of aesthetic properties demand what one might term a *straight response*: a reply that challenges the contextualist conclusion drawn from them by Levinson. When it comes to the other cases, the sonicist should get her objection in earlier, refusing to accept the way in which the contextualist describes them.

9.4 Artistic, Representational, and Object–Directed Expressive Properties

Let us start by focusing on works' artistic properties. Levinson's examples are designed to demonstrate that pairs of acoustically indistinguishable works may yet differ in their artistic properties, and hence that acoustic equivalence is insufficient for work-identity. We have met one such example already: according to Levinson, there exists a possible world in which Mendelssohn's composition of the *Midsummer Night's Dream Overture* (1826) is joined by the composition, in 1900, of a work sonically indistinguishable from it. Whilst a sonicist will insist that Mendelssohn and our *fin-de-siècle* composer compose the same work, Levinson claims that this cannot be so: Mendelssohn's work, by virtue of the time at which he was working, has a property that its doppelgänger does not: namely, originality (1980b: 70).

To return to a putative counter-example briefly introduced in §9.3, Brahms's Piano Sonata Op. 2, Levinson says (1980b: 70–1), is *Liszt-influenced*, a fact that should come as no surprise given Brahms's identification with Liszt's circle of composers, the 'Musicians of the Future'. However, now consider a possible world just like the actual world but with one difference: in this world Beethoven composed an exact sonic double of the work later composed by Brahms. Evidently, argues Levinson, since Beethoven preceded Liszt, his work cannot be Liszt-influenced, and hence, by Leibniz's Law, the work composed by Beethoven is distinct from that composed by Brahms, thereby disproving sonicism.

So how should a sonicist respond? To be sure, *if* works genuinely possess artistic properties such as these, Levinson's examples reveal sonicism to individuate musical works too crudely. But the antecedent of this conditional may be denied and, by contrast with Wolterstorff's response to Levinson's doppelgänger thought-experiments, such a denial need not lack motivation. For one thing is clear: as Levinson himself admits, there is 'some plausibility' (1980b: 72) in taking apparent artistic (though not aesthetic or expressive) properties of works to be disguised properties of persons and their compositional acts. After all, one's purpose in making artistic ascriptions to works would seem to be that of highlighting features of the compositional process, placing this process in context, or else evaluating the composer's achievement; so it is quite natural to construe such ascriptions as attaching to composers, rather than to their works. Furthermore, if the moral of this book's first seven chapters is correct—and we should regard works of music as abstract, structureless, eternally existent types—then there would seem to be a serious question as to the intelligibility of attributing properties such as *being Liszt-influenced* and *being original* to works of music. To be sure, a composer can be influenced by Liszt, or be highly original, in his composing of a certain piece of music; but it is not clear what it would be for an *abstract, eternally existent entity* to be *itself* original or influenced by Liszt. Here, perhaps, we have a case in which philosophical theory should prompt us to revisit assumptions that have we have hitherto accepted unreflectively.

Nonetheless, Levinson has two objections to this strategy for dealing with those of his examples that exploit putative differences between sonic doppelgängers' artistic properties. First, he argues that artistic attributions made of works of music are 'as direct and undisguised as attributions typically made of composers' (1980b: 72); second, he claims that artistic attributions to works are, if anything, more basic than such attributions made of composers. As he puts it, 'the composer is original because *his works* are original; his works are not original because *he is*' (1980b: 73).

However, neither of these responses quite succeeds. It is certainly true that, syntactically speaking, 'Brahms's Second Piano Sonata is Liszt-influenced' looks to be an attribution of a property to a work: it seems to wear its logical form on its sleeve. But we are well aware that surface form may mislead as to logical form; and in this case we should have severe misgivings about whether a type is the sort of thing that can be influenced by Liszt. For something to be influenced by Liszt is either for its *behaviour* or its *nature* to be so influenced. Clearly, since works of music are not the kinds of thing that can exhibit behaviour, the former cannot be true. But, given the arguments of Chapters 1–7, neither can a work of music have aspects of its nature influenced by Liszt. Works of music are types, and types, we have noted, are modally inflexible: it is impossible for them to differ in their intrinsic properties (i.e. in their nature). Consequently, since works of music are types, it follows that their nature cannot be influenced by the actions of composers. It was *Brahms* who was so influenced in his composition of his Second Piano Sonata, not the sonata itself.

Furthermore, it is by no means obvious that we should accept Levinson's claim that composers are original because their works are. Here is another explanation. For a composer to be original is for her to have performed original *actions* of a certain kind: that is, for her to have been the first to compose works with a certain combination of acoustic and aesthetic properties. But it does not follow from this that the objects of these original actions—the works composed—are literally original. For it is a familiar fact that many of the predicates true of a composer's act of composition are not true of the thing composed: the compositional act, but not the work, is spatially located, may have lasted for months, and so on. Originality is just one more property possessed by composers' actions, but not by their works. And the same goes for *being visionary, being influential, being skilful,* and the rest. The crucial point, then, is that Levinson is mistaken in thinking that it is possible for a pair of works to be sonic doppelgängers that yet differ with respect to the artistic properties they possess. Works do not possess such properties.

As it happens, essentially the same response, it seems to me, can be made to the contextualist who tries to imagine possible worlds in which sonic equivalents differ in their representational properties. Consider, once more, Honegger's *Pacific 231*. This, we are told, represents a steam locomotive in motion: something that a piece composed in the fifteenth century could not do, even if it were sonically indistinguishable from *Pacific 231*. A vehicle of representation (a word, picture, or piece of music) cannot represent something before that thing has even been conceived of. However, it is my contention that works of music do not possess representational properties; hence examples of this kind, like those that exploit putative differences in works' artistic properties, fail to go through. In a possible world in which *Pacific 231* and its fifteenth-century sonic double have both been composed, it is not that the former, but not the latter, *represents* a steam locomotive. On the contrary, *both Pacific 231* and its fifteenth-century sonic double *sound like* such a machine; yet *neither represents* such a thing, and hence there is no obstacle to identifying them.

Lest it be thought that such a claim is an off-the-cuff response to a philosophical difficulty, it should be made plain that the denial that music is a representational art-form has plenty of independent motivation. First of all, we should be clear that the mere fact that *Pacific 231* resembles a steam locomotive in motion should not be taken to show that the work thereby represents such a thing. As Scruton reminds us, resemblance is a symmetric, reflexive relation; representation is neither (1997: 122). Besides, the case of pictorial representation counsels us to avoid such a conflation, since a picture's visually resembling an object is neither necessary nor sufficient for it to represent that object. That it is unnecessary is demonstrated by the fact that many non-naturalistic paintings do not look like the things they represent. That it is insufficient is demonstrated by resemblance's symmetry: the fact that the represented object resembles the picture every bit as much as does the picture the object.

So what is the feature or features possessed by pictures that music lacks? When we view the *Mona Lisa*, we see things *in* the picture: it presents her as having certain properties. Why should we deny that, analogously, we hear things *in Pacific 231*? The answer is that genuinely representative media express thoughts, but that music does not. The *Mona Lisa* presents a woman as being *thus-and-so*: as being enigmatic, haughty, and such like. *Pacific 231*, though it undoubtedly *imitates* a steam locomotive in motion, does not express thoughts about such a thing. Representation, as Scruton puts it (1997: 63 n. 14) is 'essentially propositional': its content can be put into words. Music, by contrast, cannot express propositions about an object; it can only mimic it.

There are two reasons for this. First of all, the putative thoughts expressed by pieces of music are insufficiently determinate to have a propositional content and, hence, to be thoughts-proper. *Pacific 231* merely sounds like a steam locomotive; it does not express a determinate thought about such a thing. And the same goes for other apparent cases of musical depiction, such as the bird-calls in Beethoven's Pastoral Symphony. There is nothing that can be expressed by a 'that'-clause.

The second reason becomes apparent once we take up the perspective of the listener. In authentically representational media our interpretation of an object's representational content is constrained: there exist conventions that determine that it is one particular thought that is being expressed rather than another. This is particularly clear when it comes to language, of course, but it also applies to the case of pictorial representation: to fail to see the *Mona Lisa* as depicting an enigmatic woman is to misunderstand it. But no corresponding phenomenon exists in the case of music. A reputed case of musical representation—such as Debussy's *La Mer*—is such that someone who failed to pick up on its purported representational character at all, or perhaps took it to represent something else (say the swelling and subsiding of someone's emotions in a state of great passion), would not be taken to have *got the piece wrong*. As Scruton puts it,

> Of course, to hear with understanding you must perceive the musical movement: those vast heavings of bottomless sound which can indeed be likened to the swell of the sea. But you do not have to hear this movement as the movement of the sea or even to notice its likeness. You may hear it as you hear the movement in Chausson's *Poème* for violin and orchestra, or the movement in a Bach prelude: as a purely musical phenomenon, to which you attach no subject in your thoughts. (Scruton 1997: 131)

The same goes for *Pacific 231*: one *may* notice that it resembles the sounds made by a steam locomotive; but one *need not* do so in order to understand the piece musically. This can only mean that the piece *intimates* or *suggests* a steam locomotive, as opposed to representing one.

Naturally, the dispute does not end here, however. When it comes to the first style of argument against the thesis that music cannot express thoughts—the claim that music fails what we might call *the determinacy requirement*—Aaron Ridley has two replies. First, he suggests that any indeterminacy is *apparent* only. The bell-like sounds in Debussy's *La Cathédral Engloutie*, he suggests (2004: 57), *do* express a thought, the thought in question being something along the lines of <Here is the sound of bells chiming; it gets louder and clearer and then falls away>.[10] Presumably, the same goes for *Pacific 231*, its engine-like sounds expressing a thought such as <Here is a steam locomotive starting up, increasing in speed and then gradually coming to a stop>. Second, Ridley suggests that the philosopher who claims that music fails the determinacy requirement falls foul of a *reductio*: if music fails to meet this requirement, then so must painting. Ridley is prepared to grant that 'music doesn't have the capacity, in the relevant sense, to offer full stops or to "complete" thoughts' (2004: 58); but he claims that the same goes for painting. Quoting with approval Stephen Davies's claim that '[p]ictures are said to be worth a thousand words just because there need be no end to the description of the way a subject is represented' (Davies 1994: 88 n. 10), Ridley concludes that *both* music *and* painting fail to meet the determinacy requirement and hence, that such a requirement can only be a philosopher's tendentious concoction.

But not so fast. It is agreed that a sequence of sounds in *La Cathédral Engloutie sounds like* the chiming of bells getting louder and clearer, and then fading away; but it can only be a contrivance to suppose that these sounds express <Here is the sound of bells chiming; it gets louder and clearer and then falls away>. At the very least, in order to express this thought, a medium must contain the following: conventions that determine that certain elements within the medium express the individual concepts of which the thought is composed, and conventions which determine how the expression of such a thought is derived from the arrangement of such basic elements. But there is no reason to believe that such conventions exist.

---

[10] I follow Paul Horwich (1998) in writing '<*p*>' for 'the proposition that *p*'.

In particular, Ridley has no answer to the question of which features of the sound-sequence in *La Cathédral Engloutie* express the concepts <sound>, <here>, and <falls away>. The sound-sequence *sounds* like bells chiming louder and clearer and then falling away; it does not *represent* such a process.

What of Ridley's charge of *reductio ad absurdum*? Here, I think, he has failed to grasp the claimed nature of the difference between pictures and music. True enough, in a picture, 'there need be no end to the description of the way a subject is represented'; but this is because there may be no end to the thoughts expressed by it, not because it expresses no determinate thoughts whatsoever. Pictures plainly *do* possess the capacity to represent, since they are subject to precisely the kinds of conventions to which music is not: the arrangement of the elements in the *Mona Lisa* represents a woman as having features arranged in a corresponding way. Having said this, of course, a picture is, indeed, worth a thousand words. But this is not because pictures—as do pieces of music—fail to convey thoughts; it is because they convey so many. Music is worth a thousand words because it does not serve to express determinate thoughts; pictures are worth a thousand words because they may convey a thousand determinate thoughts.[11]

Ridley thus fails to convince with his first reply to our claim that music is non-representational. And the same goes for his second. Our claim, remember, is that it is quite possible for a musically sensitive listener to take a piece to represent something totally different from its presumed content or, indeed, nothing at all; and, what is more, that such an interpretation would not be regarded as being mistaken. Ridley's response to this claim is to argue that it begs the question by presuming an account of musical understanding that rules out the possibility of music's being representational from the very beginning (2004: 59–60). But this charge is misleading. It is true that once the (modified) acousmatic account of our musical experience I recommended in §8.3 is in place, music cannot be seen as representational. If our interest in music *as music* lies in sounds' acoustic features and organization—in intra-musical, rather than extra-musical, relations—then understanding a work will not require us to have knowledge either of the sounds' origin or of what they are supposedly *about*. But, having said this, the argument for musical works' being non-representational does not proceed

---

[11] As Scruton puts it, 'we do not see the *Mona Lisa* as face-like: we see it as a face. We are not delighting in imitation, but in the portrait of a lady, about whom we have a thousand thoughts' (1997: 121).

in this fashion. For it is independently plausible to think that someone who failed to recognize the sonic resemblance between *Pacific 231* and a steam locomotive would not thereby have failed to understand *the music*. The account of musical understanding that enshrines this intuition reinforces this claim but does not feature in the argument for it. The point is this: someone who failed to make the connection between *Pacific 231* and a steam locomotive would surely not have missed out on anything *musical*; and this suggests that music does not have a representative function. Naturally, we may accept that a piece of music may serve to *suggest*, or *intimate*, things beyond its sonic boundaries, especially in conjunction with a suggestive title; but suggestion and intimation are not representation, as Davidson has reminded us (1978: 262). Likewise, listening to a piece of music may bring it about that we have certain thoughts, but this does not entail that the music *transmits* such thoughts: a bump on the head may cause us to think of many things, but such an event does not have representational content. The same goes for music.

Ultimately, then, there is no mileage in Levinson-style thought-experiments that aim to propel us towards contextualism by pointing to worlds in which sonically indistinguishable works nonetheless differ in their supposed representational properties. Such cases are flawed from the start, since musical works do not represent.

Finally, and unsurprisingly, I suppose, I take it that something similar should be said about putative counter-examples to sonicism that invoke object-directed expressive qualities. Let us return to our earlier example, imagining a world in which Marsalis, as he did actually, composed *In This House, On This Morning* in 1992, and yet a sonically indistinguishable piece was composed by a German artist in the sixteenth century. The former work, it may be argued, possesses an expressive property that the latter lacks—namely, that of being expressive of pride in the experience of African Americans in the Deep South—hence the two works cannot be identical. If works are genuinely expressive of object-directed emotions, then cases such as these—cases that prove the contextualist's point by demonstrating that acoustically indistinguishable pieces may yet differ with respect to their object-directed expressive properties—are easy to construct.

However, at this point, we should heed the conclusion drawn from the previous discussion. For if, as we agreed a moment ago, works of music cannot represent, then they cannot express emotional states involving particular objects. A musical work could only express an emotion directed at a particular object, if the work determinately *picked out* the emotion's object; and a work could only do this, if, *per impossibile*, it could represent that object. Given that works of music do not have representational properties, examples in which sonic doubles differ with respect to their object-directed expressive qualities simply cannot get started. Works of music are unable to express emotions directed at specific objects.

This conclusion is fine as far as it goes: one more element of the contextualist's potential arsenal of thought-experiments has been defused. Nonetheless, a question remains: which expressive properties *can* be possessed by pieces of music? Infamously, Hanslick concludes that music is incapable of expressing emotions of *any kind* (1986: 9): convinced both that all emotions are object-directed and that music cannot represent, he concludes that music cannot be expressive. Such a move, however, is surely too extreme to be plausible: descriptions of music as 'sad', 'triumphant', 'exuberant', 'joyous', 'despairing', and the like are so deeply engrained in our critical vocabulary that treating such descriptions as misconceived can only be accepted as a last resort.

Given that this is so, two alternative positions seem more attractive. The first is suggested by Daniel Putman (1987), who claims that certain types of emotion (e.g. joy, anger, despair, etc.) are such that their tokens need not be object-directed, and that these, but only these, emotion-types may be expressed in music. As he, himself, puts it, 'those same emotions that *require* objects in non-musical contexts are those which pure instrumental music cannot express' (1987: 57). The problem with this, however, is that music seems capable of expressing a richer set of emotions than Putman's account allows for. Specifically, it seems that works of music *can* express what are commonly termed the *higher* emotions—emotions such as hope, disappointment, and pride—even though these emotions are such that any instance of them must be object-directed. Passages in *In This House, On This Morning* are, it seems to me, expressive of pride, and Levinson (1990b) has mounted a convincing case for Mendelssohn's *Hebrides* Overture being expressive of hope.

Here, then, we have a puzzle: how can a work of music be expressive of a higher emotion if the tokens of such emotions are necessarily object-directed? Since music cannot represent objects in the world, a musical work could not specify the higher emotion-token's object and hence, it appears, could not express the higher emotion itself. Fortunately, however,

Levinson suggests a way out of this impasse (1990*b*: 347–51). Only *tokens* of higher emotion-types attach to specific objects, of course. Whilst, e.g. the feeling of pride I have at *t* is directed at a certain object, fact, or event (e.g. Eleanor's musical achievement), pride itself—the emotion-type—possesses mere object-directedness in the abstract. This being so, it is possible for a work of music to be expressive of a higher emotion in the following way: even though the music cannot identify an object of the emotion, it can, nevertheless, get across both the *kind* of emotion involved (via its distinctive cognitive or non-cognitive markers) and the impression that this emotion is object-directed. The listener thus hears the music as expressive of, say, hope by virtue of recognizing this kind of emotion in it whilst *imagining* it to have *some object or other*. Consequently, the music expresses the higher emotion even though it does not present that emotion as being directed at a particular thing. As Levinson explains,

the fact that music lacks resources for directing such specific imagining or invest-ment of identity is in no way prejudicial to its possibly being capable of supporting the hearability of such an emotion in it, and of sustaining the degree of less precise imagining that such hearability arguably *does* require. When we hear a passage as expressive of α we in some fashion imagine that α is being expressed, but without imagining in any definite way either the subject or the object of the α involved. (Levinson 1990*b*: 349)

Needless to say, such an account preserves our sense that music can express a rich variety of emotions, including emotions whose *instances* must all be object-directed, yet does so in a way amenable to the sonicist. *In This House, On This Morning*, the sonicist can say, is indeed expressive of pride; but it does not express pride *in the Black Americans of the Deep South*. As a result, Marsalis's work and its imagined sonic doppelgänger turn out *not* to differ in their emotional content. We can thus dismiss this case, and other such cases, intended to show that there can be numerically distinct sound-alikes that differ with respect to the object-relating higher emotions that they express.[12] This is because those works of music that express higher emotions do so without their emotional content being directed at an object.

---

[12] Which, no doubt, in part explains why Levinson himself restricts his use of such thought-experiments to cases in which sonically indistinguishable works (supposedly) differ with respect to their artistic and aesthetic features.

9.5 Aesthetic and Non-Object-Directed Expressive Properties

Up to now, our response to the contextualist's thought-experiments has been to protest that such cases are ill-formed. The contextualist's attempt to prove her case by imagining possible worlds in which there are sonic equivalents that differ with respect to their artistic, representational, or object-directed expressive properties founders on the fact that works of music do not genuinely possess such properties. All in all, the cases we have considered thus far cannot disprove the sonicist's account of work-identity: nothing the contextualist has said so far undermines the sonicist's claim that W and W^* are one and the same work of music just in case they do not differ with respect to the acoustic properties normative within them.

But it is plain to see that the sonicist cannot so easily shrug off Levinson-style thought-experiments that apparently see sonic duplicates differing with respect to their *aesthetic* and *non-object-directed* expressive properties. For it is undeniable that works of music can genuinely be *coherent, flamboyant, upsetting, anguished,* and the like. Given that this is so, what can stop the contextualist from describing a possible world in which a pair of works are acoustically indistinguishable but in which, due to differences in the musico-historical matrices in which their respective composers were situated, the pair fail to share the same aesthetic properties? Such cases, we have noted, are easy to construct, and all seemingly point in the same direction: towards the thesis that acoustic indistinguishability is insufficient for work-identity. Clearly, the threat to sonicism from this direction is real enough.

Nonetheless, it is my contention that the moral Levinson draws from such thought-experiments is incorrect. Specifically, he is wrong to view them as providing counter-examples to the sonicist's account of the individuation of musical works. The sonicist, we shall see, can stick out her chin and deny that the cases are genuine counter-examples to her thesis. She can insist, in other words, that there is no genuine variance in aesthetic qualities and, hence, that the imagined situation is really one in which a single work is composed twice.

So let us return to the cases in question. As I noted in §9.3, Levinson claims that a possible world in which Schoenberg composes *Pierrot Lunaire* (1912) and in which Strauss composes the aurally indistinguishable piece

*Pierrot Lunaire** (1897) is a world in which the latter is the more bizarre, upsetting, anguished, and eerie. Likewise, in a possible world in which Stamitz's composition of a certain symphony is joined by a contemporary composer's composition of a sonically indistinguishable piece, the latter's work, so it is said, is *funny—kitsch*, even—at the very places in which Stamitz's is *exciting*. In both cases there exist two sonically equivalent works of the same category that differ aesthetically, such a difference being the result of the respective composers' occupancy of distinct regions of musico-historical space. The examples reputedly demonstrate that a work's aesthetic properties 'are dependent on more than the sound structure contained' (1980b: 68). Specifically, they are taken by Levinson to show that a work's aesthetic properties also depend upon the context in which it was composed and, hence, that hearing a work correctly requires one to hear it 'in a way that reflects its provenance and musico-historical position' (Levinson 1990c: 226). To fully understand a work, says Levinson, one must perceive it 'against a musical tradition, a field of current styles and an *œuvre*' (1980b: 70).

Levinson's idea, then, is that his examples demonstrate the truth of a specific metaphysical thesis (viz. that a work's aesthetic properties are in part determined by contextual features) that, in turn, entails a thesis concerning the nature of musical appreciation (viz. that hearing a work correctly requires the listener to place it in its musico-historical context). However, in my view, this account of what it is to appreciate a piece of music aesthetically is simply too demanding of us to be plausible, thereby revealing as unsustainable the metaphysical thesis that entails it.

The thesis that understanding a work of music *as music* requires the listener to hear it against a background of knowledge of the musico-historical context in which it was composed conflicts head-on with the doctrine of moderate empiricism that we found so plausible in §8.2. There, to recap, it was argued that the aesthetic appraisal of a work requires us merely to use our ears (and be cognizant of the category of artwork it falls under). The work's aesthetic properties are there to be heard in it; and in order to get our minds round these features, we do not need to bring to bear a raft of information concerning the composer's *œuvre* and influences, or the point in musical, social, and cultural history in which the work was composed. As an example of this, consider Miles Davis's *Kind of Blue*: perhaps the summation of the development of modal jazz.[13] Much work has been done placing the work in its musico-historical context: explaining how its composition developed out of Davis's be-bop, *Birth of the Cool*, and early modal periods, placing it in the history of jazz, and even acquainting the reader with the work's political and social setting.[14] But reading such (undoubtedly, fascinating) work, one is struck by how irrelevant it is to the question of the work's aesthetic merit. In order to appreciate *Kind of Blue* as a work of music, one need not have internalized information concerning musical, cultural, and political history up to 1959, and one does not even *need* to know anything about the development of Davis's *œuvre* or the musical influences upon him. Rather, one must be sufficiently familiar with, and sensitive to, the music itself: *how it sounds*. This, in turn, requires one both to have listened to and appreciated music of this kind, and to be the possessor of an appropriate critical vocabulary: in the case of *Kind of Blue*, for example, one must be able to distinguish jazz based on scales from chords-based jazz. Of course, the kind of contextual knowledge highlighted by Levinson *may, as a matter of fact*, help to supply the listener with the musical ear needed to hear *Kind of Blue* as it should be heard, but there is no reason to think that such knowledge is necessary.

To recapitulate, this is not to deny that such contextual matters are of concern to the music scholar; it is to insist that such questions are of art-historical interest and do not touch upon the work's aesthetic qualities. As I pointed out in §8.2, it follows that much of what comes under the heading of 'music criticism' is either intellectual biography or the sociology of music, but this should not unnerve us: it should come as little surprise that a practice that has developed organically in our culture should combine elements from disparate disciplines. In this respect, music criticism is like the (unfairly maligned) discipline of Cultural Studies.

Returning now to Levinson's thought-experiments, what should we conclude from this reassertion of the truth in moderate empiricism? The sonicist, should, I think, be bullish. Given the intuitive force behind moderate empiricism, she should insist that genuinely *aesthetic* properties (i.e. those *heard* in the work) *cannot* vary in the cases imagined by Levinson. Works of music (i.e. works of the same artistic category) cannot differ aesthetically without sounding different. So, when it comes to the imagined

---

[13] Here I treat *Kind of Blue* as a work in itself, as opposed to being a collection of five works. Nothing of import hangs on this decision.

[14] Notably by Kahn (2000) and Nisensen (2000).

possible world containing *Pierrot Lunaire* and *Pierrot Lunaire**, for example, we should insist that Schoenberg's work and Strauss's work are equally upsetting, anguished, and eerie. And the same goes for *bizarreness*, if this property is understood aesthetically rather than artistically. If Schoenberg's piece is bizarre, and bizarreness is a property that is genuinely heard in the music, then Strauss's piece cannot have this quality to any greater or lesser degree than Schoenberg's. It is, no doubt, true that *the scoring of such a work by Strauss in 1897* would have been more bizarre than Schoenberg's act of composition some fifteen years later: but such a difference is an *artistic* one (ultimately, a difference in the respective compositional acts, and not in the compositions themselves), so does not concern us here. When it comes to truly aesthetic qualities, Schoenberg's work and Strauss's work are on a par, and thus we have no reason to deny that they are identical.

What this example illustrates is how Levinson's interpretation of his thought-experiments often depends upon a reading of the properties in question that veers between the aesthetic and the artistic. To see this, just consider, once more, the possible world in which a contemporary composer composes a work sonically indistinguishable from a Stamitz symphony. In such a world, does Stamitz's work really differ *aesthetically* from that of the composer we may Christen 'Damitz'?[15] Well, we might want to agree with Levinson that Stamitz's work is more *exciting* than Damitz's (1980b: 71); but it seems to me that if we make such a claim, we are using 'exciting' to express an artistic property, not an aesthetic one. The reason why we may claim Damitz's composition to be less exciting than Stamitz's is, I take it, that the use of 'Mannheim rockets' and the like by a twenty-first-century composer is *unoriginal* and *derivative*: artistic properties both. If by contrast, we understand 'exciting' to express an aesthetic property—an audible feature of the music—then the two pieces are equally exciting. Likewise, the fact that an audience would find Damitz's, but not Stamitz's, use of Mannheim rockets funny indicates that it is not Damitz's *music per se* that is thought to be funny—an audience, after all, could not tell the 'two' works apart—but the fact that someone could unironically compose such music in the modern world. Once more, the appearance of an aesthetic difference is apparent only: the difference is really artistic, and artistic properties are really properties of composers and their actions.

---

[15] Kivy came up with the initial baptism of this character (1987: 247).

It is important to be clear that I am not suggesting that *every* claimed aesthetic difference between Levinson-style sonic doppelgängers is really artistic. My point is this: *either* the putative aesthetic differences highlighted by Levinson are disguised artistic differences, and thus differences in the composers' respective compositional acts, and not their works; or else the properties he focuses on are *shared* by the sonically indistinguishable works, and hence do not undermine the thesis that these works are numerically identical. In fact, most of the claimed differences between the 'pair' of works in the Schoenberg/Strauss thought-experiment fall into this second category. Levinson claims, for instance, that Strauss's *Pierrot Lunaire** is more eerie, anguished, and upsetting than Schoenberg's *Pierrot Lunaire* (1980b: 70). But, as I have suggested already, the sonicist should just deny this. Given that these properties are authentically aesthetic, they can only be possessed to the same degree by *Pierrot Lunaire* and *Pierrot Lunaire**. The reason for this is simple: a work of music's aesthetic properties are audible in it—they are features of how the work sounds—and so, since the works are sonically indistinguishable, one cannot be more eerie, anguished, or upsetting than the other.

What *is* true, of course, is that the original audience for Strauss's imagined *Pierrot Lunaire**, in 1897, would have *found it* more eerie, anguished, and upsetting than did the original audience of Schoenberg's *Pierrot Lunaire*, in 1912. But it does not follow from this that the one work *really is* more eerie, anguished, and upsetting than the other. For, as Levinson himself has urged (1990c: 226), a work's eeriness, for example, should not be equated with its eeriness *to its original audience*, but with its eeriness to an audience that *hears it correctly*. Where Levinson and I differ is over what such correct listening requires. Whilst Levinson insists that an audience can listen to a work correctly only if it listens to the work in a way that reflects its provenance and musico-historical position, I deny this. Such knowledge is not required to hear the music *as music*. Rather, to listen correctly is to hear it as it should be heard by someone with maximally developed discriminative abilities, discernment, and sensitivity. Such a listener would not distinguish *Pierrot Lunaire* and *Pierrot Lunaire** aesthetically.

This, then, is the sonicist's reply to the claim that there can be sonically indistinguishable works of music that nonetheless possess different aesthetic attributes. If the attributes in question really *are* aesthetic, we should hold fast to the (well-motivated) doctrine of moderate supervenience, and just rebut the suggestion that any such aesthetic differences are possible.

Having said this, the contextualist will not be finished just yet. My defence of moderate empiricism comes down to this: since a work of music's aesthetic properties are heard in it, and since Levinson's 'sonic doppelgängers' sound exactly alike, such sound-alikes cannot vary with respect to their aesthetic properties, and hence should be treated as numerically identical. This, however, presupposes that there does not exist another way of understanding 'how a work sounds' that allows for sonic doppelgängers to differ, in some sense, in how they sound.

In fact, Levinson suggests just such an approach, arguing that there exist two senses of 'how a sound sounds' (1990a: 398 n. 16). According to the narrower understanding of this phrase—that which informs the notion of an acoustic property that I have been using in this book—two sounds sound the same just in case they are aurally indistinguishable: just in case, that is, the two sounds are indistinguishable to a hearer 'given just the sounds and no other information' (1990a: 398 n. 16). But, Levinson continues, there is a broader understanding of 'how a sound sounds' such that two aurally indistinguishable sounds might nonetheless sound different. The crucial idea in this latter notion is that two aurally indistinguishable sounds might in this second sense sound different to a hearer if they are heard against different backgrounds of information. And, presumably, the contextualist will claim that it is precisely when there exists a sonic difference in this broad sense between sonic sound-alikes (narrowly construed) that the application of variant aesthetic predicates to them will get a grip.

So here is what a contextualist could now say about *Pierrot Lunaire* and *Pierrot Lunaire**. Contrary to what the sonicist supposes, the claim that these works may differ in their aesthetic properties need not amount to a denial that aesthetic properties are genuinely heard in them. For if a listener hears the two works whilst knowing that they were composed in different musico-historical contexts, the two works will, in the broad sense just introduced, *sound different* to her. Indeed, as Levinson himself puts it, *'perceived against a musical tradition, a field of current styles, and an oeuvre'* (1980b: 70; my italics), *Pierrot Lunaire** *sounds* more eerie, anguished, and upsetting than does Schoenberg's work. In the possible world in which both works exist, once an audience member is aware of the different times at which they were composed, and is able to bring to bear some knowledge of Strauss's *œuvre*, she will *hear* its sonic make-up as 'doubly extreme' (Levinson 1980b: 70). This, and other such properties of the work, are perceivable in it when contextual information about the piece forms the background against which the work is heard; and it is this phenomenon that grounds the variance in aesthetic properties between works that do not differ sonically in the narrow sense.

Furthermore, the contextualist might well supplement this position with an accusation: to wit, that the bullish stand I take against the moral that Levinson draws from his thought-experiments sees me operating with a double standard concerning what can be heard in a work. To recap, in §8.5 I argued that instrumentalism can be avoided, if we grant, for example, that a passage of piano-like sounds produced by a Perfect Timbral Synthesizer may, in fact, be heard by its audience *as played by a piano*. This way, I claimed, it is possible for an audience to detect in the work precisely those aesthetic properties that Levinson takes to be contingent upon the sounds actually being produced by a piano. But, my accuser will insist, once I have granted that an audience may hear a performance *as* a piano performance, it is inconsistent of me then to deny (as I have) that there is a sense in which *Pierrot Lunaire* and *Pierrot Lunaire** may yet sound different. For if an audience can hear a passage *as* produced by a piano, it can surely hear two qualititatively identical works as, respectively, *composed by Schoenberg* and *composed by Strauss*; and if this is possible, then, as Levinson suggests, it follows that the audience may hear differing aesthetic qualities in exact sonic duplicates.

In my view, however, the sonicist's decision to stand firm in the light of thought-experiments such as the 'Stamitz/Damitz' and '*Pierrot Lunaire*/*Pierrot Lunaire**' cases remains justified; nor does it require the sonicist to work with a thinner conception of what can be heard in a work than was offered in Chapter 8. To see this, let us, first of all, run through the details of the Levinsonian reply. Its leading idea is that knowledge of a work's co-ordinates in musico-historical space enables the listener to *hear* features of the work that would remain undetected otherwise. Now, only if these features are genuinely heard, and not ascribed on the basis of an interpretation of what is heard, will they count as genuinely aesthetic. But the problem is that inexorable pressure mounts on us precisely to deny that such differences are genuinely heard. To see this, imagine a case in which a listener hears a performance that she correctly takes to be of *Pierrot Lunaire**: one in which the performers work with a score causally-intentionally linked to Strauss's imagined compositional act. According to the contextualist, she hears the piece against the backdrop of its place in musico-historical space, and, in doing so, hears it as strongly eerie and anguished. Now compare this with a situation exactly the same as before except that unbeknownst to our auditor, the performers are actually performing *Pierrot Lunaire*, the piece by Schoenberg. Clearly, since the two performances are aurally indistinguishable, and since she takes them both to be performances of Strauss's piece, the contextualist must hold that her judgement of what she hears as eerie and anguished will remain constant across the two cases. Equally, according to the contextualist, in the second case the auditor makes a mistake: *Pierrot Lunaire* is less eerie and anguished than Strauss's piece. So, granted that a mistake has been made, what is its nature? It is at this point that the implausibility of the contextualist's position becomes evident. For, given that she holds both that aesthetic properties are perceptual and that the auditor has made some kind of error in her aesthetic judgement, she must take the error to be a perceptual one: the auditor's mistaken belief that the performance is of *Pierrot Lunaire** must lead her to *fail to hear the piece as it really is*. But, intuitively, no such *perceptual* error is made: the two performances are aurally indistinguishable—that is, they could be switched without the audience hearing any difference—and the listener hears them as such. Her mistake in the second case, if she can be said to make one, could only be a failure to *interpret* what she hears correctly. There is no sense in which a pair of aurally indistinguishable works of music may nonetheless 'sound different': *Pierrot Lunaire* and *Pierrot Lunaire** cannot *sound* anything other than *equally* eerie and anguished.

Given that this is so, how can the contextualist preserve her claim that the imagined piece by Strauss is more eerie and anguished than the sonically indistinguishable work by Schoenberg? Specifically, what could she say about the second case described in the previous paragraph? Well, when it comes to this case, she *could* claim that the auditor's mistake consists in her hearing the work as composed by Strauss, but that, nonetheless, and as a result of hearing the music as composed by Strauss, the auditor gains some insight into Strauss's (sonically indistinguishable) work.[16] However, this response fails to convince. First, it does not deliver what is needed: an error in *perception*. The error in question looks like a mistaken *assumption*: namely, that the performers are performing Strauss's work. Second, a counter-intuitive consequence of this response is that an audience can detect the aesthetic (i.e. perceptual) qualities of one work (*Pierrot Lunaire**) by listening to another (*Pierrot Lunaire*). This is a most perplexing result: if a work's aesthetic

---

[16] This move was suggested to me by David Davies.

properties are properties that can be heard in it, it is mysterious how one could detect such properties of a work by listening to another work entirely.

Having rejected this move, it looks like the only way of preserving the idea that the sonic duplicates may differ with respect to their aesthetic properties is by denying that such aesthetic properties are a species of perceptual property at all. But such a position—the contextualist's last possible bolthole—is too far-fetched to be defensible. The idea that we cannot *hear* the anguish or the excitement in a piece, or that we cannot *hear* that a particular passage is scintillating, runs contrary to our deepest pre-theoretic intuitions. The sound of a work of music does not provide *evidence* that it is eerie, or anguished, or scintillating: such properties are directly perceived in it. The aesthetic predicates *we* apply to works express perceptual properties.

But what of the charge of inconsistency on the sonicist's part? Can one simultaneously accept that an auditor can hear the sublimity and cragginess in a performance of the *Hammerklavier* by virtue of hearing it *as produced by a piano*, yet deny that an auditor can hear a passage of *Pierrot Lunaire** as 'doubly extreme', eerie, and upsetting by virtue of hearing it *as composed by Strauss*? Yes. My suspicion is that to 'hear a work as composed by Strauss' can only be to hear it whilst *believing* it to have been, or *interpreting* it as, one of Strauss's compositions. This is because, in doing what we might describe as 'hearing a work as composed by Strauss', we are, in fact, making a *conjecture* or entertaining a *hypothesis* about what is heard. The passage's constituent sounds do not present themselves to our sensibility as a passage of Strauss—this is something we *infer* from their character.

But does not the same go for the case in which we hear a passage of music as produced by means of a piano? No; and the reason for this returns us to the observation that we conceptualize the tone colours of sounds by making reference to the sounds' customary origin. In paying attention to sounds' timbre, we conceive of them in terms of the way in which they are typically produced: so, for example, in taking notice of the qualitative character of a certain sound, we think of it as the kind of sound produced by an oboe playing a middle C. Given that this is so, it is true to say that sounds, when heard by the experienced listener, typically present themselves as having been produced in a certain kind of way (even if it turns out that they have been produced by some other, non-standard means). That is to say, we *can*, and *do*, for instance, hear a passage of music as having been produced by means of a piano because, in taking in the sounds' tone colours, we take them to be piano-like. This is not a hypothesis based on what we hear; it is part of the content of our auditory experience.

This loophole having been closed, my original point stands: sonically indistinguishable works of music cannot differ aesthetically; so we should simply deny that Levinson's thought-experiments provide authentic examples of such a phenomenon. Indeed, *none* of his thought-experiments has the power to shift us from the intuitive way of individuating works of music recommended by the (timbral) sonicist.

9.6 Conclusion: The Place of Context

Sonicism stands: W and W^* are numerically identical musical works just in case they have exactly the same acoustic properties normative within them. There is no contextualist argument that should bring us to deny that acoustically indistinguishable works of music are anything other than identical. That said, it is important to understand that the simple view by no means denies a significant role to contextual factors in the composition and appreciation of music. As we noted in §5.4, the type/token theory and its corollary, musical Platonism are quite compatible with an acknowledgement that a composer's occupancy of a location in musico-historical space figures in an explanation of why she composes the pieces she does. However, the crucial point is this: although matters of context are causally relevant to a composer's composition of a work, it does not follow that such features need figure in our favoured account of the identity conditions of works of music.

Equally, and as we saw in §9.5, it is possible that gaining detailed knowledge of a work's provenance may help the listener to develop the capacity to hear a piece as it should be heard; but such a route to becoming a sensitive auditor is not essential: someone could come to understand a work of music merely by dint of listening to other such works and thereby developing appropriate critical faculties and a feel for the music. We thus have no need to abandon our wholly sonicist approach to the individuation of musical works. The role of context, once properly understand, is revealed as bearing no influence on matters ontological.

Having made this point, my defence of the simple view has come to an end. Both of its constituent theses are *prima facie* correct, and no argument considered in this book succeeds in dislodging either of them. In particular, musical Platonism, together with its consequent account of composition as creative discovery, is quite defensible; whilst there is little bite to the objections made to a properly formulated sonicism by contextualists and instrumentalists. When it comes to the ontology of music, the simple view is not merely a serious player: it is the best game in town.

Bibliography

Anderson, J. (1985). 'Musical Kinds'. *British Journal of Aesthetics* 25: 43–9.

Armstrong, D. M. (1989). *Universals: An Opinionated Introduction*. Boulder, Colo.: Westview Press.

——(1991). 'Classes Are States of Affairs'. *Mind* 100: 189–200.

Bachrach, J. (1971). 'Type and Token and the Identification of a Work of Art'. *Philosophy and Phenomenological Research* 31: 415–20.

Beardsley, M. (1958). *Aesthetics: Problems in the Philosophy of Criticism*. New York: Harcourt, Brace and World.

Bennett, J. (1988). *Events and their Names*. Cambridge: Cambridge University Press.

Blackburn, S. (1984). *Spreading the Word*. Oxford: Oxford University Press.

Burgess, J., and Rosen, G. (1997). *A Subject With No Object*. Oxford: Clarendon Press.

Caplan, B., and Bright, B. (2005). 'Fusions and Ordinary Physical Objects'. *Philosophical Studies* 125: 61–83.

—— and Matheson, C. (2004). 'Can a Musical Work be Created?'. *British Journal of Aesthetics* 44: 113–34.

——(2006). 'Defending Musical Perdurantism'. *British Journal of Aesthetics* 46: 59–69.

Carruthers, P. (1984). 'Eternal Thoughts'. In C. Wright (ed.), *Frege: Tradition and Influence*, 1–19. Oxford: Blackwell.

Child, W. (1991). 'Review of Charles Travis (ed.), *Meaning and Interpretation*'. *Mind* 100: 162–71.

Collingwood, R. G. (1938). *The Principles of Art*. Oxford: Oxford University Press.

Cox, R. (1985). 'Are Musical Works Discovered?'. *Journal of Aesthetics and Art Criticism* 43: 367–74.

——(1986). 'A Defence of Musical Idealism'. *British Journal of Aesthetics* 26: 133–42.

Currie, G. (1989). *An Ontology of Art*. Basingstoke: Macmillan.

Danto, A. (1963). 'What We Can Do'. *Journal of Philosophy* 60: 435–45.

——(1965). 'Basic Actions'. *American Philosophical Quarterly* 2: 141–8.

——(1981). *The Transfiguration of the Commonplace*. Cambridge, Mass.: Harvard University Press.

Davidson, D. (1963). 'Actions, Reasons and Causes'. *Journal of Philosophy* 60. Repr. in his *Essays on Actions and Events*, 3–19. Oxford: Clarendon Press, 1980.

Davidson, D. (1967a). 'Causal Relations'. *Journal of Philosophy* 64. Repr. in his *Essays on Actions and Events*, 149–62. Oxford: Clarendon Press, 1980.

——— (1967b). 'The Logical Form of Action Sentences'. In N. Rescher (ed.), *The Logic of Decision and Action*. Pittsburgh: Pittsburgh University Press. Repr. in his *Essays on Actions and Events*, 105–48. Oxford: Clarendon Press, 1980.

——— (1969). 'The Individuation of Events'. Repr. in his *Essays on Actions and Events*, 163–80. Oxford: Clarendon Press, 1980.

——— (1971). 'Agency', Repr. in his *Essays on Actions and Events*, 43–62. Oxford: Clarendon Press, 1980.

——— (1978). 'What Metaphors Mean'. *Critical Inquiry* 5. Repr. in his *Inquiries into Truth and Interpretation*, 245–64. Oxford: Oxford University Press, 1984.

Davies, D. (2004). *Art as Performance*. Oxford: Blackwell.

Davies, S. (1994). *Musical Meaning and Expression*. Ithaca, NY: Cornell University Press.

——— (2001). *Musical Works and Performances: A Philosophical Exploration*. Oxford: Oxford University Press.

Dodd, J. (2000). 'Musical Works as Eternal Types'. *British Journal of Aesthetics* 40: 424–40.

——— (2002). 'Defending Musical Platonism'. *British Journal of Aesthetics* 42: 380–402.

——— (2004). 'Types, Continuants, and the Ontology of Music'. *British Journal of Aesthetics* 44: 342–60.

——— (2005). 'Critical Study: Artworks and Performances'. *British Journal of Aesthetics* 45: 69–87.

Dummett. M. (1986). 'Frege's Myth of the Third Realm'. In his *Frege and Other Philosophers*, 249–62. Oxford: Clarendon Press, 1991.

Dunn, J. M. (1990). 'Relevant Predication 2: Intrinsic Properties and Internal Relations'. *Philosophical Studies* 60: 177–206.

Fine, K. (1995). 'Ontological Dependence'. *Proceedings of the Aristotelian Society* 95: 269–90.

Fisher, J. A. (1991). 'Discovery, Creation, and Musical Works'. *Journal of Aesthetics and Art Criticism* 49: 129–36.

Frege, G. (1918). 'Thoughts'. Repr. in N. Salmon and S. Soames (eds.), *Propositions and Attitudes*, 33–55. Oxford: Oxford University Press, 1988.

Godlovitch, S. (1998). *Musical Performance: A Philosophical Study*. London: Routledge.

Goehr, L. (1992). *The Imaginary Museum of Musical Works: An Essay in the Philosophy of Music*. Oxford: Clarendon Press.

Goodman, N. (1968). *Languages of Art*. Indianapolis: Bobbs-Merrill.

Grossmann, R. (1992). *The Existence of the World*. London: Routledge.

Haack, S. (1978). *Philosophy of Logics*. Cambridge: Cambridge University Press.

Hanslick, E. (1986). *On the Musically Beautiful*, trans. G. Payzant. Indianapolis: Hackett.

Horwich, P. (1998). *Truth*, 2nd edn. Oxford: Oxford University Press.

Howell, R. (2002). 'Types, Indicated and Initiated'. *British Journal of Aesthetics* 42: 105–27.

Hugly, P., and Sayward, C. (1981). 'Expressions and Tokens'. *Analysis* 50: 181–7.

Janaway, C. (1999). 'What a Musical Forgery Isn't'. *British Journal of Aesthetics* 39: 62–71.

Kahn, A. (2000). *Kind of Blue: The Making of the Miles Davis Masterpiece*. London: Granta.

Kaplan, D. (1990). 'Words'. *Proceedings of the Aristotelian Society* supp. vol. 64: 93–121.

Kim, J. (1976). 'Events as Property Exemplifications'. In M. Brand and D. Walton (eds.), *Action Theory*. Dordrecht: Reidel. Repr. in C. MacDonald and S. Laurence (eds.), *Contemporary Readings in the Foundations of Metaphysics*, 310–26. Oxford, Blackwell, 1998.

Kivy, P. (1983). 'Platonism in Music: A Kind of Defense'. *Grazer Philosophische Studien* 19: 109–29.

——— (1987). 'Platonism in Music: Another Kind of Defense'. *American Philosophical Quarterly* 24: 245–52.

——— (1988). 'Orchestrating Platonism'. In T. Anderberg, T. Nilstun, and I. Persson (eds.), *Aesthetic Distinction*, 42–55. Lund: Lund University Press. Repr. in his *The Fine Art of Repetition*, 75–94. Cambridge: Cambridge University Press, 1993.

——— (2002). *Introduction to a Philosophy of Music*. Oxford: Oxford University Press.

Kripke, S. (1980). *Naming and Necessity*. Oxford: Blackwell.

Latham, A. (2002). *The Oxford Companion to Music*. Oxford: Oxford University Press.

Levinson, J. (1980a). 'Autographic and Allographic Art Revisited'. *Philosophical Studies* 38. Repr. in his *Music, Art and Metaphysics*, 89–106. Ithaca, NY: Cornell University Press, 1990.

——— (1980b). 'What a Musical Work Is'. *Journal of Philosophy* 77. Repr. in his *Music, Art and Metaphysics*, 63–88. Ithaca, NY: Cornell University Press. 1990.

——— (1987). 'Artworks and the Future'. In T. Anderberg, T. Nilstun, and I. Persson (eds.), *Aesthetic Distinction*, 56–84. Lund: Lund University Press. Repr. in his *Music, Art and Metaphysics*, 179–214. Ithaca, NY: Cornell University Press, 1990.

——— (1990a). 'Authentic Performance and Performance Means'. In his *Music, Art and Metaphysics*, 393–408. Ithaca, NY: Cornell University Press, 1990.

Levinson, J. (1990b). 'Hope in *The Hebrides*'. In his *Music, Art and Metaphysics*, 336–75. Ithaca, NY: Cornell University Press, 1990.

—— (1990c). 'What a Musical Work Is, Again'. In his *Music, Art and Metaphysics*, 215–63. Ithaca, NY: Cornell University Press, 1990.

—— (1992a). 'Critical Notice of Currie's *An Ontology of Art*'. *Philosophy and Phenomenological Research* 52: 215–22.

—— (1992b). 'Review of D. M. Armstrong's *Universals: An Opinionated Introduction*'. *Philosophical Review* 101: 654–60.

Lewis, D. (1968). 'Counterpart Theory and Quantified Modal Logic'. *Journal of Philosophy* 65: 113–26.

—— (1973). *Counterfactuals*. Oxford: Blackwell.

—— (1976). 'The Paradoxes of Time Travel'. *American Philosophical Quarterly* 13: 145–52, Repr. in his *Philosophical Papers*, ii. 67–80. Cambridge: Cambridge University Press, 1986.

—— (1983). 'Survival and Identity', Appendix B. In his *Philosophical Papers*, i. 76–7. Oxford: Oxford University Press.

—— (1986). *On the Plurality of Worlds*. Oxford: Blackwell.

Loux, M. (1998). *Metaphysics: A Contemporary Introduction*. London: Routledge.

Lowe, J. (1995). 'Ontological Dependency'. *Philosophical Papers* 23: 31–48.

Margolis, J. (1980). *Art and Philosophy*. Atlantic Highlands, NJ: Humanities Press.

McDowell, J. (1980). 'Quotation and Saying That'. In M. Platts (ed.), *Reference, Truth and Reality*, 206–37. London: Routledge.

—— (1983). 'Aesthetic Value, Objectivity, and the Fabric of the World'. In E. Schaper (ed.), *Pleasure, Preference and Value*, 1–16. Cambridge: Cambridge University Press.

—— (1985). 'Values and Secondary Qualities'. In T. Honderich (ed.), *Morality and Objectivity*, 110–29. London: Routledge.

McGinn, C. (1983). *The Subjective View*. Oxford: Clarendon Press.

Morris, M. (forthcoming). 'Doing Justice to Works of Music'. In K. Stock (ed.), *Philosophers on Music*. Oxford: Oxford University Press.

Nisensen, E. (2000). *The Making of Kind of Blue: Miles Davis and his Masterpiece*. New York: St Martin's Griffin Press.

Oliver, A. (1996). 'The Metaphysics of Properties'. *Mind* 105: 1–80.

Pearce, D. (1988). 'Intensionality and the Nature of a Musical Work'. *British Journal of Aesthetics* 28: 105–18.

Predelli, S. (1995). 'Against Musical Platonism'. *British Journal of Aesthetics* 35: 338–50.

—— (2001). 'Musical Ontology and the Argument from Creation'. *British Journal of Aesthetics* 41: 279–92.

_____ (forthcoming). 'Authenticity and Interpretation: Musical Performances from a Particularist Standpoint'. In K. Stock (ed.), *Philosophers on Music*. Oxford: Oxford University Press.

Prior, A. N. (1963). '*Oratio Obliqua*'. *Proceedings of the Aristotelian Society* supp. vol. 37: 115–26.

Putman, D. (1987). 'Why Instrumental Music Has No Shame'. *British Journal of Aesthetics* 27: 55–61.

Quine, W. V. O. (1948). 'On What There Is'. Repr. in his *From a Logical Point of View*, 1–19. Cambridge, Mass.: Harvard University Press, 1953.

_____ (1955). 'Quantifiers and Propositional Attitudes'. Repr. in his *The Ways of Paradox and Other Essays*, 185–96. Cambridge, Mass.: Harvard University Press, 1966.

_____ (1958). 'Speaking of Objects'. In his *Ontological Relativity and Other Essays*, 1–25. New York: Columbia University Press; 1969.

_____ (1960). *Word and Object*. Cambridge, Mass.: MIT Press.

_____ (1969). 'Ontological Relativity'. In his *Ontological Relativity and Other Essays*, 26–68. New York: Columbia University Press, 1969.

_____ (1985). 'Events and Reification'. In E. LePore and B. McLaughlin (eds.), *Actions and Events: Perspectives on the Philosophy of Donald Davidson*, 162–71. Oxford: Blackwell.

Ridley, A. (2004). *The Philosophy of Music: Themes and Variations*. Edinburgh: Edinburgh University Press.

Rohrbaugh, G. (2003). 'Artworks as Historical Individuals'. *European Journal of Philosophy* 11: 177–205.

_____ (2005). 'I Could Have Done That'. *British Journal of Aesthetics* 45: 209–28.

Rudder Baker, L. (1997). 'Why Constitution is Not Identity'. *Journal of Philosophy* 94: 599–621.

Rudner, R. (1950). 'The Ontological Status of the Esthetic Object'. *Philosophy and Phenomenological Research* 10: 380–88.

Rumfitt, I. (1993). 'Content and Context: The Paratactic Theory Revisited and Revised'. *Mind* 102: 429–54.

Ryle, G. (1949). *The Concept of Mind*. London: Penguin.

Scruton, R. (1997). *The Aesthetics of Music*. Oxford: Oxford University Press.

Sharpe, R. A. (1979). 'Type, Token, Interpretation and Performance'. *Mind* 88: 437–40.

_____ (1995). 'Music, Platonism and Performance: Some Ontological Strains'. *British Journal of Aesthetics* 35: 38–48.

_____ (2001). 'Could Beethoven have "Discovered" the Archduke Trio?'. *British Journal of Aesthetics* 41: 325–7.

Sibley, F. (1959). 'Aesthetic Concepts'. *Philosophical Review* 68: 421–50, Repr. in A. Neill and A. Ridley (eds.), *The Philosophy of Art: Readings Ancient and Modern*, 312–31. Boston: McGraw-Hill, 1995.

Sider, T. (2001). *Four-Dimensionalism*. Oxford: Oxford University Press.

Simons, P. (1982). 'Token Resistance'. *Analysis* 42: 195–202.

Smith, P., and Jones, O. R. (1986). *The Philosophy of Mind*. Cambridge: Cambridge University Press.

Snoeyembos, M. (1979). 'Art Types and Reductionism'. *Philosophy and Phenomenological Research* 39: 378–85.

Strawson, P. F. (1974). 'Aesthetic Appraisal and Works of Art'. In his *Freedom and Resentment and Other Essays*, 178–88. London: Methuen.

Thomasson, A. (1999). *Fiction and Metaphysics*. Cambridge: Cambridge University Press.

Thompson, J. J. (1998). 'The Statue and the Clay'. *Philosophical Perspectives* 32: 149–73.

Trivedi, S. (2002). 'Against Musical Works as Eternal Types'. *British Journal of Aesthetics* 42: 73–82.

Van Inwagen, P. (1990). 'Four-Dimensional Objects'. *Noûs* 24: 245–55.

Walton, K. (1970). 'Categories of Art'. Philosophical Review 79, Repr. in A. Neill and A. Ridley (eds.), *The Philosophy of Art: Readings Ancient and Modern*, 332–54. Boston: McGraw-Hill, 1995.

—— (1988). 'The Presentation and Portrayal of Sound Patterns'. In J. Dancy, J. M. E. Moravcsik, and C. C. W. Taylor (eds.), *Human Agency: Language, Duty and Value*, 237–57. Stanford, Calif.: Stanford University Press.

Wiggins, D. (1980). *Sameness and Substance*. Oxford: Blackwell.

Williams, B. (1978). *Descartes: The Project of Pure Enquiry*. Harmondsworth: Penguin.

Wittgenstein, L. (1953). *Philosophical Investigations*, trans. G. E. M. Anscombe. Oxford: Blackwell.

—— (1980). *Remarks on the Philosophy of Psychology*, ii, trans. C. G. Luckhardt and M. A. E. Aue, ed. G. H. von Wright and H. Nyman. Oxford: Blackwell.

Wollheim, R. (1968). *Art and its Objects*. Harmondsworth: Pelican.

Wolterstorff, N. (1970). *On Universals*. Chicago: University of Chicago Press.

—— (1980). *Works and Worlds of Art*. Oxford: Clarendon Press.

—— (1991). 'Review of Currie's *An Ontology of Art*'. *Journal of Aesthetics and Art Criticism* 49: 79–81.

Zemach, E. (1970). 'Four Ontologies'. *Journal of Philosophy* 67: 231–47.

—— (1986). 'No Identification without Evaluation'. *British Journal of Aesthetics* 26: 239–51.

—— (1989). 'How Paintings Are'. *British Journal of Aesthetics* 29: 65–71.

Index

Action-Type Hypothesis, Currie's
167–82
aesthetic properties 6, 96, 127, 169, 170,
172, 175, 177, 185, 206, 207, 213,
250, 251, 253–6, 258, 266–8,
270–4
  and aesthetic empiricism 169–78,
205–12
  and supervenience 209–12
  and taste 209
  as response-dependent, yet
objective 214, 233–5
analogical predication 4, 46–7, 50–1,
83–5, 93–4, 100, 181, 185
artistic properties 225–6, 228, 239, 241,
250, 251–252
  not genuinely possessed by musical
works 228–9, 255–9, 269
associate-function from properties to
types 49, 59–60
Anderson, James 100–2
anti-realism, musical 25–31
Armstrong, D.M. 92
  on the existence conditions of
properties 65–6

Bachrach, Jay 22–3
basic actions theory 192–4
Beardsley, Monroe 205
Bennett, Jonathan 13
Blackburn, Simon 133
Bright, Bob 189
Burgess, John 13–14, 16

Caplan, Ben vii, 4, 13, 162, 189
  on musical perdurantism 157–8
  on objects featuring causally in events
15
  on the modal argument against the
set-theoretical account of works of
music 18
Carruthers, Peter 58–9
categorial question in the ontology of
music, the 8
  and repeatability 3, 5, 10–11, 144

and the type/token theory 5–6, 16, 37,
82, 92, 97, 143
  introduced 1–2
Child, William 235
Collingwood, R.G. 26–30
composition 5, 81, 87, 91–2, 245
  and the (misleading) analogy with
scientific experimentation 170–2, 174
  and the role of interpretation in
performance 140–2
  as contextually conditioned 123–7
  as creative discovery 4–5, 35, 56, 69,
106, 112–21, 135, 150, 181, 276
  as involving choice 122–3
  as the selection of certain properties of a
descriptive sound event-type as
normative 100–2
  as the specification of a recipe for
producing properly formed
tokens 110–11
  Levinson on 128–34
Contextualism 103, 127–8, 186, 239, 263
  and doppelgänger thought
experiments 7, 185, 240–1, 249–75
  and Levinson's conception of musical
works as indicated types 242–9
  and the notion of a musico-historical
context 241–3
  formulated 203
  timbral sonicism defended
against 239–75
Continuant View, The 5, 9, 11, 31, 142,
143–66, 168
Cox, Renée 26–9, 99, 122, 124
criticism, the nature of 206–7, 268
Currie, Gregory 4, 5, 9, 102, 143, 183,
184, 186, 188, 200, 202, 207, 209, 212,
218, 244
  and his action-type hypothesis 167–82
  and Levinson's notion of an indicated
type 246–7

Danto, Arthur 190, 243
Davidson, Donald 13, 15, 189, 249, 263
  and 'basic actions' theory 192–4